The Psychology And Dynamics of Human Energy

How Aligning Energy to Impact
can Transform the Workplace

THE CHOIR PRESS

First published in the United Kingdom in 2025 by
The Choir Press

ISBN 978-1-78963-519-5

Dedication

This book is dedicated to those talented people around the world who are using The GC Index to change the world for the better. We call them GCologists!

They are: corporate leaders, HR leaders, learning and development specialists, organisational development and change experts, occupational psychologists, executive coaches, well-being gurus and management consultants.

They all share the same drive: to make the world of work a better place for their clients.

Acknowledgements

Special thanks to:

Teresa Shaw for continued *Play Maker* inspiration.

Nathan Ott for continued *Polisher* perseverance.

Gemma Roszkowski for unfailing *Game Changer* creativity.

All the wonderful contributors to this book for their unfailing commitment and belief in what's possible.

About the Authors

Dr John Mervyn-Smith

John is a co-creator of The GC Index and director of The GC Index Ltd. He is an author, broadcaster and keynote speaker with an expertise that reflects a hybrid career as an academic, clinical and occupational psychologist. He is an Associate Fellow of the British Psychological Society and a Chartered Clinical Psychologist. He has published on subjects from leadership to well-being.

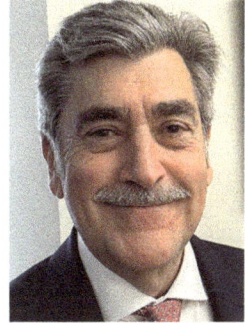

Ruth Baily

Ruth is Founding Director of The Cause Effect, a leadership development and coaching practice specialising in engaging individuals, teams and organisations with creative ideas, science, and new ways to think about their challenges through the power of emotional intelligence. Ruth is famous for her engagement and creativity, and a deep curiosity into the science of emotion and what makes each of us thrive in our own unique way.

Peter Donovan

Peter is Managing Partner at Top Gun Ventures (TGV). He brings a powerful combination of years of business experience, creative rigour, and insightful perspective to help us understand the Energy for Impact that drives business growth. The outcome is a practical approach that business leaders, teams and organisations can employ to effectively attain their chosen business growth strategies.

Andrew Dyckhoff

Andrew has worked in a variety of roles from CEO, to administrative, finance, marketing and front-line sales, working with different cultures (North America/Europe/Asia). He has led consumer and healthcare businesses from large corporate to start-up and worked in the leadership space for the last 15 years. He is passionate about energising and re-energising people and their organisations.

Simon Etherington

Simon is responsible for growing The GC Index into a global brand with a goal to profile 10% of the world's population. Simon joined The GC Index in 2018. Prior to joining The GC Index, he held senior executive roles at other partner-focused businesses including Executive Board Member of SAP UK and Managing Director of Sitecore UK.

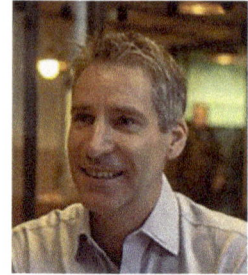

John and Natalie Franklin-Hackett are the co-owners of Frankly Farm Tours in Broseley, Shropshire – an open farm tourist attraction established in 2022. John is an accredited GCologist and has been working with The GC Index in the context of his other career as a consultant since 2016. Natalie was previously an assistant headteacher in an inner city primary school in Coventry.

John Frost

John is a professional leadership coach, GCologist and the bass player in Rebel and the Banned. He has delivered leadership development programmes across different cultures in Europe, North America and Asia. He has a particular interest in enabling personal, team and organisational impact using the leadership lenses of consciousness, connection, curiosity, collaboration and compassion.

Shann Janse van Rensburg

Shann is a change consulting specialist who helps teams to navigate change and develop greater impact to unlock their potential to bring about lasting change, using tools like The GC Index. With 20 years of experience in multiple industries on the African continent, Shann's work focuses on out-of-the-box learning through doing and laughter, to developing leaders to manage change and thrive in an ever-changing landscape.

Vanda North

Vanda is a raving Game Changer specialising in starting businesses, effective brain function, resilience and neurodiversity. She has 58 years of experience culminating in eight books; the training of many people from all over the planet; and is still learning. Her current main interests are neurodiversity and peak performance.

Nathan Ott

Nathan is the Chief Polisher at The GC Index specialising in helping teams and organisations to maximise the impact all of their people can make. With over 25 years of experience, he has co-written and published groundbreaking work to include 'The DNA of a Game Changer 2015', 'The DNA of a Game-Changing Team 2016' and the book *Coaching Me, Coaching You … Ahaa*. Their work centres on one key focus of empowering more than 10% of humankind to make their best impact in their world.

Georgina Pawley

Georgina is the Founder of Impactful Coaching, where she is an executive coach and professional well-being specialist. With 20 years of experience, she has coached hundreds of executives through career transition internationally. Her work focuses on supporting organisations in enhancing leadership impact and collaboration, as well as career fulfilment and accelerated growth.

Simon Phillips

Simon is the Founder of The Change Maker Group and is known as The Change Man by his clients. He specialises in helping executives, teams and organisations to thrive on change and transformation. He has written and contributed to seven books on personal development and change and supported clients globally during his time with Accenture and independently.

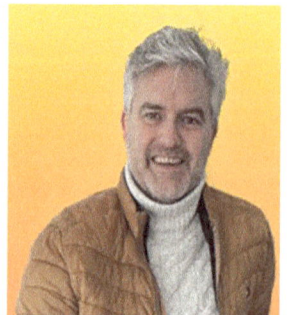

Roxana Radulescu

Roxana is a learning and development practitioner, leadership and career growth certified coach, and TEDx speaker specialised in helping mid-career individuals and teams boost communication, leadership and performance. With more than 15 years of experience, she has authored leadership programmes on award-winning platforms and is a regular guest speaker and facilitator on leadership topics.

Mark Savage

Mark is a trusted commercial board level executive with 19 years' enterprise and 15 years' B2B SME experience. Mark specialises in business consulting and leadership development. He is an executive coach and a full member of the International Coaching Federation, the Association of Business Mentors and the Institute of Directors. He is also a global accredited Master GCologist with The GC Index.

Jill Whittington

Jill is a coach, mentor, trainer, consultant. She has five decades of groundbreaking business change experience across all sectors. Jill specialises in resilience and demystifying change, is passionate about the power of the brain and remains curious about neuroscience. She lives her dream by supporting others to achieve theirs.

Contents

Introduction   xv

Section 1: Understanding Energy for Impact   1

Chapter 1   *A Psychological Perspective on the Expression of*
            Human Energy from Freud to the Present Day   3

            A brief overview of the history of the most significant
            thinking in this area and how this culminated in the
            development of The GC Index.
            Dr John Mervyn-Smith

Chapter 2   *The GC Index and Energy for Impact*   18

            The history and science behind the development of
            this groundbreaking organimetric profiling individual
            Energy for Impact.
            Dr John Mervyn-Smith

Section 2: Individuals at Their Most Productive at Work   37

Chapter 3   *Harnessing the Power of Flow and Energy for Impact*   39

            A 'deep dive' into the connection between our Energy for Impact
            and the coveted state of 'flow', and its relevance for both
            individual and team success.
            Roxana Radulescu

Chapter 4   *Playful Vitality – Unleashing Energy Through*
            Recreation   79

            An exploration of the links between play, energy and
            creativity at work.
            Shann van Rensburg

Chapter 5   *The Power of Your Mind to Optimise Your GCI Profile*
             for Greater Impact, Energy and Success   98

             A practical guide for individuals on how to effectively manage
             their energy in the workplace.
             Jill Whittington and Vanda North

Chapter 6   *The Entrepreneurial Couple*   122

             An inspiring story of one couple's journey from despair to joy …
             with the help of The GC Index.
             John and Natalie Franklin-Hackett

Chapter 7   *Energy for Sales*   149

             A practical understanding of the sales dynamic through the
             lens of The GC Index.
             Mark Savage

**Section 3: Collective Energy for Impact: Teams at Their
Most Effective**   169

Chapter 8   *Energy for Impact in Teams*   171

             In this chapter, the focus is upon how talented individuals can
             make a collective impact in teams.
             Nathan Ott

Chapter 9   *Energy for Impact in Projects and Processes*   182

             The concept of Energy for Impact helps us to understand how
             individual energies align with various tasks and stages within a
             project, and can provide profound insights into why some
             projects succeed while others fail.
             Simon Etherington

Chapter 10   *Keeping the Band Together*   194

At the heart of this exploration is the view that great art
'connects' with people and to do so, those making that art
must feel connected to each other.
John Frost

Chapter 11   *The Origin of Energy in Work Teams*   218

High-performing teams are those that recognise and cultivate
individual and collective energy with a focus upon a shared ambition to thrive as a team, not just survive.
Ruth Baily

**Section 4: How Impactful Leaders Channel Energy into
Organisational Performance**   235

Chapter 12   *Leadership and the Expression of Energy*   237

The link between leadership and energy and why energy
matters. Key insights from research and practice with practical
pathways to translate insight into individual and organisational
impact.
Andrew Dyckhoff

Chapter 13   *The Drive for Business Growth*   257

Understanding the energy that drives business growth. A
practical approach for business leaders, teams and
organisations to employ in order to effectively achieve their
chosen business growth strategies.
Peter Donovan

Section 5: Channelling Energy for Effective Organisational Change   303

Chapter 14   *Dynamic Flow and The GC Index*   305

A breakthrough in productivity and energy management – the key ingredient to human engagement, impact and efficient productivity.
Simon Phillips

Chapter 15   *Harnessing The GC Index to Understand CIO Impact, a Case Study*   328

The ways in which The GC Index can inform decisions when it comes to talent management within organisations. These decisions are crucial to the success and longevity of organisations large and small.
Georgina Pawley

Introduction

By Dr John Mervyn-Smith

'Radiators and drains'

Like many 16-year-old boys I was restless, easily bored and more at home on the sports field than in the classroom. As you might imagine then, the thought of being stuck in a drab assembly hall on a sunny summer's day for the school's annual prize-giving filled me with dread. We have probably all experienced the mind-numbing boredom that such events can induce.

With low expectations set, my headmaster did not disappoint, droning on for what seemed like an eternity. However, what was to follow was startling, an epiphany perhaps. The guest speaker was also a head teacher, and her message was compelling, her energy infectious.

Her message was:

> 'There are two types of people in this world, "radiators and drains".'

I can't remember the details of her proposition; her energy and presence was enough to convince me. It's a statement that has stayed with me even though I'm generally not seduced by binary views of the world.

I got the message, and it was a challenge of a sort. She wanted each and every one of us to recognise that we have the capacity, and potential, to generate energy in our world and for others around us, and, equally, to drain others of energy. She wanted us to see that we have a choice in this.

This view of energy and how we choose to use it, has fascinated me ever since; in some ways it seems so simple and yet, with thought, becomes complex.

The simple bit: we all seem to know when we have energy and, conversely, we all seem to know when we haven't. Over time, and with growing self-awareness, we may come to recognise our own idiosyncratic manifestations of energy.

As we will see in the coming chapters, recognising and understanding individual differences when it comes to the manifestation of energy has been a preoccupation of many psychologists. You will have your own 'markers' of when you have energy and when you don't.

And then the concept of energy starts to become a bit more complex: we may begin to recognise those experiences and situations that 'give' us energy and those that 'deplete' us, but we don't always know why.

We may recognise when we're 'pretending' to have energy when we don't, and what this 'costs' us, or indeed, when we are 'suppressing' energy when we consider it inappropriate to express it.

The chapters that follow will shed some light upon the complex ways in which human beings express their energy within the workplace and present the reader with a framework and language – The GC Index – for understanding how people can manage and develop these expressions as they seek to have an impact within their world.

Section 1:

Understanding Energy for Impact

Chapter 1

A Psychological Perspective on the Expression of Human Energy from Freud to the Present Day

A brief overview of the history of the most significant thinking in this area and how this culminated in the development of The GC Index.

Dr John Mervyn-Smith

An evolutionary perspective

Let's go back to basics and ask the question 'why do human beings need energy?'

The pregnant mother will often delight at the first kicks of her child to be. She is bringing a new life into the world and what could be more confirming of that life.

The relevance of these kicks become more apparent when the newborn begins to crawl, their leg movements propelling them across the floor. These movements are instrumental in developing spatial awareness and the precursors of standing, walking and running.

Observing young children learning to walk illustrates a strong drive for potency: they get up, flop back down and then get up again. Without this drive the infant is vulnerable: the world would become a very threatening place without these very basic actions needed for 'flight' and 'fight'.

Humans have the luxury of mastering these actions over many months while giraffes, for example, are walking upon wobbly legs within an hour of being born. Giraffes, like many other animals, are 'prey animals' and they need to be able to move with the pack, especially when they are under attack. The survival imperative means that they have evolved to act with speed and this takes energy.

With human beings, this drive for mastery continues and many will delight in seeing the extent to which the complex action of walking becomes a Florence Griffith Joyner or a Usain Bolt, setting world records for running fast. Their actions, ultimately, give us collective hope in the ability of the human species to survive and thrive. Thriving, excelling, is a demonstration of the human potential to survive through developing our capabilities, learning from, and adapting to, a changing world.

These actions of fight and flight are key to humans surviving and thriving, and these actions are fuelled by energy channelled into what we would typically call drive or motivation.

The paradox, of course, is that this human drive for mastery may come to destroy the human species: we can become complacent in our belief in our collective ability to master our world with science and technology, and we are witnessing this with our global management of a climate crisis rapidly reaching a point of no return but with a view that someone will come up with the magic answer.

Fight and flight are designed then, to help us to manage and eliminate threat and can be evidenced as energy for action fuelled by biochemical, physical and physiological changes.

These behaviours in the animal world can be quite dramatic when we witness, for example, the stampedes on the African Savanna as zebras are being pursued by cheetahs. And the energy that is required to fuel these behaviours seems obvious when we conjure up images of buck deer locking horns to determine mating rights.

We also know that 'flight' doesn't always work; it doesn't always eliminate the threat in a way that 'freeze' behaviour can.

This YouTube video provides a dramatic example of the benefits of 'freeze' behaviours in the animal kingdom: https://www.youtube.com/watch?v=-QgglTik6G4

For human beings these behaviours of fight, flight and freeze are usually more subtle – shaped by social and cultural norms and expectations – and not always manifest as action even though that suppression of action will take energy. Moreover, these behaviours can be both adaptive and maladaptive for people in terms of the ways in which they support survival and nurture thriving.

In Table 1 (see overleaf) I have presented some examples of human 'fight', 'flight' and 'freeze' behaviours in a work context with possible consequences. You will note that, dependent upon circumstances, behaviours could fit into more than one category: they can be adaptive in the short term but maladaptive in the long term and, potentially, vice versa.

Charles Darwin sought to capture the principle inherent in the relationship between these behaviours and survival with this paraphrase:

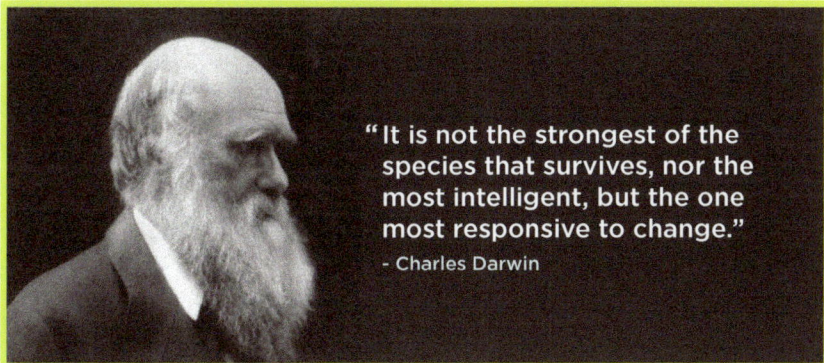

"It is not the strongest of the species that survives, nor the most intelligent, but the one most responsive to change."
- Charles Darwin

BEHAVIOURS	ADAPTIVE	MALADAPTIVE
'FIGHT'	• Leading with visions of success. • Building alliances with others. • Learning new skills and acquiring new knowledge as a way to meet the demands of a job. • 'Putting in the hours' in order to meet expectations of performance. • Competing for profile and recognition. • Getting promoted. • Working at being indispensable.	• Working harder but not 'smarter'. • Winning at other's expense: getting to the 'top' of the organisation makes us less vulnerable, we're in charge, or are we? • Bullying: showing someone 'who is boss'. • Empire building: protecting ourselves from the threat of others. • Taking credit for others work/ideas.
'FLIGHT'	• Getting away from 'toxic' cultures that undermine self-esteem. • 'Cutting losses' when there is a misalignment of expectations.	• Avoiding conflict and confrontation. • Avoiding dependence upon others. • Passive aggressive behaviours such as 'switching off' in meetings. • Avoiding 'being seen'.
'FREEZE'	• Avoiding change for the sake of change?	• Hypervigilance when it comes to getting things wrong. • Not speaking out; standing out. • Procrastination.

Table 1: Fight, flight and freeze behaviours

Given the complexity of these behaviours, it is not surprising that the ways in which human energy is shaped, and manifest, has received attention from some of the great minds in the world of psychology over the last 100+ years and their influence remains with us today.

A psychodynamic view of energy

In 1874, the concept of 'psychodynamics' was proposed with the publication of 'Lectures on Physiology' by German physiologist Ernst Wilhelm von Brücke.

Influenced by the physicist Hermann von Helmholtz, one of the formulators of the first law of thermodynamics, he presented the view that all living organisms are energy systems and governed by this principle.

In 'Lectures on Physiology', he went on to propose the then radical view that the living organism is a dynamic system to which the laws of chemistry and physics apply.

At this time, Brücke was tutoring a first-year medical student at the University of Vienna called Sigmund Freud. Freud, in turn, was influenced by this new 'dynamic physiology'.

In 1920 Freud presented his views on the now familiar model of the Id, Ego and Superego in the essay 'Beyond the Pleasure Principle'. He went on the develop his thinking in a 1923 publication: *The Ego and the Id*.

Like much of Freud's work, his proposal was compelling, controversial and, as we will see, influential.

Freud describes the Id as 'the great reservoir of libido', the energy of desire, usually seen as the energy of sexual desire, that underpinned the drive for constant renewal of life or more broadly we might argue, the survival of the species. His view of a death drive or instinct, Thanatos, came later.

On the assumption that the Id, in social animals such as humans, needs to be regulated by social norms if it is to find acceptable expression, Freud described the regulators of this expression as the Ego and Superego, functions of the psyche developed through socialisation.

Moreover, this approach to understanding the ways in which the expression of energy is shaped, underpins much of our thinking about the nature of individual differences in the form of personality.

Freud's thinking was criticised by those who saw the model as beyond scientific confirmation. Nonetheless, others were influenced by his thinking.

In that same decade Carl Jung published 'On Psychical Energy' (1928) in which he presented his views upon how individual differences – 'personality' – are a reflection of the ways in which activities differentially give us energy or deplete us.

The Myers-Briggs Type Indicator grew from this view and, necessarily, the many subsequent derivatives of the MBTI.

In 1957 Eric Berne presented his model of ego states – 'Parent', 'Adult', 'Child'. Berne trained as a psychoanalyst and his thinking clearly reflects this and, within it, Freud's influence.

His model of ego states underpins Transactional Analysis, an approach to therapy that readily maps onto Freud's model of Id, Ego and Superego: Id = Free Child; Ego = Adult; Superego =Parent.

Berne's model has provided a very practical and enduring approach to focusing upon developing adaptive behaviours in relationships, as well as a framework for thinking about the origins of maladaptive behaviours; those behaviours that lead to dysfunction and emotional distress. Coaches, counsellors and psychotherapists for the last six decades will have found value in Berne's approach.

Energy as motivation

Maslow's (1943) 'Hierarchy of Needs' gives us a contrasting view of how human energy is shaped. It focuses, in a positive way, upon the human drive to channel energy into meeting basic and aspirational needs in contrast to the psychodynamic view of energy distorted and/or suppressed in ways that can lead to pathological outcomes.

Nonetheless, what the psychodynamic and Hierarchy of Needs approaches share is the view that energy not requited can lead to the subjective experience of frustration, a sense of deprivation. The notion that frustration is 'energy that can't go where it wants to' also features below in the exploration of the practical applications of The GC Index.

Maslow's Hierarchy of Needs is often portrayed in the shape of a pyramid (see Figure 1 below), with the most fundamental needs at the bottom, and the need for 'self-actualisation' at the top.

Essentially, the idea is that an individual's most basic needs must be met before they become motivated to achieve higher-level needs. Even though the ideas behind the hierarchy are Maslow's, the pyramid itself does not exist anywhere in Maslow's original work.

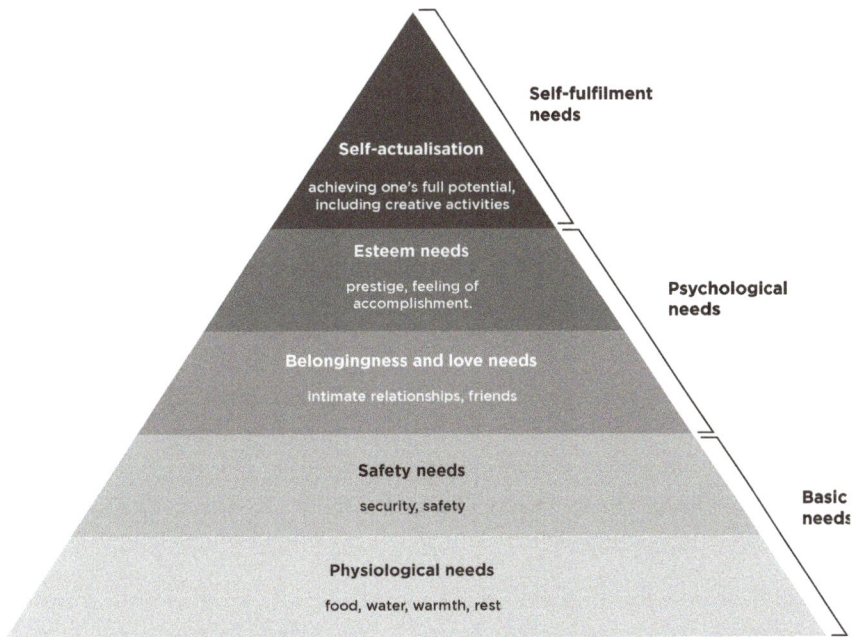

Figure 1: A representation of Maslow's Hierarchy of Needs

The most fundamental four layers of the pyramid include what Maslow called 'deficiency needs' or 'd-needs': esteem, friendship and love, security, and physical needs. If these 'deficiency needs' are not met the individual will, the argument goes, feel anxious and tense.

Deprivation is what causes deficiency, so when one has unsatisfied needs, this motivates them to fulfil what they are being denied. Maslow's idea suggests that the most basic level of needs must be met before the individual will strongly desire (or focus motivation upon) the secondary or higher-level needs.

This is then a model that describes the journey from surviving to thriving, and the overlaps between this and the 'fight-flight' approach to understanding human behaviour are evident. It adds to our understanding of how human beings channel their energy in ways that shape behaviour.

In the next chapter we will see how Maslow's view of self-actualisation has much in common, conceptually, with a GC Index view of Energy for Impact.

Herzberg's 'Motivator-Hygiene Theory' (1987) develops Maslow's thinking within a work context.

Herzberg's Motivator-Hygiene Theory, also known as the 'Two-factor theory of job satisfaction', proposes that 'hygiene factors' don't motivate people per se, but if they are not in place, they can undermine motivation. These factors could be anything, from clean toilets and comfortable chairs to a reasonable level of pay and job security.

The model takes a view of satisfaction and dissatisfaction that arises in jobs, and which are not affected by the same set of needs, but instead occur independently of each other. Herzberg's theory challenged the assumption that 'dissatisfaction was a result of an absence of factors giving rise to satisfaction'.

So motivational factors will not necessarily lower motivation but can be responsible for increasing motivation. They include, he suggests:

Intrinsic factors:

> *'Orientations toward money, recognition, competition, and the dictates of other people, and the latter includes challenge, enjoyment, personal enrichment, interest, and self-determination.'*

Extrinsic factors:

> *'Doing something because it leads to a distinct outcome, some-*
> *thing external you expect to receive, and the latter refers to doing*
> *something because it is inherently interesting or enjoyable, an*
> *internal reward.'*

Herzberg's 1968 publication 'One More Time: How Do You Motivate Employees?' had sold 1.2 million reprints by 1987 and was, at that time, the most requested article from the *Harvard Business Review*.

Herzberg's drivers or motivators readily equate to Maslow's needs for esteem and self-actualisation presented in a work setting; we see in his thinking the ways in which energy is channelled into making work satisfying and fulfilling.

Moreover, the approach brings a practical focus to understanding what 'self-actualisation' means to an individual in their world of work.

Similar thinking will have shaped the emergence of the concept of 'the psychological contract' and employee engagement surveys; theories and practice designed to support and develop the engagement and motivation of people at work in the hope of increasing productivity and retention.

While this thinking can bring a practical approach to shaping an individual's Energy for Impact, it also highlights the complexity of human motivation, the number of intrinsic and extrinsic variables that can play a part in motivating or demotivating all of us.

Energy channelled into learning and adaptation

To revisit Darwin's proposal noted above:

> *'It is not the most intellectual of the species that survives; it is not*
> *the strongest that survives; but the species that survives is the*
> *one that is able best to adapt and adjust to the changing environ-*
> *ment in which it finds itself.'*

Darwin (1859)

Given Darwin's emphasis upon the importance of adaptation for survival in a changing world, it's not surprising that the themes of learning, adaptation, change and growth have been the subject of enquiry for many psychologists and philosophers.

The equation is this:

- Survival requires the efficient and effective use of energy, energy fuels survival.
- This efficient and effective use of energy is reflected in the human ability to learn, adapt and master the world.
- That process of learning is shaped by many variables that humans experience as thinking, feeling and doing.

For the American psychologist George Kelly part of the complexity of how we learn is a product of how we make sense of our world. Efficient learning, in part, assumes the potential to make sense of patterns and trends in our world and to use our understanding to make predictions about future events. This assumption of causality is the basis for learning, adaptation and, potentially, growth.

In 1955 Kelly published *The Psychology of Personal Constructs*. The main thrust of his proposition was that human beings can be likened to 'amateur scientists' who seek to make sense of our social world. This 'making sense' then, would be more likely to be experiential and unique rather than wholly derived.

Given this, our view of others would be unique, meaning that the perception of another's personality would be 'in the eye of the beholder' and this unique view would shape our predictions about others and our interactions with them.

Take, by way of illustration, the theme of trust. Making judgements about whether or not we can trust someone can be key to both surviving and thriving.

We may base that judgement on a few, very superficial constructs such as the shape of someone's ears having 'learned' that people with certain shaped ears cannot be trusted. This approach to learning is limiting in terms of missed opportunities and leaves the learner vulnerable should this view of causality not be reliable.

A complex set of constructs using, for example, eight constructs to determine someone's trustworthiness, may also be less than optimal, leading to indecision and passivity, not the basis for thriving.

It's possible to see, from this very brief description, how Personal Construct Theory lends itself to a range of psychotherapeutic interventions, cognitive behavioural therapy (CBT) for example. People could, given the theory, potentially, change their view of the world and in so doing change the way they interact with, think about and feel about others and their reactions to them.

This very positive view of human nature takes on a broader horizon in the world of enquiry known as Social Learning Theory.

Social Learning Theory was influenced by the work of behavioural psychologists in the 1950s and 1960s and was pioneered by Albert Bandura. For Bandura the question went beyond 'how do people make sense of the world?' to 'how does sense-making shape the ways in which people learn?'

Bandura rejected the simplistic behaviourist notion that human learning could be explained by the processes of Pavlovian or operant conditioning alone. His view was that learning needed to take account of the complexities of human cognition.

As with Freud's notion of Id, Ego and Superego, we have seen how Social Learning Theory has developed, not surprisingly perhaps, into a very complex area of enquiry.

From Bandura's early thinking developed the concept of 'self-efficacy', a key variable that influences the individual's approach to learning and acting upon that learning.

The essence of Bandura's thinking is captured in this quote:

'The development of a sense of personal agency begins in infancy and moves from the perception of the causal relationship between events, to an understanding that actions produce results, to the recognition that they can be the origin of actions that effect their environments. As children's understanding of language increases, so does their capacity for symbolic thought and, therefore, their capacity for self-awareness and a sense of personal agency.'

Bandura, 1997

So, the basic premise of self-efficacy is that 'people's beliefs in their capabilities to produce desired effects by their own actions' are the most important determinants of the behaviours people choose to engage in and how much they persevere in their efforts in the face of obstacles and challenges.

This view echoes the famous Henry Ford quote:

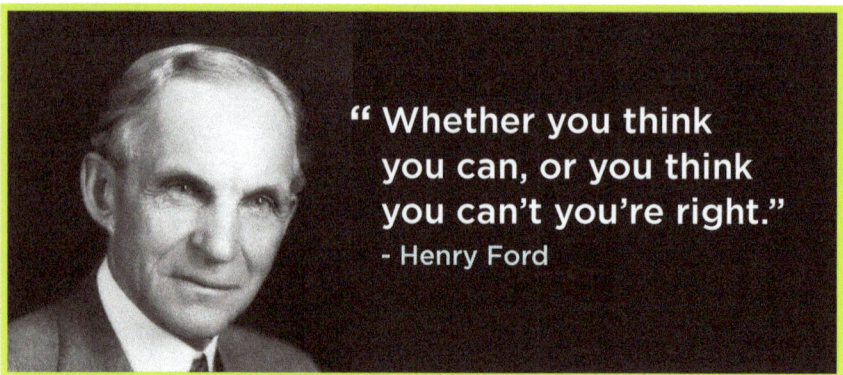

" Whether you think you can, or you think you can't you're right."
- Henry Ford

The relevance of this thinking for the ways in which people survive and thrive in their world is evident. Social Learning Theory broadly, helps us to understand the ways in which energy is channelled into learning.

Not surprisingly, this concept has been the subject of a good deal of research with the suggestion that perceptions of self-efficacy play a role in psychological adjustment, psychological problems, and physical health.

Self-efficacy then, seeks to understand the relationship between how someone responds to events based upon their anticipation of those events. Individual differences when it comes to learning from past events has been the subject of enquiry known as attribution theory and as we might expect, it has proved to be a fascinating challenge for researchers to discern how anticipatory beliefs develop from past experiences.

In psychology, the term attribution has two meanings: the first refers to explanations of behaviour; the second refers to inferences.

> *'What the two meanings have in common is a process of assigning: in attribution as an explanation, a behavior is assigned to its cause; in attribution as inference, a quality or attribute is assigned to the agent on the basis of observed behavior.'*
>
> Malle, 2011, p. 17

Put simply an attributional and explanatory style is the way in which an individual explains their circumstances to themselves and, in this sense, it's easy to see the influence of George Kelly's work on Personal Construct Theory (1963) on this line of thinking.

The theory has developed over time, shaped by influential psychologists such as: Heider (1958), Rotter (1966), Kelley (1972), Weiner (1972, 1985), Maier and Seligman (1976).

In its most developed form, attribution theory highlights three variables that will shape an individual's assumptions of causality, why events happen in their world. These are:

1. **Internal vs External Locus of Control**

   Locus of Control was originally proposed by Rotter (1966) as a generalised and enduring belief about how responsive and controllable our environment is.

   Locus of control is a continuous scale; at one end are individuals who attribute success or failure to things they perceive that they have control over, at the other end are those who attribute their success or failure to forces outside of their control: to luck and/or 'powerful others'.

2. **Stable vs Unstable (Permanence)**

   This dimension is the degree to which we attribute outcome causality to temporary or temporally fixed factors. Weiner (1972) drew a distinction between stable versus unstable causes. A stable attribution occurs when an individual believes an outcome will persist indefinitely. An unstable attribution occurs when an outcome is attributed to a transient factor, specific to a period of time.

3. **Global vs Specific (Pervasiveness)**

   This dimension was introduced by Kelley (1972) who focused on attributions of global versus specific causes for events. The global-ity dimension indicates a tendency to generalise events, with the expectation that these events will continue to occur in other aspects of life.

Here's an example of how these variables can play out in the real world: when my son failed his first driving test, he declared that he was 'unlucky' (External Locus of Control) on that particular day (Unstable and Specific). When he passed his second test, his announced that he was the best (Internal Locus of Control; Stable) driver in the world (Global).

The work of Overmier and Seligman (1967) is significant for the purpose of this book in a very particular way. They explored the role that 'Explanatory Styles' can play in mediating positive and negative mental states and, in doing so, formulated a model of 'Learned Helplessness'. This thinking evolved with the work of Abramson, Semmel, Seligman, & Von Baeyer (1978) who took the view that the attributional variables of locus of control, stability versus instability and global versus specific, would be influenced by the predispositions of optimism and pessimism.

Energy channelled into potency: Energy for Impact

The 'Learned Helplessness' model supports the evolutionary view, described above, of the importance of energy for survival. The model and associated research demonstrate the dramatic consequences that can come from believing (attributional and explanatory styles) that we cannot have an impact upon our world: that we behave as if helpless, that we lack energy and that we 'feel' depressed.

So, how can we understand energy channelled into impact, channelled in ways that leave individuals feeling potent in their world rather than help-less?

The following chapter presents that next step in this journey of enquiry into human energy with the history and development of The GC Index. The GC Index profiles individual differences when it comes to Energy for Impact, the ways in which human beings seek to have an impact in their world.

Chapter 2

The GC Index and Energy for Impact

The history and science behind the development of this ground-breaking organimetric profiling individual Energy for Impact.

Dr John Mervyn-Smith

A note about this chapter

The chapters that follow will present the ways in which The GC Index has been used to understand the varied manifestations of Energy for Impact at work for individuals, teams and organisations.

This chapter will give you an understanding of how The GC Index model works but you may want to use it for reference as you read subsequent chapters.

Research phase 1: understanding 'Game Changers'

The GC Index journey started in 2012.

Nathan Ott, director at the time of the London-based search firm eg1, had several client organisations who had expressed an interest in recruiting people who could 'drive transformational change' within organisations and as consultants to others. They wanted to know more about these individuals; how to identify, recruit and retain them.

These organisations were still suffering the after-effects of the 2008 banking crisis and wanted to find a 'competitive edge' within their markets. 'Game Changers' as they had tagged them, were seen as a possible solution.

In an evolutionary sense, this quest made sense: organisations, like all living organisms, survive and thrive when they have the capability to develop, change and adapt; Game Changers were seen as those people who could drive transformational change through creativity and innovation.

This view was also consistent with the Darwinian view of surviving and thriving discussed in Chapter 1.

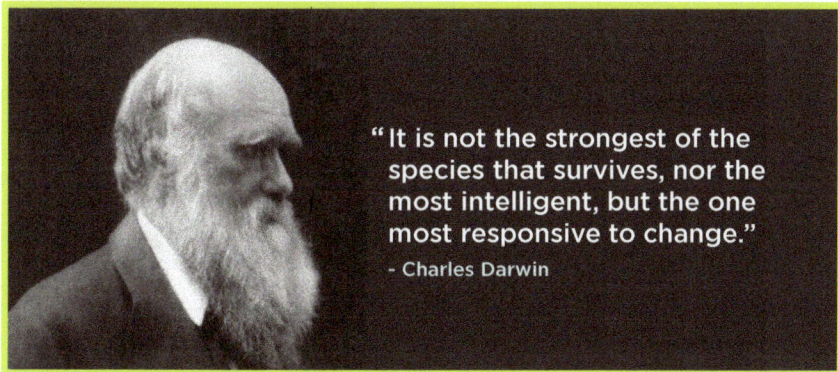

"It is not the strongest of the species that survives, nor the most intelligent, but the one most responsive to change."
- Charles Darwin

We might argue that there was enough anecdotal evidence to support the view that these people existed; the Apple video – 'Here's to the crazy ones' is an example of such evidence.

So too, was the story of Paul Buchheit, a Google engineer in 2001. It illustrates the potential and power of people to make a game-changing, transformational impact on organisations. He started using his '20% time' (the one day a week Google allowed staff to work on new projects) to develop a new product. Initially codenamed Caribou, the product was, after nearly three years of development, released as Gmail and would reinvent the entire web-based email category, capturing 53% of the market.

Gmail, at the time, was one of Google's most successful products and was not an idea formulated by management and developed in a classic top-down waterfall manner. Developing an email product was not even part of Google's corporate strategy at the time. It was one engineer's 'passion project', driven by the belief that email services should be better.

It is an example of how one Game Changer can positively transform the destiny of not just one organisation but an entire industry.

Nonetheless, inherent in this interest were the assumptions that these individuals existed in the 'real world of work' and given the tag of Game Changer, that they had defining and differentiating characteristics.

These two questions became the focus for a series of research projects funded by eg1 and supervised by me.

The methodology for this research was influenced, in part, by the work of researchers like Warren Bennis and Burt Nanus who developed our understanding of leadership and, specifically, what leaders actually do with an emphasis upon observation and deduction.

This approach seeks to understand the world as it actually is, rather than seeks to impose conceptual models upon it. It's an approach that allows data to shape our understanding rather than have our understanding shape the data.

Given the broad methodological approach then, our questions for exploration were:

- Do these individuals who drive transformational change through creativity and innovation – people tagged as Game Changers – exist in the corporate world?
- If they do, what characteristics differentiate them from their colleagues?
- Can we assess these characteristics in a meaningful way, a way that can support the identification, recruitment, retention and development of these individuals?

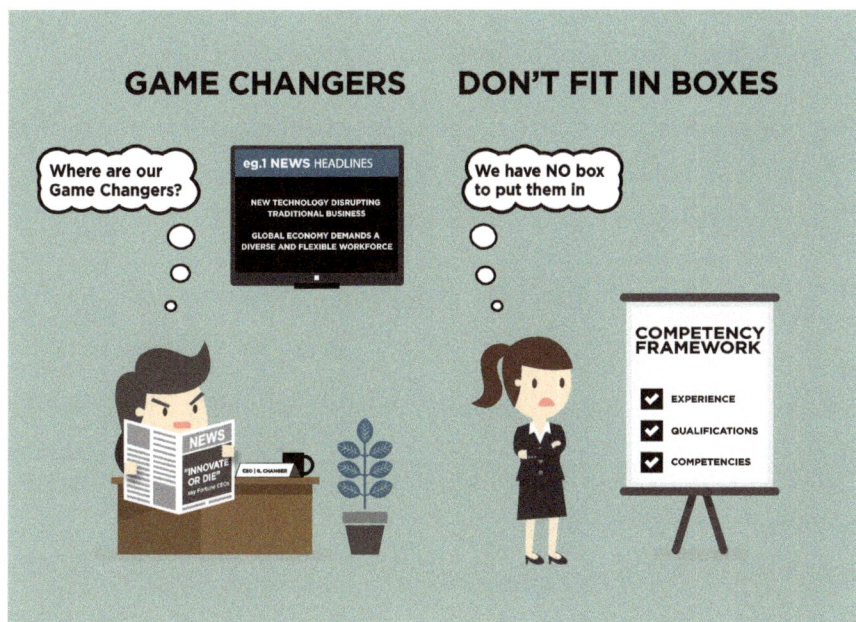

The research methodology together with the full results are described in the study: 'The DNA of a Game Changer'. It can be downloaded from www.TheGCIndex.com.

In brief, and consistent with a belief in a deductive approach to scientific endeavour, we gathered data from hundreds of 1:1 interviews using a data capture methodology based upon a repertory grid approach that reflects the essence of George Kelly's Personal Construct Theory. We wanted to capture people's experience of Game Changers, if, indeed, they had them!

The key findings to emerge from this first phase of our research, and presented in Duke University's Corporate Education Journal *Dialogue* were as follows:

1. Game Changers do exist in the corporate world, working at all levels of an organisation; this was what our interviewees reported.
2. Game Changers are different: they have characteristics that differentiate them, in a statistically significant way, from colleagues described, in our interviews, as 'high potentials' and successful

senior executives. Our interviewees' descriptions of Game Changers created a convergent and coherent picture.

The characteristics described by our interviewees seemed to 'cluster' into two main constructs: imagination and obsession.

- Imagination: a capacity for original ideas; the ability to see possibilities that others don't.
- Obsession: an obsessive, compulsive nature that drives them to turn ideas into reality.

You may recognise these qualities in people you know or have worked with, or perhaps yourself. We did at the time of doing the research: James Dyson's book *Against the Odds: An Autobiography* (1997) certainly brought these qualities to life.

Dyson challenged all the rules to achieve success and, in his words:

> *'The key to success is failure … not other people's failure but how you respond to failure yourself.'*

Giving up was never an option for Dyson; he believed in something and was going to make it happen.

There was also Maxine Clark in our thoughts. She was the founder of Build-A-Bear Workshop who features in *The Transformative CEO: Impact Lessons from Industry Game Changers* by Jeffrey J. Fox and Robert Reiss.

Maxine talked about how she followed her dream with passion. She says:

> *'When a 10-year-old girl innocently asked, "Why can't we make our own teddy bears?", the lightbulb flashed. My dream for Build-A-Bear Workshop was born. Every adult I asked about the idea said it would not work.'*

So, the headline view from 18 months of research suggested that Game Changers were imaginative and obsessive! Not a surprising outcome perhaps, but in line with my experience of science in the sense that, more often than not, it supports a 'common sense' view rather than reveals a counter-intuitive truth.

A trawl of the literature also revealed that much had been written on the topic of imagination and much on the topic of obsession. Of more interest was the fact that we didn't come across any research that gave us a picture of how these constructs interacted. We were left with the view that it was possible to be imaginative but not obsessive and vice versa and with only anecdotal views, like those above, of how the constructs 'came together'.

Moreover, one aspect of the original challenge on understanding Game Changers remained: 'how could we help organisations to identify, recruit, manage and nurture them?' It was not enough to say that they are imaginative and obsessive, we wanted to find a more sophisticated way of measuring these characteristics.

Consistent with the tradition of psychological research, we sought a way of measuring these individual differences through subjective self-report; a questionnaire.

Our literature review helped Nathan Ott and I to prepare a series of questions designed to measure these two constructs. We wanted to test the hypothesis that Game Changers would see themselves as imaginative and obsessive and, if they did, shed more detail upon associated characteristics.

Research phases 2 and 3: the emergence of The GC Index

With a set of 58 questions for reliably measuring the two key constructs of imagination and obsession, our approach was to gather data from a sample of 400 volunteers in order to examine the distribution of responses to the questions set. This revealed a diverse set of responses: within this large group, people saw themselves differently in terms of imagination and obsession.

This initial exploration then, suggested that we may be measuring real differences. While we persisted with the hypothesis that Game Changers would see themselves as imaginative and obsessive our presentation of these data to learning and development specialists encouraged us to consider other patterns within the data. 'What does it mean,' they asked, 'if someone does not see themself as obsessive and/or imaginative?'

These questions led to a third phase of research, which consisted of adding data to our sample in order to see if we could we make any meaningful sense of why people score 'low' on imagination and/or obsession.

At this point The GC Index model developed from a factor analysis of data from an initial sample of 1000 people which was subsequently re-examined with a sample of n = 7880.[1]

These statistical analyses revealed an underlying structure within our data with four factors emerging, grouping responses of people together who saw themselves as:

- Imaginative and obsessive
- Imaginative and not obsessive
- Not imaginative but obsessive
- Neither imaginative nor obsessive.

We needed then to explore the question: does this statistical map reflect the real world? Our initial examination of the four factors suggested a tentative description of each factor that gave us a starting point for this enquiry. These were:

- Factor 1: describes people who are imaginative and obsessive who we called 'Game Changers'.
- Factor 2: describes people who are obsessive but not imaginative and who we called 'Polishers'.
- Factor 3: describes people who are imaginative but not obsessive and who we called 'Strategists'.
- Factor 4: describes people who are neither imaginative nor obsessive and who we called 'Implementers'.

---

[1] This was the beginning of The GC Index framework and its technical development, which is described in more detail in 'The GC Index: The Technical Story So Far' which is available via info@thegcindex.com on request.

This representation of the data at this point in our research is presented in Figure 1 below.

THE GC INDEX: PROCLIVITIES

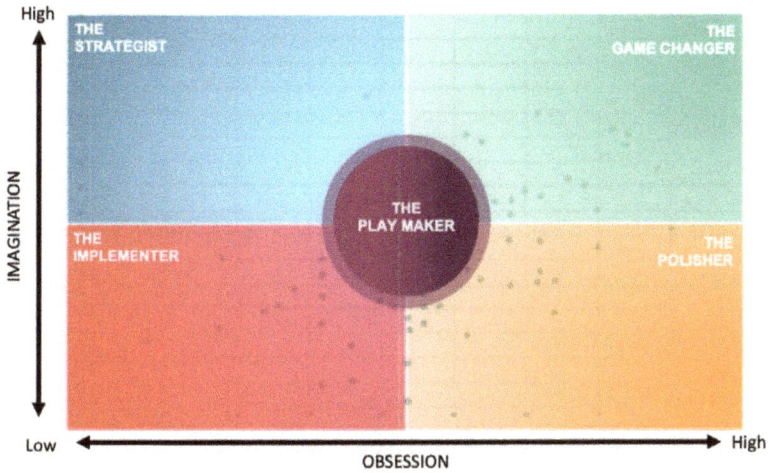

Figure 1: The GC Index model at the end of research phase 2

Phase 3 of our research consisted of series of focus groups which were then used to test the veracity of the model. More specifically we invited groups of people to review their profiles to emerge from the question-naire; to explore its accuracy and to add comments to the ways in which these constructs were manifest in their day-to-day lives. From these focus groups we learned:

1. There was a high degree of convergence between their profiles and the ways in which they behaved day to day; people saw their profiles as accurate.
2. The ways in which people described the manifestation of the char-acteristics led to the view that, in broad terms, the instrument was measuring individual differences when it comes to Energy for Impact: the ways which people like to make an impact upon their world. I will discuss this finding in more detail below.
3. That the model was incomplete. A number of individuals whose profiles plotted midway on both dimensions of imagination and

obsession, described the influence of their relationships upon the manifestation of their energy in these areas. Whether or not they were imaginative or obsessive or a mixture of both, they described how these characteristics would be shaped by a need for a degree of harmony in their relationships, a need for cohesion and groups and often manifest as an inclusive and involving approach to working with others. Given their descriptions, we called these individuals 'Play Makers'.

Figure 2 below was the culmination of these early phases of research. We, along with The GC Index community, have continued to develop an understanding of the ways in which the five GC Index proclivities are manifest. This understanding is the focus for the remainder of this book.

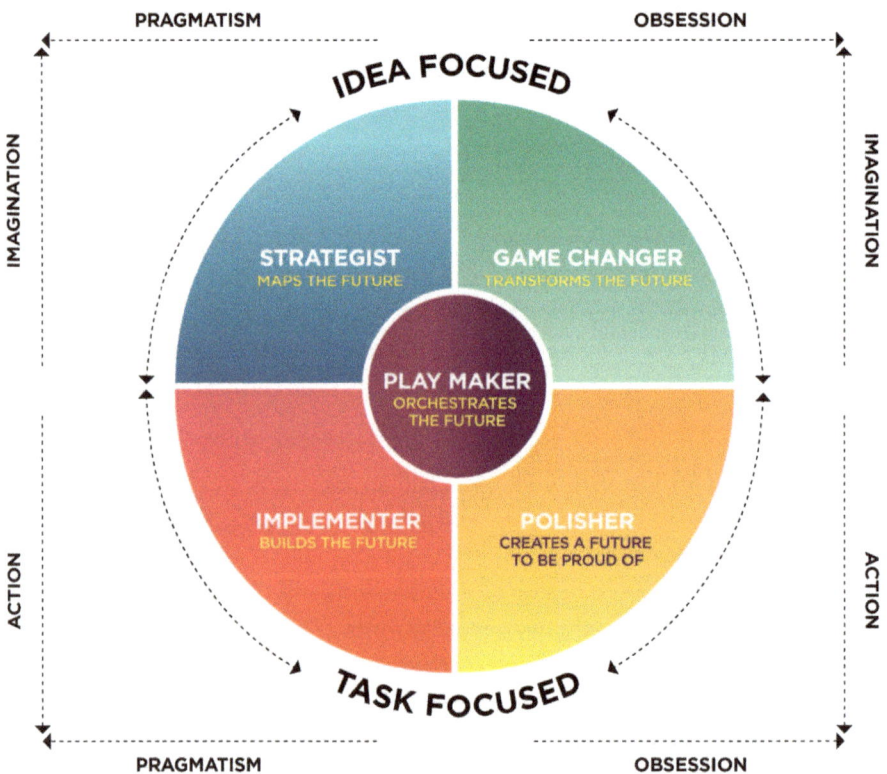

Figure 2: The GC Index model at research phase 3

The framework describes five proclivities that reflect individual differences when it comes to channelling energy, the basis for making an impact.

The GC Index then, measures proclivities not competence.

These five proclivities suggest individual differences in the following ways:

Strategists

- Bring energy to making sense of patterns and trends in events and data, looking for causal relationships.

Game Changers

- Bring energy to new ideas and possibilities, to original thinking.

Play Makers

- Bring energy to seeking consensus in groups that leads to a sense of cohesion.

Implementers

- Bring energy to delivering tangible outcomes.

Polishers

- Bring energy to review, learning, continuous improvement, and the pursuit of excellence.

Energy for Impact

Consistent with the nature of scientific enquiry perhaps, a journey that started with a desire to understand Game Changers led to an understanding of the expression of human energy. As noted in Chapter 1, this interest in human energy is not a new one but this research gave us a new perspective. This evolving view of our understanding is presented in broad summary on page 28.

Understanding the psychology of energy: a historical journey

UNDERSTANDING THE PSYCHOLOGY OF ENERGY- AN HISTORICAL CONTEXT

PSYCHODYNAMIC ENERGY	ENERGY AS PERSONALITY	ENERGY AS MOTIVATION	ENERGY AS SELF EFFICACY	ENERGY AS WELLBEING	ENERGY FOR IMPACT
The energy of neuroses	Approach and avoidance behaviours	'Surviving and Thriving'	Learning and adaptability	Energy correlates of mental health	Energy for Impact
• Freud (1923)	• Jung • Berne	• Maslow • Herzberg	• Bandura • Rotter • Dweck	• Seligman	• The GC Index (2013)

The GC Index framework then measures and describes five proclivities: five different ways in which people are inclined to make an impact and contribution.

These five proclivities are described in more detail below. As you read about the behaviours associated with each proclivity, bear in mind that these behaviours are a product of an individual's assumptions about the world, their values and beliefs, 'internal dialogue' – what people say to themselves about their actions and impact upon the world. See Figure 3 below.

STRATEGIST
MAPS
THE FUTURE

THE GC INDEX PROCLIVITIES

RESULTING IMPACT

A STRATEGIST'S DRIVERS ARE:

1. **They need to make sense of events in their world.**

   · A Strategist will look for patterns and trends in their world in order to correlate events in a way that helps them to predict the future in a way that makes sense to them.

2. **They need for things to be predictable.**

   · A Strategist assumes causality between events – "if this, then that". Ambiguity makes them feel uncomfortable.

   'The past shapes our future'

POSITIVE IMPACT:

• At their best they will create compelling visions for the future.

• They can bring direction and focus to action in a purposeful way; they bring the 'why' of action.

• They bring structure and order to what might otherwise be chaotic situations.

NEGATIVE IMPACT:

• Once they have made up their mind the Strategist's need to make sense may mean that they are no longer open to the influence of others; they will be seen as rigid in their opinions.

• They can slow down action with their need to get their own clarity.

• They may struggle to just 'try things and see what happens'.

GAME CHANGER
TRANSFORMS THE FUTURE

THE GC INDEX PROCLIVITIES

A GAME CHANGER'S DRIVERS ARE:

1. The need for creative expression; to express their ideas, thoughts and feelings in an uncensored way.

   • They see possibilities which might seem unrealistic or intangible to others.

2. The freedom to be expressive in a way that brings about change.

   • Game changers work best in a 'safe to fail' cultures that encourages experimentation in innovation and creativity.

   'Freedom is the oxygen of possibilities'

RESULTING IMPACT

POSITIVE IMPACT:

• They are possibility-centred. They see possibilities in ways that others often don't.

• They generate original ideas that can be creative, supporting transformational change.

• They can help organisations to reinvent themselves with their creative ideas.

NEGATIVE IMPACT:

• They can see things with such clarity that they can become fixated with turning an idea into a reality; this can be disruptive.

• They may struggle to accept that an idea may not be relevant or timely when it comes to organisational objectives.

• They can lose interest and become visibly bored when the strategic details are being articulated.

PLAY MAKER
ORCHESTRATES THE FUTURE

THE GC INDEX PROCLIVITIES

A PLAY MAKER'S DRIVERS ARE:

1. They take responsibility for building cohesion in teams.

   • Play Makers have strong values about the importance of the group.

2. Valuing others.

   • Play Makers care that people are valued for the contribution they can make and the contribution that they could make.

   'One for all and all for one'.

RESULTING IMPACT

POSITIVE IMPACT:

• They build cohesion in a way that is inclusive and involving.

• They build consensus in a way that drives individual and collective performance through collaboration.

• They can challenge colleagues to be at their best and having the 'tough conversations' when colleagues are 'letting the side down'.

NEGATIVE IMPACT:

• They fail to align the needs of the individual with the needs of the group.

• They seek cohesion even if it is built upon an illusion of harmony rather than healthy conflict.

• They can be perceived to be abdicating personal responsibility when insisting on collaboration.

IMPLEMENTER
BUILDS
THE FUTURE

THE GC INDEX PROCLIVITIES

RESULTING IMPACT

AN IMPLEMENTER'S DRIVERS ARE:

1. An impatience to achieve results.

   • Implementers are driven to make a tangible impact upon their world; to get things done

2. The value based upon pragmatic outcomes.

   • They don't allow perfection to be the 'enemy of good enough'.

   'Just do it'

• **POSITIVE IMPACT:**

   » They effectively deliver tangible outcomes that support organisational goals.

   • They bring focused energy and urgency to action.

   » They help teams to convert strategic plans into plans of action.

NEGATIVE IMPACT:

   • They are busy 'doing their own thing', not aligned to team objectives.

   » Their urgency for action undermines debate and decision making.

   • They stifle the development of others in their urgency to get started.

POLISHER
CREATES A FUTURE
TO BE PROUD OF

THE GC INDEX PROCLIVITIES

RESULTING IMPACT

A POLISHER'S DRIVERS ARE:

1. That things can always be better.

   • Polishers struggle to settle for 'good enough' and will set high standards for themselves.

2. 'If I'm going to do this, I'm going to do this brilliantly'.

   • Polishers have energy for review, learning, continuous improvement and the pursuit of excellence.

   'If a job is worth doing it's worth doing properly'.

POSITIVE IMPACT:

   • They focus upon innovation through continuous improvement and the 'pursuit of excellence'.

   • They can inspire others to greater things when they set high standards for themselves and others.

   • They are role models for review, learning and development.

NEGATIVE IMPACT:

   • They inhibit others with a critical and demanding nature.

   • They allow 'perfection to be the enemy of good enough'.

   • They procrastinate when they feel things are not 'good enough'.

Figure 3: The GC Index proclivities

We have with The GC Index then, a more detailed and refined way of understanding the ways in which human beings channel energy but a way that is consistent with the core principles described above, namely that the human need to be potent – to survive and thrive – takes different and definable forms.

Energy for Impact, learning, motivation and personality

So, The GC Index view of Energy for Impact has grown from, and is consistent with, over a 100 years of enquiry in the world of psychology into the nature of human energy.

If we use this understanding of people as a starting point, it also helps us to link the model to past-thinking on personality and motivation. This relationship is presented in Figure 4 below, reproduced with permission from its creator Shantonu Chundur.

This example will help us to explore the point here: two individuals have similar GC Index profiles; they both have a strong Implementer proclivity: they bring energy and urgency to getting things done in a task-focused way. Can we assume that their Implementer actions reflect the same motives? The diagram below highlights that actions are the product of a complex set of motives, and this is the picture that has emerged from exploring with people the underlying drivers of their GC Index proclivities.

More specifically, our two Implementers may *look alike* and while they will often report some shared drivers, they will also report different ones. So, for example, while Implementers will often report shared values such a belief in 'good enough' delivery or valuing the 'tried and tested' one might report that they are motivated by a strong sense of responsibility, another needs for control or 'personal glory'.

With all five proclivities we can speculate about the underlying drives and motivations. Our interest was in describing behaviours, so The GC Index is presented as an organimetric which measures Energy for Impact. We feel this is a critical difference when comparing to typical psychometrics measuring personality. Moreover, we shall see in coming chapters the relevance to organisations of being able to measure the collective Energy for Impact of teams and groups.

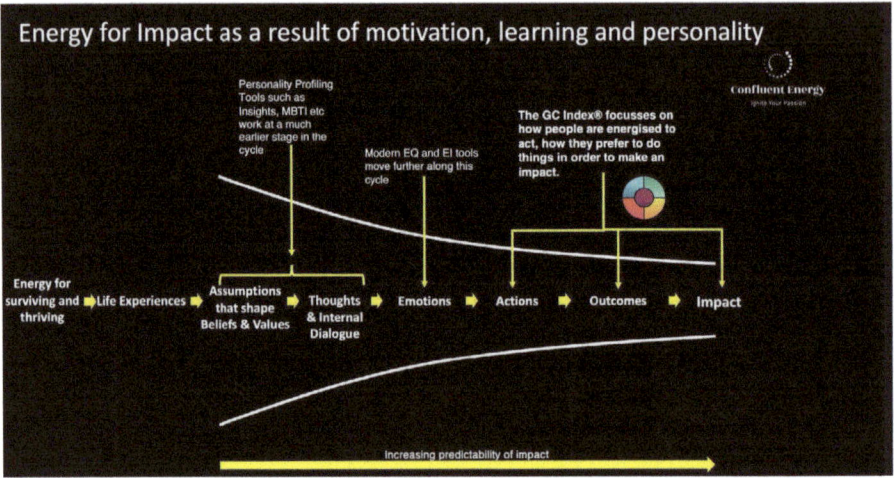

Energy for Impact as a result of motivation, learning and personality

Figure 4: A representation of the relationship of GC Index Energy for Impact with aspects of personality

An example of The GC Index profile

At this point an example profile may help you to crystallise your understanding of The GC Index and give you a more concrete sense of how it works.

The mechanics of a GC Index profile: in the profile for Joanna (below) you will see a score in the 1–10 range (a STEN score) for each of the five proclivities. The scores are based upon a normal distribution of raw scores responses to the 58-item questionnaire and are, largely, independent of each other. This means that there are 80,000+ different combinations of scores.

The scores reflect the strength of that proclivity: a high score suggests a strong Energy for Impact for that proclivity; a low score suggests a weak Energy for Impact for that proclivity. The scores do not reflect competence.

In Figure 5 (opposite) I have presented Joanna's profile. She is in the early stages of her career in a customer-services role in an energy company. She had thrived in her previous role trouble-shooting high-profile customer complaints: she had enjoyed the pace of the action (Implementer) and the contribution that she was making to the company's visionary purpose (Strategist).

She enjoyed the pressure to come up with creative solutions to practical problems (Game Changer/Implementer); she was thriving and seen as a future company leader. In her new role she was struggling. Rather than being 'out and about' fixing problems, she was working on her own in an office, focused upon checking detailed customer-service contracts. The role, which would lend itself to a Polisher proclivity, was depleting her, not feeding her.

Her manager was concerned by her loss of energy for the job but she, and Joanna, used her profile to understand what was happening and find a practical solution. Joanna's story is not an untypical one and demonstrates the utility of The GC Index for understanding Energy for Impact.

In the chapters that follow you will be presented with a number of different GC Index profiles reflecting the many and varied manifestations of human beings' Energy for Impact

Figure 5: Joanna's GC Index profile

Bibliography and References (Chapters 1 and 2)

Abramson, L. Y., Seligman, M. E. P., and Teasdale, J. D., 'Learned Help-lessness in Humans: Critique and Reformulation', *Journal of Abnormal Psychology*, 87, 1978, pp. 49–74

Bandura, A., *Self-Efficacy: The Exercise of Control*, W. H. Freeman, New York, 1997

Bennis, W., and Nanus, B., *Leaders: The Strategies for Taking Charge*, Harper & Row, New York, 1985

Berne, E., 'Ego States in Psychotherapy', *American Journal of Psycho-therapy*, 11 (2), 1957, pp. 293–309

Dyson, J., *Against the Odds: An Autobiography*, Orion Business, 1997

Freud, S., 'Beyond the Pleasure Principle', *Standard Edition*, Vol. 18, Hogarth, London, 1920, pp. 7–64

Heider, F., *The Psychology of Interpersonal Relations*, John Wiley & Sons Inc., 1958

Herzberg, F., 'One More Time: How Do You Motivate Employees?', *Harvard Business Review*, 46, 1968, pp. 53–62

Herzberg, F., Mausner, B., and Snyderman, B., *The Motivation to Work,* (2nd edn), John Wiley & Sons Inc., New York, 1959

Jung, C. G., 'On Psychical Energy', A paper in: Jung, C. G., *Contributions to Analytical Psychology*, Harcourt, Brace and Company, 1928

Kelly, G. A., *A Theory of Personality: The Psychology of Personal Constructs*, W. W. Norton, 1955

Kelly, H. H., *Causal Schemata and the Attribution Process*, General Learn-ing Press, Morristown, NJ, 1972

Malle, B. F., 'Attribution Theories: How People Make Sense of Behavior', Chadee, D. (ed.), *Theories in Social Psychology*, Wiley-Blackwell, 2011, pp. 72–95

Maier, S. F., and Seligman, M. E. P., 'Learned Helplessness: Theory and Evidence', *Journal of Experimental Psychology*, 105, 1976, pp. 3–46

Maslow, A. H., 'A Theory of Human Motivation', *Psychological Review*, 50, 1943, pp. 370–396

Mervyn-Smith, J., and Ott, N. O., *Coaching Me Coaching You*, self-published, 2018, The GC Index Ltd, ISBN-13: 978-1-5272-2713-2, ISBN: 1-5272-2713-8

Overmier, J. B., and Seligman, M. E. P., 'Effects of Inescapable Shock Upon Subsequent Escape and Avoidance Learning', *Journal of Comparative and Physiological Psychology*, 63, pp. 23–33, 1967

Rotter, J. B., 'Generalized Expectancies for Internal Versus External Control of Reinforcement', *Psychological Monographs*, 80 (1), 1, 1966

von Brücke, E. W., 'Lectures on Physiology', 1874

Weiner, B., *Theories of Motivation: From Mechanism to Cognition*, General Learning Press, Morristown, NJ, 1972

Weiner, B., *An Attributional Theory of Motivation and Emotion*, Springer Verlag, New York, 1985

Section 2:

Individuals at Their Most Productive at Work

Chapter 3

Harnessing the Power of Flow and Energy for Impact

A 'deep dive' into the connection between our Energy for Impact and the coveted state of 'flow', and its relevance for both individual and team success.

Roxana Radulescu

Flow

I was mesmerised watching the artistic skating championships as a teenager. Actually, I think I was mesmerised watching any kind of high-level sports competition, starting with gymnastics (not surprising, since I'm Romanian born).

I was born after Nadia Comaneci got the first ever 'perfect 10' in gymnastics, but re-watching the routine that she did back then might just fascinate you today, as much as it did others watching her in 1976, during the Olympics in Montreal.[2]

So, starting with gymnastics as a child, and then continuing with skating as a teenager, I realised I was mesmerised by some of the performances I was watching.

Talking about the Olympics, I vividly remember watching the performance of the Japanese figure skater Yuzuru Hanyu, and feeling like I was there, on the ice, with him. I also remember his short interview after the performance, and the reporter asking him, 'What did you say to yourself to keep going over there?' to which he said, 'Well, I don't know, I don't know what I did there, I just know I felt great just being there and skating.'[3]

---

[2] Nadia Comaneci – first perfect 10 in history (1976 Montreal), https://www.youtube.com/watch?v=4m2YT-PIkEc

[3] Yuzuru Hanyu (JPN) – Gold Medal, Men's Figure Skating, Free Programme, PyeongChang 2018, https://www.youtube.com/watch?v=23EfsN7vEOA

To me, watching him skate felt like I was 'flowing', too. And I caught myself thinking: 'So that's how you do it!' I'm not sure I was clear about what I meant when I said that, but I realised later that what I meant was 'that's how you tap into your power to perform at your best'.

That triggered my curiosity on what makes people set high standards and deliver at high standards, while enjoying what they're doing, making a difference, showing us something that has never been done that way before: making a difference their way and loving it!

And you know how the story goes: what you focus on, expands. For me, that meant that now I could always see and feel when people were in flow.

I could feel the flow in an actor's performance, for example, as I was also getting into a state of flow just watching that performance.

Watching a band on stage performing their songs in a way they hadn't before and which made them feel in flow, also reached me in the audience differently; to me they were transformed, different from what I knew about them.

I also recall watching a tennis game between Simona Halep and someone else; I don't remember who, but that's not the point. It was a game Simona was serving in, and I could see her focused and enjoying her game – maybe because it was a joy to just watch her play. So, she kept serving and playing, running for the ball, scoring points, and getting ready to serve again. At one point the umpire intervened and said, 'Ms Halep, that was the last point of this game, no more serves left.' She reacted with an 'Oh!' and a smile and headed towards her bench. She was so focused on her game that she never paid attention to the scoreboard, and would have kept going if it had not been for the umpire's intervention.

And, of course, I couldn't help noticing it in those close to me: my husband, who's an IT guy, and who can work for hours on end in front of a screen to get something fixed for someone at the other end of the screen. The world could 'crumble' and he wouldn't know. Those are moments when I can say anything to him and he would totally agree with me.

My visual artist child, drawing or painting something he wants to do, responding to my question 'are you going to eat something?' with a telegraphic 'no, no, not now, later, need to do this'.

My performing artist whom I didn't even recognise there on the stage, being transformed and transported into a role and taking the audience with him.

And me – but I will tell you that story when we look at the elements of flow later on in this chapter.

Because, yes, all these examples describe what we call the state of 'flow' which, as defined by psychologist Mihalyi Csikszentmihalyi, is 'the state in which people are so involved in an activity that nothing else seems to matter; the experience itself is so enjoyable that people will do it, even at great cost, for the sheer sake of doing it.'

But that's not all, there's more to it! You might also know it as 'optimal experience', 'being in the zone', 'peak experiences', 'runner's high', 'being unconscious', 'the forever box', etc.

And, in this chapter, we delve into the profound link between our Energy for Impact and the coveted state of flow, examining its relevance for both individuals and teams.

As we explore the concept, we'll start with individuals and look at what happens when we align our innate proclivities with our tasks and objectives, and how that might make us more likely to attain a state of flow.

We'll then extend this understanding to teams, where members can collectively recognise and leverage each other's unique Energy for Impact, fostering seamless synchronisation. We'll delve into how this alignment might foster collaborative flow states within the team, and yield heightened creativity, productivity, and a strong sense of unity.

Let's get to it.

Flow definition

Having worked in international law firms for more than 15 years, one of the things I've learned is: you need to define things before you start talking about them.

So, let's make sure we know what we're talking about. The concept of flow was introduced by psychologist Mihaly Csikszentmihalyi in his book, *Flow: The Psychology of Optimal Experience*, and refers to a mental state of complete absorption in an activity. In this state, individuals are fully immersed and focused on the present moment, experiencing a sense of energised focus, full involvement, and enjoyment in the process of the activity. It is characterised by peak focus, productivity, and a deep sense of enjoyment and effortlessness.

Elements of flow

The key characteristics of the flow state include (and we'll look at an example of these further on):

- Intense Concentration:
- Individuals in a state of flow are deeply engaged and concentrated on the task at hand. They may be unaware of their surroundings. Individuals are so engrossed in the activity that they become one with what they are doing, leading to a sense of effortless involvement.
- Clear Goals:
- Flow often occurs when individuals have clear, achievable goals and immediate feedback on their performance. This allows for a sense of progress and accomplishment.
- Loss of Self-consciousness:
- In a flow state, individuals are not overly concerned about how they are perceived by others. They are immersed in the activity, and their focus is on the task itself.
- Distorted Sense of Time:
- Time may seem to pass quickly in a state of flow. Individuals may not be aware of how much time has passed because they are fully engaged in the present moment.

- Intrinsic Motivation:
- Flow is often associated with activities that are intrinsically rewarding, where the activity itself is enjoyable and satisfying.
- Balance of Skill and Challenge:
- Flow tends to occur when the level of challenge in an activity is well matched with an individual's skill level. If the challenge is too high, it can lead to anxiety; if it's too low, it can result in boredom.

Csikszentmihalyi's research suggests that achieving a state of flow can contribute to increased happiness, creativity, and overall well-being.

Other research by Deloitte[4] suggests that flow states at work increases productivity and engagement.

For this particular chapter, let's also define productivity and engagement from a workplace perspective:

Productivity = A measure of economic performance that compares the amount of goods and services produced (output) with the number of inputs used to produce those goods and services.

Engagement = Describes the level of enthusiasm and dedication a worker feels towards their job.

Looking at these two definitions, one question that comes to mind is: what if the 'number of inputs' is defined as the level of 'effort' and energy we put into our work?

And what if this input was perceived as effortless, rather than effortful?

What if our input was more often filled with enthusiasm, motivation and enjoyment, rather than the good old 'work hard' or 'hustle'?

And what if we knew what naturally makes us feel motivated, energised and valued?

---

[4] 'How to design work for flow', 18 November 2022, https://action.deloitte.com/insight/3036/infographic:-how-to-design-work-for-flow

Effortless vs effortful

Well, I'll start. Let me share what I noticed about myself and what makes me feel motivated and engaged, and which kind of energy gets me into a state of flow.

Early in my career I was what they called an IT trainer at the law firm I was working for. This meant that every week I had short training sessions on different topics that would help both lawyers and business services use the system with more ease and not waste time figuring out how things work by themselves.

Now, I had to design these sessions. And almost every time I was designing a training session, I was in flow in accord with the definitions above.

What got me into flow was not the actual session design, but the image I had in my mind about how this session can be different, unexpected and memorable for them (that was my own clear goal).

So, I would think of ways to make it fun, surprising, in any case, not mainstream. I had the freedom to design these sessions my way and, for me, this was how I was contributing best to helping people: helping them get out of their day to day in a short training session about a potentially boring topic that ended up being surprisingly fun.

I remember in one session I was going to show them the 'sort' function or something similar in Excel and I started with 'please pay attention because this is extremely difficult to do, but so helpful especially in due diligence reports,' and then went on with 'Ready? What you need to do is first click here and then here, and it's all done for you.'

I remember people chuckling, reacting with 'phew' or 'ha-ha, not sure I can do it' or 'Roxana, you gave us a scare!'

Later in my learning and development years, as I was designing soft skills programs, I was getting into flow states almost every time I was designing a new program or changing one that I had designed before to make it better (as in more intriguing, captivating, surprising, memorable).

The memorable part for me was important because I wanted learning to stick – my clear goal again, and, in a way, my own individual feedback. This was going to be as good as it could be for me if I knew, at the end of designing that session, that it had high chances of fulfilling my goal: what people do with it afterwards. And for them to do anything with it, they need first to remember. And they won't remember much if they don't feel it one way or another.

It is the initial goal that kicked in the flow state for me. I am not a process person. But the goal is what helped me enjoy the process. And I was getting completely lost in the design process, looking for videos, creating exercises – I especially loved creating them from scratch instead of looking them up, handouts, slides, rehearsing, all of it. I could do this for hours on end and not feel like I was working!

It was all there:

- ✓ the Loss of Self-consciousness: I was totally immersed in the activity.
- ✓ the Distorted Sense of Time: totally unaware of how much time has passed and not even caring about it.
- ✓ the Intrinsic Motivation: the entire exercise felt so rewarding, I felt like I was directing a theatre play that no one had done before.
- ✓ the Balance of Skill and Challenge: because yes, it was a new challenge every time I was creating a new program. I had the skills, but did I really have the right skills to create something that's never been done like that before?

It's interesting to note how the sense of enjoyment and effortlessness, and the imposter syndrome can coexist!

Because it felt like I was having so much fun doing what I was doing, because it felt easy, it also felt … wrong, somehow too good to be true. I remember I was feeling guilty for not 'really working'!

This entire process did not feel serious, painful, or boring. It certainly did not feel like hard work. So, was it really work? Well, that's where my own feedback (and subsequently the learners' feedback) helped me reconcile this.

It helped me to understand and challenge this cultural value, perhaps, that 'work' must feel effortful.

My presentation skills workshop was filled with movie references and fun exercises. One of the voice exercises was people reading excerpts from monologues in famous movies (I think I've read one from *Erin Brockovich* so many times as an example that I used to know it by heart – and so did the participants!).

We were doing diction and breathing exercises, just like actors would do to prep before a scene. We were role playing short team meeting presentations, watching videos (one of which was Ellen DeGeneres' speech at the Oscars, the first one she gave).

And I knew, looking at the final 'product', that it was going to 'stick'. That it was different, entertaining as well as filled with practical learning points that people will remember and apply. I remember the last 'dress rehearsal' before the first workshop felt exciting, exhilarating; it felt like I was right before an Olympic race and I was ready for it. That was my own internal feedback.

One of the lawyers told me at the end of our sessions: 'I've been to other presentation skills workshops before, but this one was so different, I'll remember what we did here for a long, long time, it was really good!'

And that was the external feedback that got me back into flow each time I was designing a new learning experience.

And yes, other people remembered the same workshop because they disagreed so much with what they had to do in it! Some of them refused to take part in some exercises, and that was just fine. Nothing was compulsory. But here's the trick: it was especially these people that I found, at the end of the workshop, when they were delivering their own presentations in front of the group, who used all the exercises and techniques so well.

I remember one of the more senior lawyers came to me and said, 'I didn't see the point of what we were doing at times, but it all makes sense now; I'll take those exercises with me and practise with my kids, they're fun!' I remember I was shocked – and happy to hear it – because she had been giving me 'the look' so often during the workshop and had barely partici-pated in the exercises but was present for the entire time.

This also helped me understand that 'memorable' has an upside and a downside, and that people are going to be ready or not ready, willing or not willing, and that if the dots connect at the end, then I've done my job right!

This is the kind of feedback that also helped get me into flow whenever I had to design new workshops, thinking about 'how can this be different to anything they'd done before?'

Energy for Impact

'Optimal experience is a form of energy, and energy can be used either to help or to destroy.

'The optimal state of inner experience is one in which there is order in consciousness. This happens when psychic energy or attention is invested in realistic goals and when skills match the opportunities for action. The pursuit of a goal brings order in awareness because a person must concentrate attention on the task at hand and momentarily forget everything else. These periods of struggling to overcome challenges are what people find to be the most enjoyable times of their lives. A person who has achieved control over psychic energy and has invested it in consciously chosen goals cannot help but grow into a more complex being.'

Mihalyi Csikszentmihalyi, Flow: The Psychology of Optimal Experience

Research by The GC Index shows[5] (also see Section 1, Chapter 2) that people differ when it comes to their proclivities for making a positive impact on their world.

---

[5] The GC Index, https://www.thegcindex.com/

I noticed this when I was in a flow state dealing with the design process described above: the strong desire to create a learning experience in a way that was unique, never done before, memorable and fun, to help people connect dots and be able to apply it in their world – I had no 'scientific' angle on that.

I later discovered through my exploration of The GC Index, that this is called Energy for Impact, that it is different from one individual to another, and it does not depend on personality, but rather upon a unique combination of proclivities and skills.

The way to measure your specific Energy for Impact is to use The GC Index (where the GC stands for 'game changing') – a people and organisation assessment tool that identifies where individuals and teams naturally want to make an impact and contribution in their world.

When we align individuals and teams to roles/tasks where they are naturally engaged and energised, we end up with both higher employee satisfaction and higher productivity.

I believe that the reasons for this are related to the ways in which perceive our world, our values and beliefs, with what we say that 'makes us tick'. And what makes us 'tick' is our specific Energy for Impact.

In all my examples of what resulted in a flow state when designing learning experiences, what made me enjoy that process so much was my desire, perspective and drive to make that experience different, surprising, memorable and fun (or at least playful).

Years later, as the Chief Game Changer of All Personal[6], a partner organisation to The GC Index, I found out that my Energy for Impact is that of a Game Changer/Strategist. See Figure 1 below.

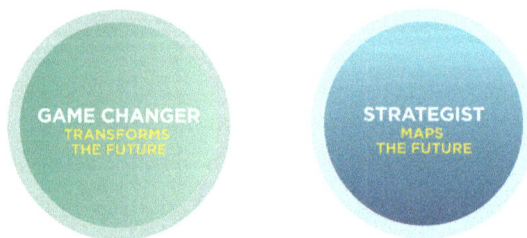

Figure 1: My GC Index profile

---

[6] All Personal – Leadership and Team Coaching and Training, https://personalskillscoach.com/

This profile means that, at my best, I bring creative ideas and possibilities (Game Changer) to shaping future purpose and direction (Strategist). To be at my best, I also need to ensure that I have the skills to engage people with my ideas, especially those who will make them a reality.

Through my understanding of The GC Index and of my profile specifically, I also found out that Game Changers have the imagination to 'see' what is possible in ways that others often don't. That they're not constrained by the 'tried and tested' and often challenge and question 'received wisdom' and traditional ways of doing things. I found out that there's a sense of playfulness in Game Changers, too; for me that's about pushing the boundaries of what is possible.

And I also discovered that my Strategist proclivity helps me see these creative possibilities within a strategic context, appreciating how they can support the achievement of strategic goals; I need to take a 'big picture' view.

Or, to share a different 'picture' of a Game Changer (GC)/Strategist, here are the sketches that my visual artist kid drew for me before one of the workshops I delivered to a team going through change:

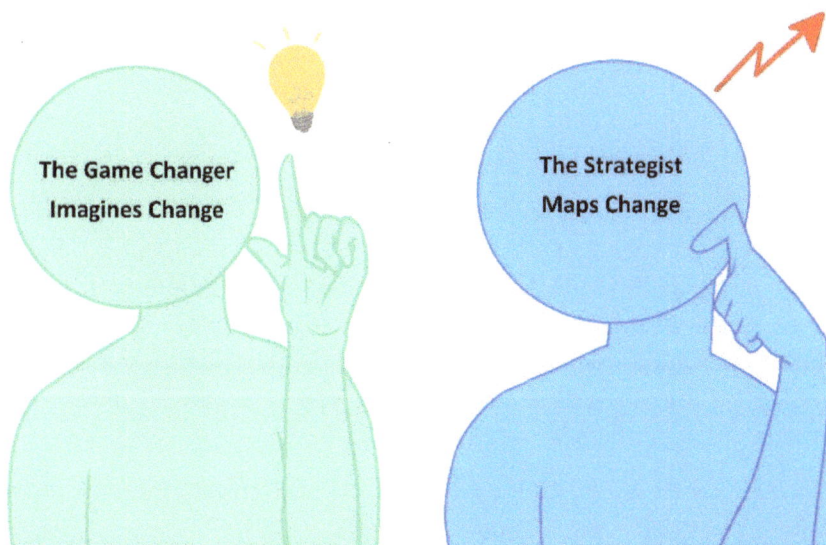

The Game Changer
Imagines Change

The Strategist
Maps Change

The suggestion is then, that the way in which any one of us gets into a flow state is different, reflecting the unique nature of our Energy for Impact.

Having noticed the connection between my own Energy for Impact and what made me get into flow, I was curious to see what the connection between energy (for impact or not) and flow is for other individuals This all makes perfect sense to me now, thinking back to why I enjoy doing what I do so much: making learning and coaching experiences memorable, and helping people connect dots – the GC/Strategist at work!

Learning experiences get me into flow when I design them, because my goal is for them to make a difference in people's lives. I love coaching because each coaching session is different from the previous one, even with the same client; it's all about exploring perspectives that have not been explored before and helping people 'connect their own dots'. As a Game Changer/Strategist, how could I NOT love it?

That's when I feel I'm at my best and what I also want to be appreciated for. This also explained why the feedback I received on my presentation skills training made me feel even more motivated and valued: because it was underlining how the training was different and memorable, and how it helped participants 'connect dots' for themselves.

As a Game Changer/Strategist that's one great piece of feedback to receive.

Now, that same piece of feedback might leave you feeling completely indifferent!

If so that's because, I would suggest, your Energy for Impact is different; what you naturally focus on that's valuable to you is different, the way in which you make a difference is different. (By the way, The GC Index generates 90,000+ different combinations for describing an individual's Energy for Impact; rather than 'putting you in a box', it gives you a window through which to see your world.)

The exploration asks: 'Can we understand any individual's flow state in terms of their GC Index Energy for Impact?'

Individual Energy for Impact and flow

As a Game Changer/Strategist, the most important questions to me in my life are: 'why not?' (Game Changer) and 'why?' (Strategist).

Given this, I'll pose the question: 'why is Energy for Impact and flow with tasks important to us, anyway?'

In his *Forbes* article, 'Is The Secret To Ultimate Human Performance The F-Word?'[7], Steven Kotler (author, journalist and Director of Research for the Flow Genome Project) sums up some strong benefits of being in flow:

'Technically, flow is defined as a peak state of consciousness where we feel our best and perform our best. [...] as was learned from one of the largest psychological studies ever conducted, the people who have the most flow in their lives are the happiest people on Earth.

'In a 10-year McKinsey study[8], top executives reported being five times more productive in flow. This means, if you spend Monday in flow, you can actually take the rest of the week off and still get more done than your steady-state peers.

'While most of us spend less than five percent of our work life in flow, if that number could be nudged up closer to 20 percent, according to that same McKinsey study, overall workplace productivity would almost double.'

So maybe some other good questions to ask here would be 'why not get into flow more often?', 'what can we do to get into a flow state?' and 'how might we make that a habit that increases our overall life satisfaction?'. I mean, I don't know about you, but I would love to be included amongst the happiest people on Earth!

---

[7] 'Is The Secret To Ultimate Human Performance The F-Word?', Steven Kotler, 8 January 2014, https://www.forbes.com/sites/stevenkotler/2014/01/08/the-research-is-in-a-four-letter-word-that-starts-with-f-is-the-real-secret-to-ultimate-human-performance/?sh=df23e05227f0

[8] McKinsey study on flow: https://www.mckinsey.com/~/media/mckinsey/email/newsletters/2021-10-29a-onpoint.html

What gets us into flow seems to be strongly related to our internal motivation drivers, our values, our beliefs, our perspectives, our skills, our natural proclivities, which form our Energy for Impact (as described in detail in Section 1, Chapter 2). Here is a quick recap.

When it comes to Energy for Impact, individual differences are underpinned by our energy for original thinking – Imagination – and our drive to turn ideas into reality – Obsession.

These differences are manifest as engagement with:

1. Ideas and possibilities: Strategists and Game Changers.
2. Tangible outcomes and the pursuit of excellence: Implementers and Polishers.
3. A drive to create collaborative endeavour and collective contribution: Play Makers.

Understanding the ways in which you feel most engaged and energised when it comes to making an impact upon your world helps you identify how you can 'play to your strengths' and maximise your contribution to a role, team and organisation.

So, what if (another one of my favourite questions) we could identify all of these and help ourselves and people around us (both at home and at work) get into flow more regularly, feel that what they do is aligned with who they are?

We hear the statement: 'bring your whole self to work' a phrase stated so often and yet the 'eye-rolling' we notice the second we say it is pretty significant: it means we haven't nailed it yet. Because we've done what we've seen done over and over again: we've imposed that on people without even asking them, 'When do you feel most engaged and energised?', 'What are YOU about?', 'What matters to you?', 'When do you feel at your best?', 'What do you love being valued for?'

When do we start asking these questions? The sooner, the better!

Being a mum of two Gen Zs – a 20-year-old and a 17-year-old – the conversations with them around what makes them motivated, what gets them into flow, what they enjoy doing that stretches their abilities are so different – no surprise there, because they are different.

My 20-year-old is studying theatre and would like to pursue acting. His Energy for Impact is that of a Polisher/Strategist. See Figure 2 below.

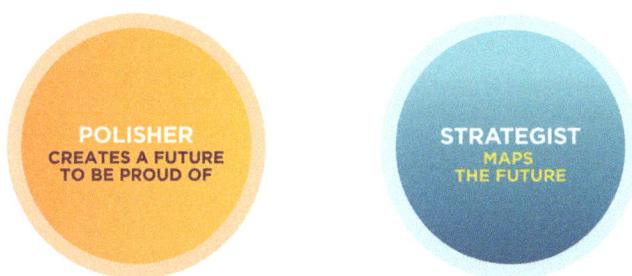

Figure 2: My son's GC Index profile

'Polishers want to see things "done well". When it matters most to them, they will be perfectionists. These qualities and inclinations, typically, lend themselves to innovation and continuous improvement.'

'Strategists are at their best when they are able to see, and clearly articulate, direction, change and action within a strategic context that takes account of operational and people needs.'

The first thing he said to me in response to the Game Changer proclivity in his profile was 'Hmm, so I'm not creative enough.' Which is what helped us have an informed and deep conversation about 'how' he can support the creative process rather than whether or not he was creative.

The other important thing he said was:

'The Polisher makes a lot of sense, though. It's always easier for me to build on someone else's idea or on something that already exists.'

In the context of changing scenes, decors, prompts and perhaps even lines, for example, that made even more sense to him. He can see how things can be improved, and he can clearly create a plan for action, while being able to explain the 'why' behind it (why one action is better than the other):

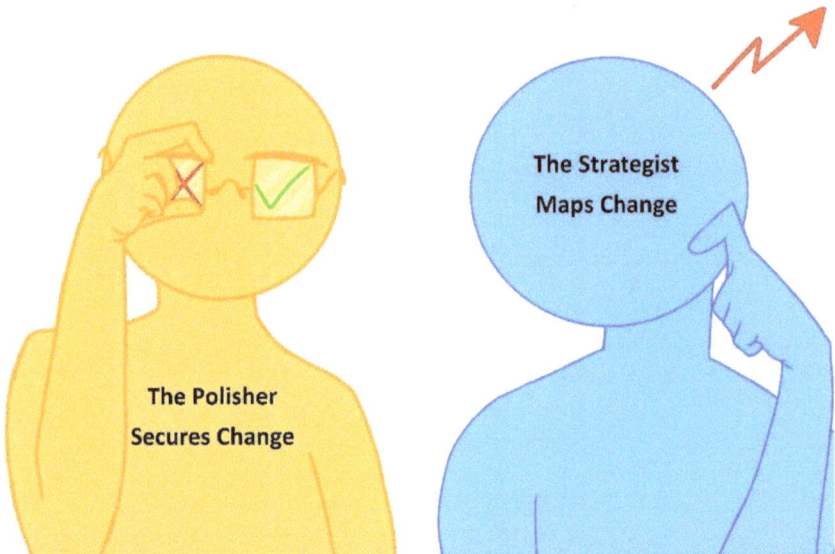

The Strategist Maps Change

The Polisher Secures Change

Now, to him, building on something that already exists is what energises him.

As a Game Changer, my preference is always to start from scratch. Give me a blank sheet of paper or tell me that we need to think about doing something and I won't bat an eyelid. Ask me to check how we can improve a process, product or idea and I'll do it because I have to, not because I feel driven to.

Knowing his Strategist proclivity was his second Energy for Impact helped him to understand why the 'bigger picture' was important to him, as well as the importance of techniques, structure and routine of actor training, for getting things done.

In his life generally, one thing he does that comes easily to him is ask the 'why' and 'how' questions and see the most effective way of doing something with a sense of purpose. The clarity with which he immediately sees the best next step in a situation is astonishing, and he's always been so confident sharing it. These behaviours reflect his Polisher/Implementer proclivities.

I remember that, on one occasion, he joined me for a workshop I was delivering at a conference in Toronto. I had a few ideas on how to arrange the props (of course we had props!) for the session. I shared the options with him, and he immediately helped decide: 'Let's use these props to bring people into the session, and stick these other props on the walls.' Clear, short, to the point. Decision making done easy – once he understood the 'why', he could clearly see the 'how' that made the experience better.

He thrives in environments that value innovation and have a 'safe to fail' culture. He has a practical approach to getting things done, but with a desire to challenge the 'tried and tested'. The Strategist in him implies a need for action within a clear strategic context, valuing the 'why' as much as the 'how'. He has a lot of energy for building upon others' ideas and is focused on developing key skills that leverage his strongest proclivities, particularly around leadership, creativity, innovation, engaging and influencing, and getting things done.

The elements that help him get into a state of flow include working on tasks that align with his proclivities for continuous improvement, strategic context, collaboration, and practical execution, all within an environment that encourages innovation and values excellence. Hence his passion for theatre, choir practice, assisting and helping his colleagues stage a show.

(Fun fact: as I am writing this, I completely forgot the time. My 20-year-old announces to me 'I'm off,' as he is getting ready to go to uni classes and then choir practice. I respond: 'Oh, right, I forgot; well, not that you're off, but what time it was.')

My 17-year-old has a different GC Index profile. He is a Game Changer/Strategist (and close Polisher) visual artist (who sketched the individual change proclivity images I've used in this chapter). What this profile helped him clarify is that

'His "above the line" profile describes someone who will have most impact when they are engaged in shaping strategy and direction with transformational ideas and possibilities. He is likely to feel most energised when engaged in "leading edge" thinking.'

He said:

'YES! It's so frustrating, I want to do so many things and never have enough time, my work has to look good, I can't paint something that's going to look horrible, I'm in 11th grade! If I don't deliver quality work now, how am I going to study art in college? What would my purpose be as an artist?'

By the way, this quote is a shorter version of the many questions he asks, among which a lot of 'why not' do this or that like this, or 'why' do we even have to?

What gets him into flow is drawing or painting, anything that has to do with creating something where he just dives into not only the artistic endeavour, but also in the process of making it better with each stroke, fine line, colour or shade – coupled with a strong need to understand the purpose of doing that! The 'WHY' is extremely important to him in mapping the journey of creating each artistic piece.

Contribution to change? It made perfect sense to him:

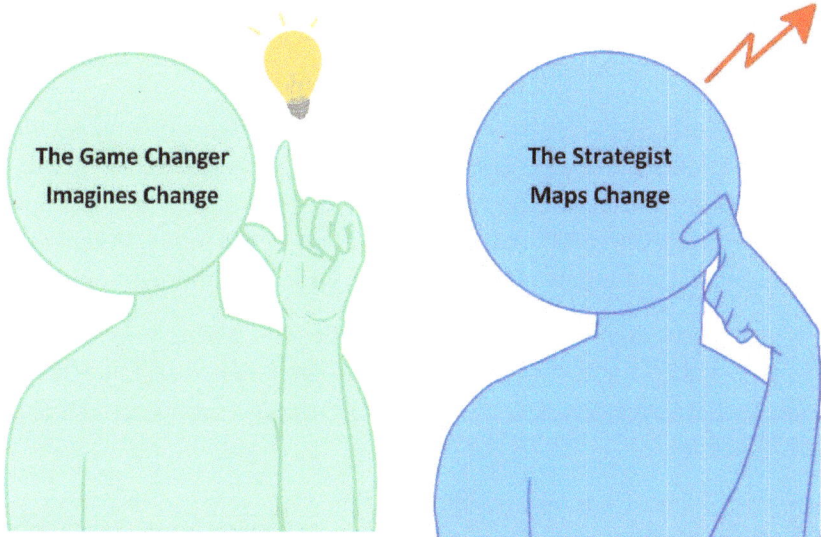

The Game Changer
Imagines Change

The Strategist
Maps Change

Now, knowing his Energy for Impact helped him understand where his energy as well as his frustration came from: 'frustration is energy that can't go where it wants to!'

As an artist, he definitely feels none of his works will ever be good enough. The feedback he gives himself when he says: 'this looks good' ends up being temporary, until he looks at the same drawing or painting a week later and declares 'this looks like doo-doo'.

This is a pattern that he's been able to somewhat reconcile knowing that, as a Game Changer, he will always have a perspective that might be different from others, that he will be able to imagine possibilities that others won't and that as a Polisher he will always strive for perfection in himself and others. The Strategist helps him understand the change that his talent and his art can create in the world, the need to create, think and act differently in order to improve what's already there. It also helps him make a plan and stick to it, so that he can conclude that something is good enough – at least for now!

This extends far beyond his artistic endeavours. He has an incessant pool of ideas and gets into flow when discussing how we can do better as a society, how we might be able to solve for inequalities and injustices out there, and how fast we need to move before it is too late. He sees the trends, patterns and solutions of how things can be done differently very clearly – and is frustrated when others don't.

With this particular teen, the high-energy conversations on various topics that affect us as a society (big picture, Game Changer thinking) and the map of what we need to do to improve (Strategist) are a state of flow in itself! And as a Game Changer, I get it: two Game Changers debating new possibilities and options means no sleep, food or water are needed!

I remember talking to a Polisher client, who was also a lawyer by trade, and who said: 'I think my boss is also a Polisher. We could talk about one paragraph for an entire day, on a quest of making it sound perfect, almost unbreakable.'

Ask two Game Changers to do this and they will run like there's no tomorrow!

Ask two Polishers and they will have the time of their lives!

What people say about their Energy for Impact and flow

Being able to understand how we can make for better conversations, motivation triggers and effectiveness is what also triggered a survey/study[9] for this chapter.

If you're one of the people who've already responded to it, thank you! Your contribution is game-changing!

If you haven't responded to the survey, just know that you still can. I've decided to leave it open so that we get continuous feedback and more data to consolidate in time. This connection between Energy for Impact and flow and what it means for us when it comes to making our stance in this world seems to be too important to confine to a set time frame.

---

[9] Energy for Impact and Flow Study: https://forms.gle/c5nSmvrFvqCoxTBo8

The connection between our Energy for Impact – innate proclivities – and flow.

So, what makes people get into flow, how is that connected to their Energy for Impact and why does that matter for individuals and teams?

Flow activities are connected to The GC Index profile in that individuals tend to experience flow when engaging in activities that align with their impact proclivities as measured by The GC Index.

We explored the connection between innate proclivities and what gets us into a state of flow in our survey.

The first question asked in the survey:

How often do you experience a sense of "flow" or being in the zone during your daily activities?
13 responses

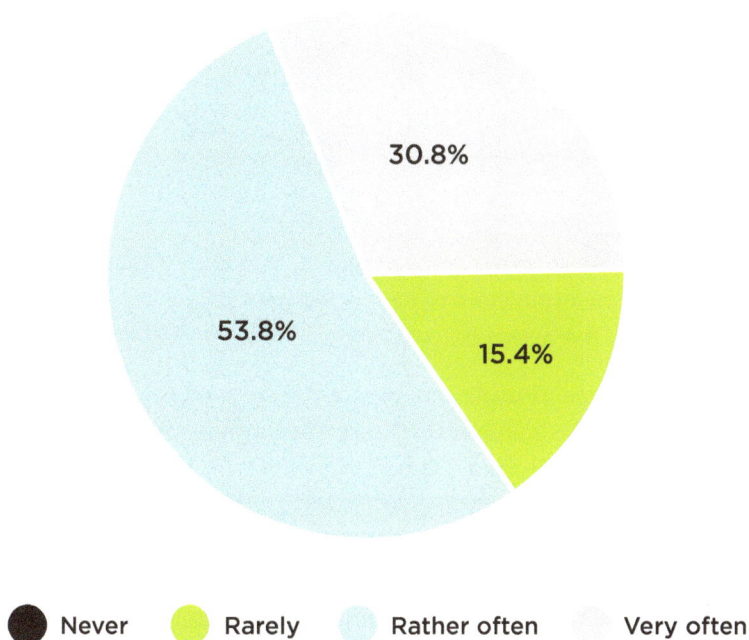

Figure 3: Survey reponses

It was encouraging to see a distribution of responses inclining towards the 'rather often' and 'very often', and that 'never' was not an option.

We also looked at the specifics of activities and what it is about those activities that makes us get into flow.

Those who took the survey and had Game Changer as their main proclivity mention several activities that get them into a state of flow:

WHAT ARE 3-5 EXAMPLES OF ACTIVITIES THAT GET YOU INTO A STATE OF FLOW IN GENERAL? 'I get into a state of flow when I … '	WHAT ARE 3-5 EXAMPLES OF ACTIVITIES THAT GET YOU INTO A STATE OF FLOW AT WORK? 'I get into a state of flow when I … '
When I'm writing, it's creative, I channel my guides and I'm using my feminine, which is flow	When I'm polishing slide decks / our course materials. It just feels right for me, I enjoy making things better
1) I do my gravity grounding technique, makes me feel connected 2) I take time to notice things, it keeps me in the present 3) I take walks in nature and focus on gratitude, manifestation	1) When mentally acute, I can write with stream of consciousness 2) I set alerts on my phone to take pause and check in with myself/energy 3) I manage my days based on energy and acuity rather than by time
– I get into a state of flow when working on an idea about a problem I want to solve – I get into a state of flow when I learn something new, and it requires creative problem-solving – I get into a state of flow when I am doing something artistic – I get into a state of flow when I am walking and able to daydream	– I get in a state of flow when I am actively working with others to solve a problem together – I get in a state of flow learning something I can creatively apply to current challenges – I get in a state of flow when I have to figure out a creative solution to a sticky problem – I get in a state of flow when I am future thinking with others on creating something new

If we're categorising these on themes, it becomes clearer that what seems to get them into a state of flow is the creativity, novelty and unpredictability behind the activities:

- Working on an idea about a problem they want to solve.
- Learning something new that requires creative problem solving.
- Figuring out a creative solution to a sticky problem.
- Future thinking with others on creating something new.
- Radical problem solving through engaging their Game Changer drive.
- Being in charge of their ideas and fully controlling them.
- Feeling that they can make a difference.

- Using their creative skills (e.g., artwork, reorganising things at home).
- Wanting to make a surprise for someone.

What factors Game Changers say help them get into flow:

'When I feel spacious, I have lots of ideas flowing, I can see possibilities of how something can be better. To create spaciousness, I call in my guides, I meditate and get quiet.'

'Think, imagine, see.'

The two Implementer/Game Changers who participated in the survey (with their second proclivity of Game Changer) seem to have done that in an efficient and effective way.

WHAT ARE 3-5 EXAMPLES OF ACTIVITIES THAT GET YOU INTO A STATE OF FLOW IN GENERAL? 'I get into a state of flow when I ... '	WHAT ARE 3-5 EXAMPLES OF ACTIVITIES THAT GET YOU INTO A STATE OF FLOW AT WORK? 'I get into a state of flow when I ... '
Activity 1: when I am cleaning my house Activity 2: when I am doing yoga Activity 3: when I am cooking	Activity 1: when I am doing a presentation Activity 2: in a breakout room Activity 3: designing a flyer
I get into a state of flow when I have the opportunity to strategise and masterplan a project, being able to draw on my experiences and collaborate to determine the most **efficient and effective path** to completion	Every example I think of is very similar to the above. Sorry!

What seems to be important for them in getting into flow in the activities they are mentioning are key themes such as:

- organisation (cleaning the house, strategising and master planning a project),
- physical activity (doing yoga),
- tangible outcomes (cooking, designing a flyer),
- efficient collaboration (in a breakout room, collaborating to determine the most efficient and effective path to completion).

Factors that Implementers mentioned are needed to get them into flow:

'A challenge, a problem to solve and authority/autonomy – not needing to play politics.'

By now I'm sure you've noticed the subtle differences in what makes us get into flow depending on what our Energy for Impact is at an individual level – which is important for what makes us feel engaged, motivated and productive, both at home AND at work.

We're not necessarily talking about completely different types of activities. We are talking about different ways to 'see' and be motivated by the same activity.

Let's continue.

There was one Strategist who responded to the survey (and their second proclivity was of Game Changer). Here is what they responded:

WHAT ARE 3-5 EXAMPLES OF ACTIVITIES THAT GET YOU INTO A STATE OF FLOW IN GENERAL? 'I get into a state of flow when I ... '	WHAT ARE 3-5 EXAMPLES OF ACTIVITIES THAT GET YOU INTO A STATE OF FLOW AT WORK? 'I get into a state of flow when I ... '
Solving puzzles, reading, runing, drawing, data manipulation	Data manipulation, problem solving, design

Which is completely in line with the Strategists' ease in seeing trends, patterns, connecting dots to plan for and understand the 'why' of now and of the future.

Perhaps unsurprisingly, Play Makers were the majority of people who offered to participate in this study. Knowing that this will serve the wider community, that their impact will help others and that they get to hear from the other respondents, too (in this book) – that must have energised them a lot as Play Makers!

Their second proclivities varied among the five GC Index proclivities, which is why I'm assuming that the Play Maker energy was the main force that pulled them into this exercise.

WHAT ARE 3-5 EXAMPLES OF ACTIVITIES THAT GET YOU INTO A STATE OF FLOW IN GENERAL? 'I get into a state of flow when I ... '	WHAT ARE 3-5 EXAMPLES OF ACTIVITIES THAT GET YOU INTO A STATE OF FLOW AT WORK? 'I get into a state of flow when I ... '
– I facilitate mindfulness activities, as I feel that I support others with their wellbeing efforts – I am with my family, spending time together, as I know time is precious and this is one way – I show them I love them, sharing the precious resource of time with them – I am with my friends, building bonds and I do something I like at work, ie, talent development and employee engagement	– I help people with talent development, as I feel I help them on their career path – With employee engagement and appreciation, as so often this can be ignored, and I think it is important to occur and helping people with diverse HR queries, as I appreciate having variety in my work and I always want to help others
– I want to organize something (gathering or event) – I have to use my creative skills (eg, artwork, reorganize things at home) – I want to make a surprise to someone	– I have to put pieces together – People and activities/projects – I am doing things that I know very well (eg, recruiting) – I have to negotiate something – most of the time I know exactly what to do and say
Writing, executing a task, nice conversation, reading something I really like	Delivery a session. Connection with others and a sense of work completed
– I play my favorite music - at home it just helps me adjust my mood for things that need to be done – I walk in the woods - I need about an hour break to clear my head to get moving – I mountain bike short escapade - like walking in the wood, this activity clears my head, helps me get calmer and more creative, I need to get a bit exhausted too	– I play my favorite music/ put my headphones on - I have working music ready to cut me off from the office sounds and help me focus – Sometimes playing favourite music is too much. Thus, I need silence and the only way to achieve it in the office is with this function in head phones – I walk in the park/wood/outside work - 20/30min break clears my mind and prepares me for work, cuts distractors – I get new ideas and reaching consensus with my project groups - gives me energy for next tasks, makes me more interested while working = helps me maintain my enthusiasm for the project
– I teach adapted chair yoga online - I become immersed in the moment, the movement, my observations, and feedback from participants – I talk to a new friend/ colleague and we are on the edge of planning a new initiative – I meet new people in the creative fields and discuss how to collaborate together – I do a jigsaw puzzle (500 - 2000 pieces). This helps my mind free up and get back into the flow	– When all the parts are working together which also means all parts of my team – Currently I am relying on partners, and contractors. When I am clear about what I want to do as far as content, my state of flow and all related activities work better – Part of getting into the state of flow is having clear strategy from my marketing strategist, and a flow sheet from my social media manager – Sometimes the needs of clients inspire my state of flow to create and provide what is needed

Some key themes for Play Makers getting into flow seem to be: mindfulness, family, friends, work, talent development, employee engagement, creativity, music, nature, and collaboration.

What Play Makers say are the factors that help get them into flow:

'Having feelings shared with and by others; having opinions being shared by others or learning by disagreeing constructively; and imagining winning the lottery and being able to do what I really want to do, having the financial means to do so.'

'Consensus within a group keeps the collaboration level on the positive level, also helps eliminate unnecessary running thoughts, helps to focus on the outcome. Feeling no anxiety, and motivation for action.'

'Taking a moment to breath/check in with what I am feeling in my body, where in my body, what the feeling is like. Deciding if I need to revisit that and give it more time to process. Choosing right action, whether it is bouncing off a new idea, revisiting a conversation for clarification, or approaching a situation that needs to come to light and find a resolution.'

We do not have any responses from a main Polisher, but we did have a Game Changer/Polisher who said that what gets them into flow is 'when I'm polishing slide decks/our course materials. It just feels right for me, I enjoy making things better.'

Their main proclivity was the Game Changer, which is where the creativity and need for high-quality work combine to allow them to enter in a state of flow.

As to everyone's responses to the question 'Have you noticed a connection between your specific Energy for Impact (GCI profile) and the way in which some activities/tasks get you into a state of flow?', most respondents were able to see that connection clearly:

'Yes, creating the space for myself, being conscious in how I choose to work, following what lights me up.'

'I've not thought much about it to make that connection.'

'Always – I am a creative thinker and like to pair with doers to make it a reality for me.'

'Yes. I like to get things done.'

'Yes, Implementer and Game Changer – as someone who is passionate about making a positive impact, I feel that when I'm helping to make positive changes, with and through others and helping to leave places and people better than I found them, I find my flow easily.'

'It did not surprise me to be a Play Maker and Game Changer, as I get my energy from people and encouraging and supporting them to be at their best.'

'Yes. For example, I can notice how "being in middle" of things is helping me to get into a state of flow. When I know things and I understand different perspectives I can use every information that I have and I do a lot of things.'

'My Play Maker is my drive when I am in flow.'

'Some of them yes, especially new ideas and reaching consensus with a working group.'

'Absolutely yes. It is very important to me to be clear about my relationships, as well as the interactions between others on my teams. When something needs to be dealt with, I tend to lose my creativity and get out of flow until the situation is resolved, at least within myself.'

'Yes, excited when I have an idea and want to get it mapped out – plan, time, resources etc.'

'I experience flow typically when working with data in line with my Strategist drive, and radical problem solving through engaging my Game Changer.'

Which leads us to the 'why' of this chapter: why is connecting energy and flow as individuals important?

The responses received suggest that it is this connection that helps us align our innate proclivities with our tasks and objectives, making us more likely to attain a state of flow.

As coined by Csikszentmihalyi, when we are in a state of flow, we experience a sense of energised focus, full involvement, and enjoyment in the process of the activity. It's when we get that peak focus, productivity, and a deep sense of enjoyment and effortlessness.

By connecting energy and flow we get to increase our levels of happiness, creativity, and overall well-being.

One last proof?

On a scale of 1 to 10 (1 lowest 10 highest) on how important the connection between energy and flow is for their overall well-being, motivation and productivity, the survey participants marked it between 7 to 10, with the majority in the 9s and 10s. (See Figure 4 below.)

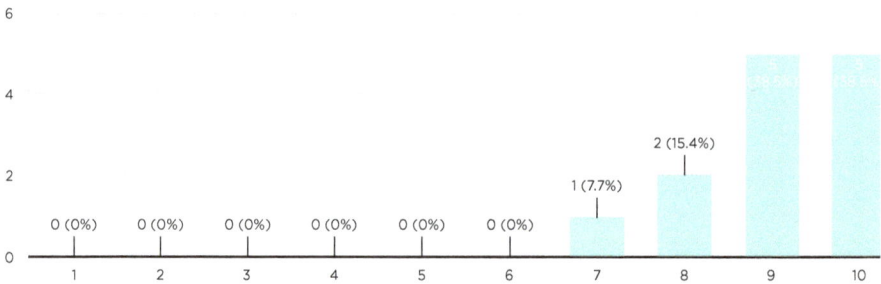

Figure 4: Survey responses

So, let's imagine this: what if we tapped more into this potential for teams, too?

Team impact and flow

'When a team experience flow collectively, they're able to "feed off" of one another's energy … When teams optimize their time by moving into periods of high focus and productivity together, they end up working like a beautifully synchronized crew team. They probably move about as quickly, too.'[10]

How does the description above of what a team in flow might look like resonate for you? Also, when is the last time you've been in a flow state as a team?

I am lucky to have experienced flow when working with my team back in my corporate days. That happened especially when we were doing our 'big picture' planning, strategising and brainstorming the goals, actions, what each of us would be responsible for. Flow was possible in that scenario because of several factors, in no particular order of importance:

- First – time – we would schedule uninterrupted time for this exercise, no distractions, all-in.
- Second – trust and psychological safety – we were a small team who trusted each other; we knew we were valuing each other's areas of expertise, valuing each other as people, we knew we could disagree, share different perspectives, and that we would be valued for it.
- Third – fun – or a sense of play, which might actually be one of the elements that helped us build trust in the first place. It helped bring a sense of ease, of relief that whatever we'd do, it won't be punished or dismissed. It brought the 'safe to fail' right into our culture as a team.
- Fourth – we were, after all, the learning and development team – and that element of learning with and from each other, the fact that we were, in fact, a learning team not just by title, but by behaviour, that was crucial in allowing us to get into flow during our planning

---

[10] 'Team flow: how to make productivity contagious' by Liz Winston, https://wavelength.asana.com/work-style-team-flow/

sessions, get creative, engaged, think 10 steps ahead, disagree or suggest changes, all that in a way that did not feel like work, but which was extremely productive for us. It's this planning that was going to deliver results for the entire organisation. It was important. It was serious business. And, at the same time, we could get into flow in this important, serious process.

Now, as an independent workshop facilitator and team coach, I have the opportunity to observe flow in other teams as well.

I remember one of the first team coaching sessions I ran, even before knowing this is what I was doing, was to help the leadership team of a non-profit organisation review and redefine their purpose, values and mission, right after the 2020 pandemic.

I believe it was one of the few times that the team had met together to discuss 'big picture' topics rather than the immediate survival ones that come due to a crisis. Needless to mention this session was virtual.

At the beginning of the session, we simply checked in with each other, where they were, what they were seeing in front of them, what their day had been like until that point. They started to relax, sharing anecdotes and chuckling at times, or sharing tough moments and offering support to one other.

Which helped get into the values conversation at a level that was deep, genuine, close to what their day-to-day was like. They were building on each other's ideas and sharing different views with ease.

We agreed on the way to de-stress a situation: make a face – either use an emoji or physically change their appearance on screen – and ask for help, to understand, to clarify, to revisit. The energy in the virtual room was catchy; you could almost distinctively see the fun vibes, the serious vibes, the disagreement vibes, the confusion vibes, the in-sync vibes.

When one of them asked for help to clarify, others would chime in. When one of them was taking too much space, others would raise their hand to speak. When one of them was sharing a new idea, the others would acknowledge it first, before agreeing or disagreeing. They were moving flawlessly through the process, just like a fine-tuned orchestra.

Why connecting Energy for Impact to flow might be the missing piece in creating sustainable, effective and happy teams

Why is tapping into the team energy and flow important?

Because, in these instances, most likely the teams don't need to re-do, revisit, re-schedule, spend countless more hours debating and discussing.

Or, if they do need to revisit and rediscuss, they have a process that allows them to move flawlessly through the nuts and bolts of getting things done.

The more teams can create this common language – verbal and non-verbal – the more they are able to get unstuck, to move forward, to be productive and motivated at the same time.

We talk about team motivation and engagement so much, and yet … there's very little focus on energy and flow in teams, and they're essential to motivation and engagement! Teams are overwhelmed by the number of meetings in a day, without feeling that they're making real progress. Actually, quite the opposite. They feel like the more meetings they have, the less they can get done. Meetings have come to be perceived as distractions from 'real work'.

What if, by tapping into this power of focus, collective Energy for Impact and flow, we could change this and actually help teams get more productive, engaged, or simply happier at work?

One thing I've noticed in team coaching sessions is that team members crave to communicate on topics that are important for them and the team, but very rarely on the team agenda. Topics like trust, accountability, values, psychological safety, impact, communication.

And yes, in the first instance, these conversations seem to not have a seat at the 'real work' table. The downside is that the more these conversations are delayed, the less productive the team is. The minute a team opens the door to bring in a creative, safe to fail, communicative, transparent space, the more productive they become, the less silos are created and the more results they see.

So, what do our respondents say about experiencing flow in teams?

First, here is what they said about how often teams they have either been on, or consulted with, actually get into flow:

How often does the team experience a state of 'flow' or optimal performance during projects?

13 responses

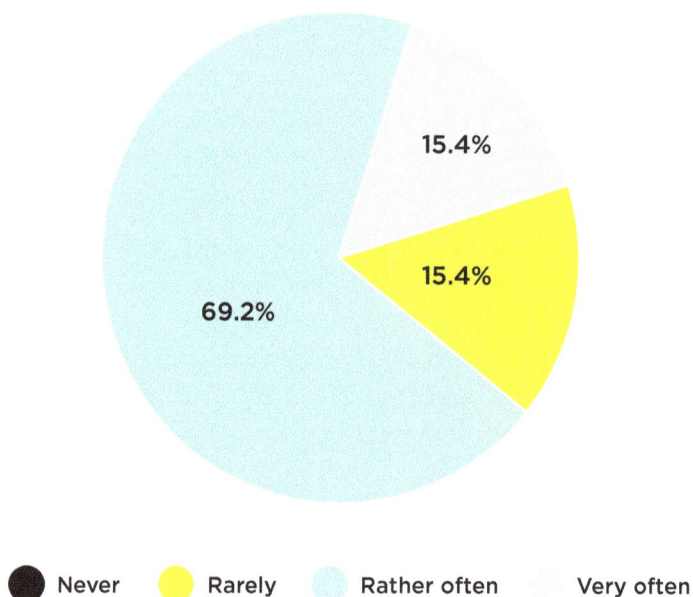

● Never ● Rarely ● Rather often ● Very often

Figure 5: Survey responses

So, it seems we are pretty good at tapping into the power of flow in teams!

What if we could move the needle even more towards 'very often'? What would that do for both productivity, well-being, motivation and engagement?

And how important would that be for teams? Pretty important if we look at these results from the same survey:

On a scale of 1 to 10, how important is team flow for productivity, engagement and motivation?

13 responses

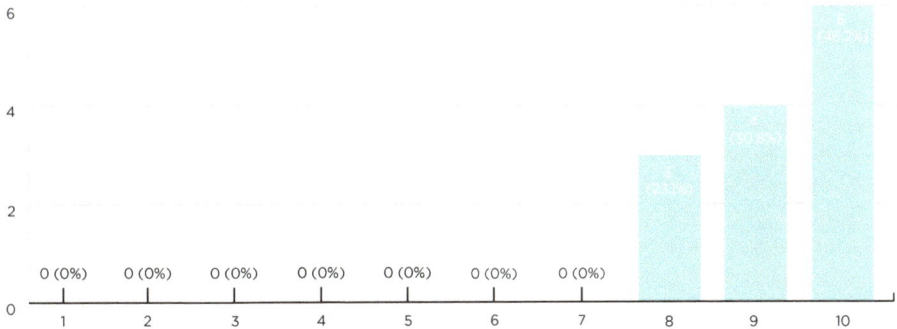

Figure 6: Survey responses

At the team level, things seem to change compared to the individual level. It seems that knowing their individual proclivities makes people more curious about finding out more about their colleagues.

Some of the differences in how they feel more motivated and productive might be that, for example, a Game Changer may be more focused on generating new ideas and driving innovation, while a Play Maker may be more focused on building relationships and facilitating collaboration among team members.

Similarly, a Strategist may be more focused on developing long-term plans and strategies, while an Implementer may be more focused on executing tasks and getting things done.

Despite these differences, there are certain activities that tend to boost the overall energy and flow of the group, regardless of individual proclivities.

These activities include having a clear direction, understanding where each team member contributes and fits, and building trust among team members.

Interesting to note that some of the things that Game Changers felt could be better are related to tapping more into their colleagues' proclivities such as Strategists (the need for direction and clarity) and Implementers (scheduling, finishing what they started).

All respondents seem to have a sense that, when everyone is trusted to do their work and the team is working towards a common goal, the team is more likely to achieve a state of flow.

Here is what respondents identified are elements that bring the team in flow or prevent that from happening, by proclivity:

WHAT IS YOUR GC INDEX (GCI) PROFILE? Please share your first two proclivities	ARE THERE SPECIFIC TEAM ACTIVITIES OR PROJECTS THAT TEND TO BOOST THE OVERALL ENERGY AND FLOW OF THE GROUP? Please share an example	WHAT CHALLENGES OR FACTORS HINDER THE TEAM'S ABILITY TO ACHIEVE A STATE OF FLOW? Please share an example
Game Changer / Polisher	When everyone is trusted to do their work, when the best team for the duration is being played. Trust is a large component, having a clear direction, everyone understanding where they contribute and they fit	Lack of trust, no clear direction
Game Changer / Polisher	Free-flow ideation and collaborative discussions	Scheduling and distractions
Game Changer / Strategist	When the team has a clear idea of the problem they are solving, the expected outcome and the ability to understand the application of the solution they need to be built will be used	Lack of clarity or too many things to focus on as they are compelled to finish what they started
Implementer / Game Changer	Don't recall	Multitasking and workload
Implementer / Game Changer	Identifying team members' strengths and likes and dislikes. Being clear on mission/objectives, deadlines and expectations and of course the why behind it all	Inconsistent leadership practices, organizational and staffing changes and unclear communication and expectations
Playmaker / Game Changer	Working collaboratively on projects energizes us, as we each have different skills and we complement each other	Outside pressures – ie, volume of work and tight / unrealistic deadlines

Playmaker / Strategist	Yes – I think that having projects with fast results is helping the team to feel like they have a purpose	With multiple implementers on the team, the hardest way to get them into the flow is when many projects are started but none have a conclusion. On the other hand, having only one game changer, this one has many ideas but most of them don't get the point of her ideas – this also interrupts the flow somehow
Playmaker / Implementer	Thinking in a collaborative manner	Polishers
Playmaker/ Polisher	Setting understandable goals (project, leadership), clear purpose, clear roles and responsibilities, backup behavior and focus on people, effective and clear communication	Miscommunication, lack of clear goals, chaos in the process - chaotic project management, lack of finding consensus within a group and forcing one sided opinion for agreement and execution

As you look at these answers, please consider: what would you respond to these two questions? What would your colleagues respond? How often are you asking these questions in your team?

Maximising team impact through flow

If you're looking for ways in which you might help your own team get into flow, these examples our participants gave on team rituals or practices that contribute to a positive energy and flow environment might inspire you.

There are certain activities that survey participants mentioned which tend to boost the overall energy and flow of the group, regardless of individual proclivities. These include:

- having a clear direction;
- understanding where each team member contributes and fits;
- building trust among team members.

'When everyone is trusted to do their work and the team is working towards a common goal, the team is more likely to achieve a state of flow.'

Similarly, all proclivities had a mix of responses when it came to elements that hinder the team's ability to achieve a state of flow. These include:

- Lack of trust;
- No clear direction;
- Scheduling and distractions;
- Multi-tasking and workload;
- Inconsistent leadership practices, organisational and staffing changes, and unclear communication and expectations;
- Outside pressures, such as volume of work and tight or unrealistic deadlines;
- Miscommunication, lack of clear goals, chaotic project management, lack of finding consensus within a group, and forcing one-sided opinions for agreement and execution;
- Interruptions or redirection of projects due to corporate urgent needs;
- Lack of direction or clarity, some people dominating, others shying away;
- Lack of interest in doing the job.

It seems that at a group or team level, the more we can help each other feel seen, included and valued, the higher the chances of getting into a state of flow collectively. That's where understanding our own and others' Energy for Impact helps us create that framework that allows us to collaborate effectively. That's where we start feeling that we are indeed speaking the same language and, even more so, trust that when I don't understand your language I can ask without feeling judged, ridiculed or punished. That when you don't 'get me', you will ask questions that help me translate the meaning of what I say or think.

This means that we are capable, as a team, of forming pathways, or patterns, that are our go-to when (not if) misunderstanding, tension or even conflict arise.

Talking about patterns in the team's energy levels and flow experiences during different phases of a project or over time, our respondents share some of their own observations of what's helpful or less so:

'The more trust in each other the greater the flow and the impact and the contribution.'

'The majority of members just want to get to the action and have a hard time staying in the creative thinking space when they have a list of things that need to get done that day.'

'Space to brainstorm and have fun.'

'Roadblocks can always be a bit challenging, especially when we have encountered them due to a failing of another department to fulfil their objectives. The lack of accountability or a sense of urgency is conveyed to our team, we respond accordingly and then the momentum fizzles with other teams or leadership.'

'Energy can fluctuate as described above, according to pressures outside of our control. Also, for change projects we may not agree with, i.e. change of employer, it may be tougher to maintain a stable and or high level of enthusiasm throughout.'

'At the beginning of a project everyone is very motivated to achieve the results and they get into the flow very fast. When they encounter bottlenecks, their level of energy decreases.'

'Planning – discussions around the topic normally are alive and with lots of disagreement. It's always project related, but sometimes team members need additional push/encouragement to deal with difficult elements.'

'Each team member, or contractor, has had their own projects. There is no issue with their time management to still do the work that I require, but there may be an energetic sense of me as the client losing that closer communication for a period of time.'

'At times frustration with being redirected on what is most urgent.'

'Losing interest is easy when they do not understand what they are supposed to achieve.'

Instead of a conclusion, an invitation

There seems to be a profound link between our Energy for Impact and the coveted state of flow. When we align our innate proclivities with our tasks and objectives, we are more likely to attain a state of flow, characterised by peak focus, productivity, and a deep sense of enjoyment and effortlessness. By connecting energy and flow, we seem to increase our levels of happiness, creativity, and overall well-being.

Our participants shared that being aware of their energy and what helps them be in flow allows them to communicate their needs clearly, minimise urgent requests, and have better well-being. It also helps them understand themselves better, trust others, and connect with others on a deeper level.

They mentioned that knowing what motivates them also helps them know what they need in order to get into flow and reduce their stress, allowing them to make the most of their quality time with family and friends after work.

This individual potential is what we each bring to our teams, too. The more we feel we have the space to use it, the more aligned, included and motivated we feel.

'Random thought – if the proclivities *are* our why's, it makes sense as to why we would draw energy from tasks that help us utilise or achieve them.
They're the things that come easily and naturally to us and in a way is the path of least resistance, right?'

By understanding and leveraging each other's unique energy for impact, teams can foster collaborative flow states, yielding heightened creativity, productivity, and a strong sense of unity, which helps increase motivation, engagement, and happiness at work.

> 'I feel that when the dominant energies cannot be utilised, we tend to give up activities that would bring us motivation and energy from that sphere, out of fear of becoming frustrated. In this case, I believe we access the following types of dominant energy to recharge ourselves.'

When a team experiences flow collectively, they are able to feed off of one another's energy, leading to increased productivity and effectiveness. From a business and results perspective, this is going to be the difference that makes the difference.

I have yet to meet a team that does NOT want to be productive, effective and feel good about the work that they do and who they do the work with.

So, I am going to leave you with this last share from one of our respondents:

> 'It's important for me is to know my team colleagues; there should be trust and confidence between us, we should understand our strong and weak sides to be able give each other a support if necessary (putting professionalism aside, we still are people, so sometimes our emotions imprint on what we do, it's good to deal with them/support each other, help overcome difficulties).'

The more we understand what makes each of us different and the value and contribution we individually bring to collective endeavours, the less frustration and the more motivation we build.

As one of my former clients said at the end of a coaching session, 'When I am motivated, I absolutely hold myself accountable to deliver the results expected of me!'

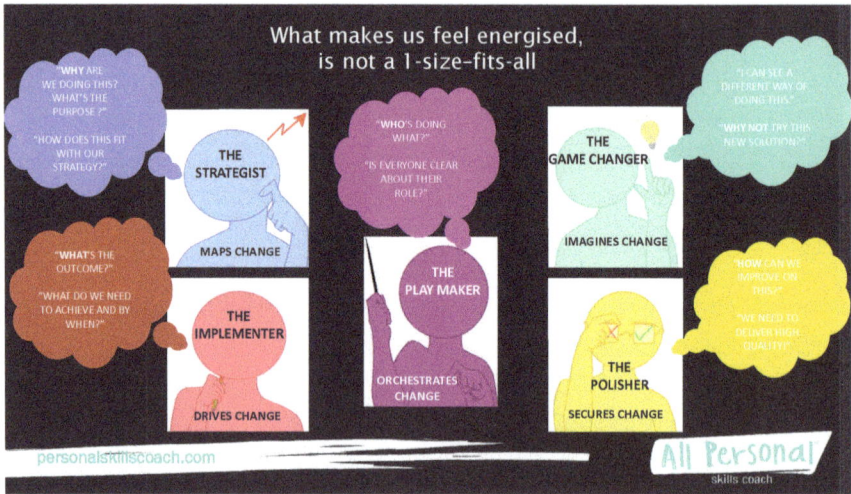

My invitation is to keep being curious about what makes people motivated, what their flow is all about, what they appreciate being valued for. Building on the hypothesis started in this chapter, we might tap further into ways of working that make us feel productive, effective, motivated, engaged and, yes, even happy at work!

Let's not make it an either/or equation any more.

The first step in that invitation is to Lead Different – lead with impact and flow!

Both for ourselves and our work and home teams!

Chapter 4

Playful Vitality – Unleashing Energy Through Recreation

An exploration of the links between play, energy and creativity at work.

Shann van Rensburg

In the tapestry of life, a vital thread, Play weaves our tales, by joy it's led. A treasure trove, both near and far, Play shapes who we become, by who we are.
In the playground of the heart and mind, Creativity and friendships there to find.
A sanctuary where dreams take flight, Play, the catalyst of untainted delight.
It fosters learning, growth, and grace, A vital rhythm in life's hurried pace. Through games and laughter, bonds grow strong, Play is where we all belong.
Amid responsibilities, a respite is there, Play nudges the spirit out of care. In its dance, lessons quietly unfold, A symphony of stories, precious like gold.
So cherish the moments from every day, For in the act of Play, we find our way. In the heart's recess, its echo will stay, A reminder of the importance of Play.

'We don't stop playing because we grow old; we grow old because we stop playing.'

George Bernard Shaw

When exactly did it become 'uncool' to play? At what point were those of us who continued to play seen as childish? Is there a linear relationship between age and play/fun/laughter?

There is so much evidence to support the value of play in physical, social, cognitive and behavioural development, yet in the 'grown-up' world only serious things are taken seriously.

As a strong advocate of play for both children and grown-ups alike, I have undertaken to explore play with a view to breaking down stigmas and to investigate the links between play, energy and productivity.

As I delve deeper, I find more questions, curiosity, slipping slides and winding turns which lead me down the proverbial rabbit hole of exploration. By its nature, I feel play is playing with me! So, I am hoping that although I am only scraping the tip of the iceberg, this chapter will stimulate playful debate, further research and entice future play advocates.

I have heard numerous anecdotes of where play in the workplace has been frowned upon. I have one of my own such examples to share. I started my career in a large corporation, managing communications and change management for their contact centre, a department usually filled with young adults working in high-pressure/emotive situations and within a rigorous structure.

In order to effectively communicate to staff, the role required creativity to find innovative ways of ensuring vital information was transferred, understood and retained amidst the 'noise'. There was no pausing of customers for scheduled meetings or to read long-winded emails. We had to use quick, fun and memorable initiatives to get our messages across in a meaningful way.

I was exposed to many leadership styles at that point. Some leaders were hugely supportive, involved and 'on board' with this approach and our communication thrived. Others saw this approach as immature and unprofessional and success was stifled. At the threat of reputational risk and soul destruction, I eventually decided to move on. This experience has been one that I have drawn on many times and one that has sparked my research and passion for introducing fun and play as a tool into the workplace.

Similar experiences have been shared by my colleagues:

'This gave us a sense of ease and flow, especially when we were doing our "big picture" planning, strategising and brainstorming the goals, actions, what each of us would be responsible for.

'That sense of play and having fun together was one of the elements that helped us build trust in the first place. It helped bring a sense of ease; of relief that whatever we do, it won't be punished or dismissed. It brought the "safe to fail" element right into our culture as a team.

'But … is fun taken seriously in the workplace? Not really. I remember one time when I had all my team gathered for a three-day team event (planning the learning strategy for the entire firm) and we were planning and strategising AND having fun. We were enjoying exploring options and solutions and laughing together in the process. It felt good, we were in "flow".

'And I remember one of my colleagues and friends came to me at the end of the day and said, "I've heard people commenting as they were passing by your office and hearing you laugh. Nothing major, just that they were wondering what's going on. Maybe tone it down tomorrow?"

'Well, I'm not sure how much we were able to "tone it down", but it hurt. Because we were serious about what we were doing, and pretty good at it, too. This reinforced the idea that somehow work, and enjoyment cannot coexist, in the corporate world at least. That we either work or enjoy ourselves, an "either/or", never an "and". An idea that I deeply disagree with to this day.'

Roxanna, in Chapter 3, reflects upon her experience of leading a learning and development team which shared core values of playfulness and fun.

Join me then, on this journey of exploration into my favourite aspects of play, namely freedom, joy, laughter and learning, as we dig into this much-debated topic of play beyond childhood, and the question of how it links to energy and our natural proclivities.

What is play?

When we look at defining play, there are numerous definitions, explanations and many associated activities.

Wikipedia[11] defines play as a range of intrinsically motivated activities engaged in for recreational pleasure and enjoyment. Mostly associated with children and juvenile-level activities but could be engaged in at any life stage.

The *Oxford English Dictionary* begins with: 'occupy or amuse oneself pleasantly with some recreation, game, exercise, etc.; do this with another; act light heartedly or flippantly'... and goes on for half a page, ending in 'play up to' and 'play with fire', followed by 16 play-prefixed words. Play is clearly a complex concept, which the more I try to 'nail down', the more complex it becomes, throwing up more questions than answers.

In trying to find out more about play, some common themes or characteristics emerged. Scholarpedia[12] summarises the top five most agreed upon of these, they fail to overtly call out the sixth, so I felt compelled to add it:

1. Play seems to be mostly self-chosen; you cannot force someone to play.
2. It is more or less self-directed, even when there are rules, the 'player' has the ability to choose to participate or not to, to follow the rules or abstain.
3. Intrinsically motivated in that we play for the sake of play, not necessarily the outcome and the means (the playing) are often more important than the ends.
4. Imaginative; for that period of play we are removed from current reality.
5. Done in an active, alert, but relatively peaceful or stress-free state, they propose that even if a play activity has the ability to cause tension you are free to choose to continue or not – suggesting that if you continue under stressful conditions, it is no longer play.
6. Pleasurable.

---

[11] https://en.wikipedia.org/wiki/Play_(activity)
[12] http://www.scholarpedia.org/article/Definitions_of_Play

These observations are, necessarily, influenced by observer bias and interpretation.

Their vagueness and the vast range of literature prompted me to look closer to home to try to define more tangible aspects of play. I looked to a sample of colleagues to assist in attempting to distil this complex topic.

Benefits, and the evolutionary purpose of play

Having always believed in the ability of play to help people (children and adults) learn, break down barriers, bring people together for a common cause and reduce the impact of stress, I posed the question 'Do you think there is a benefit to play as an adult?' to a group of peers and colleagues (n = 35?), the results were unanimous, everyone agreed that play is beneficial for adults. Thank goodness, I am not alone! But why?

See below:

Do you think there is a benefit to play as an adult?
20 responses

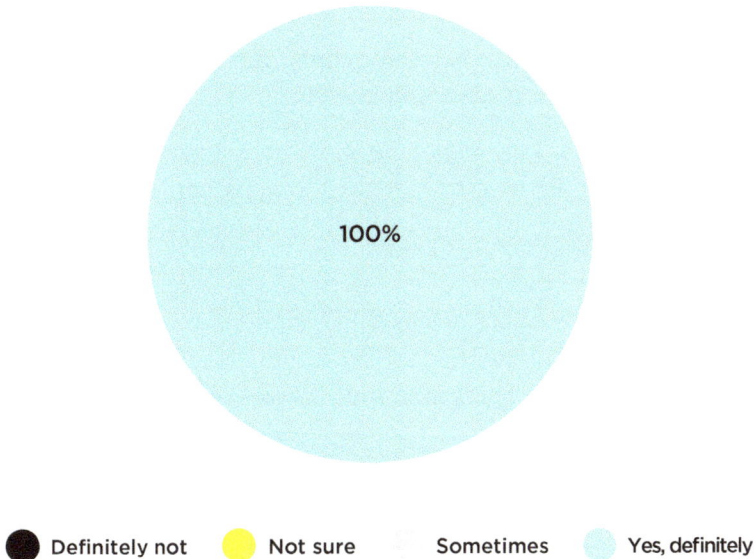

100%

● Definitely not   ● Not sure   Sometimes   ● Yes, definitely

Figure 1: Responses to the question: 'is there a benefit to play as an adult?'

So, there would seem to be no disputing the benefits of play. And drawing from various sources, some agreement to the contribution of play to:

- Increased ability to deal with stress and the capacity to cope
- Cognitive development and learning through play
- Skills development and practice
- Heightened problem solving
- Improved mood through the release of endorphins during play
- Increased energy and vitality
- Better social skills along with the ability to build/repair relationships.

Nonetheless, play remains a complex construct, and many authors on the topic have and continue to theorise over the importance and purpose of play in various aspects of our development.

Theories of play

In his psychoanalytic perspective, developed out of his clinical work with patients, Sigmund Freud emphasised the role of play in development – through play, children express themselves and their emotions.[13]

Through play, children can build emotional, cognitive and moral skills, and experience relief from anxiety and fear.[14]

Inferring from this, play could be seen as a tool for communicating. Through play we are able to express thoughts and feelings we did not even know we had.

Piaget[15] believed that play is essential for cognitive development because it provides opportunities for children to actively gain knowledge and understanding of the world. Play would allow them to practise new cognitive skills, encouraging creativity, problem-solving, and social skills. Play allows us to explore, learn and develop skills.

---

[13] https://www.theatlantic.com/magazine/archive/1987/03/the-importance-of-play/305129/

[14] https://www.irelandassignmenthelp.com/samples/theories-of-play-including-psychoanalytic-theories-research-paper/#:~:text=Freud%27s%20theory%20of%20play&text=Through%20the%20playing%20activities%2C%20the,them%20capable%20of%20communicating%20symbolically.)

[15] https://files.eric.ed.gov/fulltext/EJ1118552.pdf

Vygotsky[16] recognised how learning that occurs through play is socially constructed and does not happen in isolation of surroundings. He focused more on pretend play and emphasised the importance of the social nature of learning through play. Thus, the beginning of imagination and the ability to think creatively.

Play for these writers then serves a tangible purpose.

Friedrich Schiller and Herbert Spencer in the 1870s[17] saw a relationship between play and energy. They suggested that because children are cared for the energy that would have been needed for survival becomes surplus to requirements. So, play is a result of extra energy, not needed for survival, and is therefore released through potentially aimless, yet enjoyable activities.

This theme then, of the frivolous nature of play, the unimportance of play, is reinforced by their thinking. While other theorists have seen the role of play as the basis for developing key social survival skills. Of particular interest here is the notion of surplus energy.

Moritz Lazarus[18] takes a different view, suggesting a 'relaxation (recreation) theory of play' implying that play is restorative, with the purpose of re-energising the individual through activities that are relaxing, distracting, and de-stressing. Play replaces the energy lost through work or effort. In contrast to the surplus energy theory, play arises from an energy deficit.

The view here seems to be that play has a role in maintaining a level of energy and emotional well-being.

Dr Stuart Brown reinforces this view. He identifies play as something purposeless, all-consuming, and fun, but he goes on to say that play is anything but trivial. It is a biological drive as important to our health as sleep or nutrition.

---

[16] https://www.teachearlyyears.com/nursery-management/view/pioneering-play#:~:text=Vygotsky%20was%20probably%20the%20first,in%20isolation%20from%20their%20surrounding)

[17] https://www.csun.edu/~sb4310/theoriesplay.htm

[18] https://www.csun.edu/~sb4310/theoriesplay.htm

He asserts that play is essential to the development of social skills and adult problem solving. In his research of homicidal males, he linked play-deprived histories with the likelihood of future violence or other serious life dysfunctions. He even suggested a likeness of play deprivation, to sleep deprivation having serious negative consequences.[19]

'We are built to play and built through play.'

Dr Stuart Brown

Again, it would be remiss to champion any one of these single views, preferring a more multifaceted view; could it be all of them?

Much of the available research seems to be focused on childhood development, so it was necessary to dig deeper and make certain assumptions, when looking at adult play.

The consideration is therefore that play serves as a multifaceted tool which contributes to the survival and success of individuals and societies, promoting skills development, social bonding, cognitive abilities, stress reduction, exploration, physical fitness, emotional regulation, and cultural learning.

Is it reasonable to conclude that we can infer from childhood research and the continuous nature of individuals to grow, that play has implications for adults?

If so, then the next question that seemed relevant was: if play is beneficial in adulthood, what does that look like?

My initial methodology and hypotheses:

Play is linked to energy, energy is linked to proclivities
… where to from here?

Play in action

'The opposite of play is not work. It's depression.'

Brian Sutton-Smith

---

[19] https://www.nifplay.org/about-us/about-dr-stuart-brown/

The web is full of examples of play in the world of work; the World Famous Pike Place Fish Market, where the fishmongers' energy is so infectious, people spend their lunchtime just watching the 'show' and being drawn into the energy.

There is a reason why a whole training philosophy came out of it.

More recently VW and the Fun Theory. In a VW campaign the experimenters paint the stairs between the escalators to look like the keys of a piano and they play music when stepped on. The result – people playing music as they walked up the stairs which led to more and more people choosing to take the stairs instead of the escalator.[20]

In another initiative, dustbins in a public park were rigged to simulate the sound of something falling a far distance when people threw their trash into the bin. Once again this initiated positive behaviour change as people were encouraged to use the bin to have the sound repeated leading to more trash collected. Google VW Fun Theory to see more examples of this innovative approach.[21]

These are examples of innovative, playful ways of encouraging people to do unexciting things. You will notice how these playful strategies not only get people to do mundane or otherwise less desirable things but also how they tend to lift the individual and collective energy.

I see play as an expression of energy. I explored this theme of play as an expression of energy by asking a sample of 35 colleagues a series of structured questions about their experience of play (see below). These questions were designed to distil their views on how they see and experience play.

Within the context of The GC Index, I speculated that there may be some correlations between people's experience of play and their GC Index proclivities.

Do people with certain proclivities get 'drawn into' certain types of play and, if so, how would we understand that?

---

[20] The Fun Theory 1 – Piano Staircase Initiative, Volkswagen (youtube.com)
[21] The Fun Theory 2 – an initiative of Volkswagen: The World's Deepest Bin (youtube.com) and Speed up your life – Take the slide!, Volkswagen (youtube.com)

I hypothesised, that, for example. Play Makers would be drawn to 'social play', involving groups, teams, collaboration, play scenarios that would encourage inclusion.

I considered that Strategists would tend to engage in more structured play, board games, chess, puzzles, for example, play that would allow them to exercise their energy for looking for patterns in data and events.

I saw Implementers preferring games involving action, instant gratification, acquiring points, 'hands-on play', putting their ideas into practice, focused on achieving tangible results and being 'target-driven'.

When it comes to Polishers, I imagined energy for meticulous, detail-oriented play; crafting, fine tuning, play that involves beating your own or others' previous scores, systems or ideas, refining tactics – and winning!

And, I considered that Game Changers would seek unconventional or experimental forms of play that support their need for creative expression. Activities that challenge norms, break rules and test new approaches, free expression arts, maybe? Inventing new games, or at least new rules?

Initial findings: activities associated with play

I have presented the findings from this initial survey below (see Table 1).

Those activities most frequently associated with play were:

- Outdoors
- Reading
- Puzzles
- Sports.

Different types of play activities

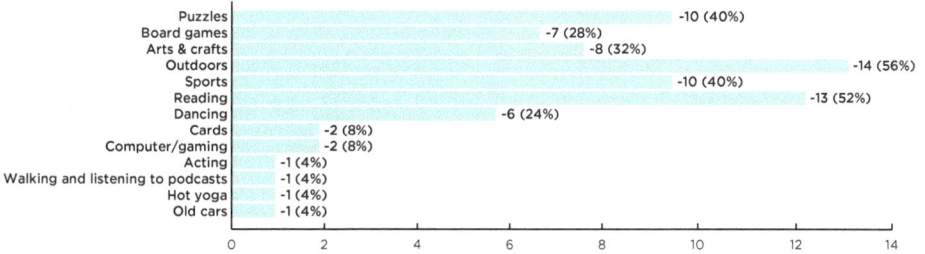

Puzzles	-10 (40%)
Board games	-7 (28%)
Arts & crafts	-8 (32%)
Outdoors	-14 (56%)
Sports	-10 (40%)
Reading	-13 (52%)
Dancing	-6 (24%)
Cards	-2 (8%)
Computer/gaming	-2 (8%)
Acting	-1 (4%)
Walking and listening to podcasts	-1 (4%)
Hot yoga	-1 (4%)
Old cars	-1 (4%)

Table 1: Responses to the question: 'what are currently your favourite type of play activities?'

Initial findings: play choices by GC Index proclivity

When I reviewed the choice of activity by GC Index proclivity no discernible patterns emerged (see Table 2).

In part, perhaps, this may reflect that 'outdoors' can be the context for a variety of activities and 'reading' could be a vehicle for interest in a variety of topics.

1ST, 2ND AND 3RD ACTIVITY CHOICES BY PROCLIVITY		
	1ST	2ND	3RD
OUTDOORS	● ● ●	● ●	
READING	● ●	● ●	●
DANCING	●		
SPORTS		● ●	● ●
PUZZLES	●		● ● ●
ARTS & CRAFTS		● ●	●
BOARD GAMES			● ● ● ●

Could some similarities be emerging? Could this support our inferences?

Table 2: When looked at per proclivity, in this relatively small sample, Game Changers chose reading and dancing as their number one play activity; Play Makers, puzzles and reading; while Strategists, Implementers and Polishers chose outdoors as their number one play activity.

This led me to wonder if it is the purpose of play that is linked to proclivity, rather than the type of play?

So, for example, does the type of reading material consumed, what we are doing in the outdoors, and which sports we choose, differ per proclivity, or does play have a purpose not directly linked to proclivity at all?

Is play linked to our proclivities then? And if so, how? The jury is still out!

A more in-depth evaluation of the associations with play

The sample group was asked how they would explain play to someone who didn't know what it was. Responses were extremely varied but contained a degree of commonality which has been represented as a word cloud.

Figure 2: Responses to the question: 'how would you explain play to someone who didn't know what it was?'

Worth noting is that fun was the most frequently mentioned (most common) characteristic of play. It was also the only characteristic mentioned across all five GC Index proclivity groups. (Enjoy, activity, exploration and letting go were also mentioned more than once.) If we summarised the concepts from the word cloud into themes, they would look something like this:

1. Enjoyment
2. Engagement, interaction and connection
3. Freedom and uninhibited expression
4. Exploration and curiosity
5. Relaxation
6. Growth.

Could some similarities be emerging? Could this support our inferences?

CATEGORY	GAME CHANGER	STRATEGIST	PLAYER MAKER	POLISHER	IMPLEMENTER
Kid's stuff	5		2	2	
Sport	5	3	1	2	
Relaxation	4	3	4	1	1
Fun & laughter	10	4	8	4	3
Friends	8	1	4	1	1
Music	4	1	2	1	
Games	8	4	5	2	
Outdoors	4	2	3	1	
Freedom	2	1		1	1
Creativity	7	3	3	1	

Table 3: Responses to the question: 'what comes to mind when you hear the word play?', categorised by the top two proclivities of the respondent.

As seen above, fun and laughter was highest for all five proclivities and games were mentioned in three proclivities, no other similarities were seen.

With this in mind, if we think about the concepts of play and fun, play is an action or behaviour, while fun may be a subjective experience or outcome that we associate with doing something positive and enjoyable.

Play can lead to fun, but not all play is fun for all people equally, we are all different. Similarly, activities that could be considered fun for some, may not involve playful behaviour.

In his book *The Fun Habit* (2003), Mike Rucker highlights research which concluded that, in line with the hedonic flexibility principle, when our mood is low, we seek out pleasure to feel better. However, if we are already feeling good or as he puts it 'our fun cup is full' we may choose to tackle useful activities that are not necessarily mood-enhancing, but will be beneficial for our longer-term enrichment.

Is this consistent with the surplus energy notion? Could it be true for those things that energise us or our proclivities?

If we know that proclivities are our natural inclinations and that, when in alignment with these natural tendencies, we are energised, could 'being in proclivity' lead us to feel good? Might this in turn lead us to be more productive?

Is it possible then, that we could be drawn to play in a way that aligns our proclivities with that activity for this purpose?

If we use the analogy of our highest proclivity being likened to the keys of a car, you can have a pretty fancy dash and all kinds of features, but without a key nothing will work. We too can achieve many things but to be energised and most impactful in a sustainable way, our highest proclivities need to be activated. Meaning we can be energised enough to fulfil tasks linked to other proclivities if our highest ones are activated. Simply put, I can 'play make' in the pursuit of a polished outcome, not for play-making sake in itself – I do things in pursuit of highest proclivities.

If all of this is true then is it possible that productivity can be achieved when my 'fun cup' is full and also when my highest proclivity(ies) is/are activated.

If we are energised by 'being in proclivity', could that lead to play? Or when we are drained of energy from doing too much that is not in line with our proclivities, do we seek play? Different proclivities manifest differently, for example, Game Changers could generate novel ideas or harvest novel ideas, Polishers could seek to polish or seek the polished. Do people either seek play or create play? Get silly versus looking for energy, gain energy or use up excess energy?

There is still much to explore then if we are to understand play through the lens of The GC Index. While this may prove to be interesting, I will close this chapter with some thoughts about a seemingly specific correlate of play: creativity.

Seeing play differently: exploring the relationship between creativity and play

Piaget was once quoted as saying:

'Play is the answer to how does anything new come about.'

Brene Brown believes that play is at the core of creativity and innovation.

Jane McGonigal, in her TED Talk 'Gaming can make a better world'[22], speaks about gaming being the answer to real-life problems through creating an epic win outcome so extraordinarily positive that you had no idea it was possible.

Through her research at the Institute for the Future, Jane believes that through online gaming we could solve real world problems like obesity, hunger, poverty, global conflict and climate change.

She adds that in games people are motivated to do something that matters, they are inspired to cooperate and collaborate; in games, people are willing to trust you with a mission perfectly matched to your level in the game, and there are plenty of collaborators to work with to achieve your mission. Find out more in her TED Talk.

When we know our proclivities and those of our colleagues then could there be some similarities to the positives Jane describes around being in a game and being 'in proclivity'. In particular, if we are 'working in proclivity' are we more likely to cooperate and collaborate based on mutual trust and respect, knowing we have collaborators to help us, and if our proclivities and skills are matched to the task are we more motivated and more likely to succeed?

---

[22] https://www.ted.com/talks/jane_mcgonigal_gaming_can_make_a_better_world?language=en

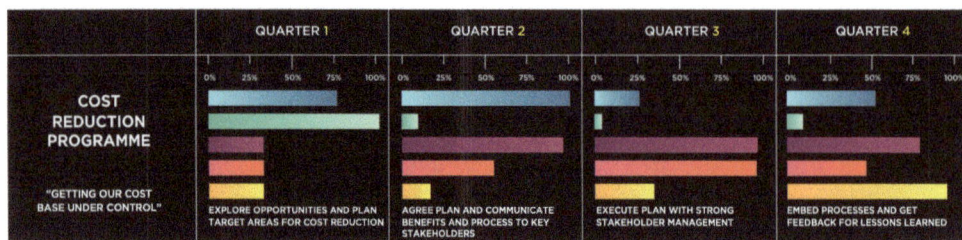

	QUARTER 1	QUARTER 2	QUARTER 3	QUARTER 4
COST REDUCTION PROGRAMME "GETTING OUR COST BASE UNDER CONTROL"	EXPLORE OPPORTUNITIES AND PLAN TARGET AREAS FOR COST REDUCTION	AGREE PLAN AND COMMUNICATE BENEFITS AND PROCESS TO KEY STAKEHOLDERS	EXECUTE PLAN WITH STRONG STAKEHOLDER MANAGEMENT	EMBED PROCESSES AND GET FEEDBACK FOR LESSONS LEARNED

Table 4: An example of designating tasks per proclivity to ensure the right proclivities are represented at the right time and for the right activities or stages of a project.

Is there a correlation between play and productivity?

Reviewstudio.com, suggests that playfulness has been linked to higher levels of creativity and innovation. The suggestion is that a different mindset is required to implement new ideas as opposed to coming up with a new idea, and play is the key.[23]

According to Britishcouncil.org, creativity begins with play.[24]

Some common threads between creativity and play:

- Freedom and exploration
- Imagination
- Problem solving
- Risk-taking and innovation
- Flow state – a highly focused, immersive state
- Positive emotions and joy
- Adaptability and flexibility.

It may be helpful here to note that The GC Index framework helps us to draw a distinction between creativity based upon original and transformational ideas and innovation, based upon continuous improvement and the pursuit of excellence. In GC Index terms, Game Changers bring energy to original thinking while Polishers bring energy to continuous improvement.

---

[23] 'The Power of Play and its Role in Creativity', Review Studio, https://www.reviewstudio.com/blog/the-power-of-play-and-its-role-in-creativity/#:~:text=The%20Creative%20Benefits%20of%20Being,innovation%20in%20humans%20is%20strong

[24] 'Creativity and pretend play', British Council, https://www.britishcouncil.org/programmes/creative-play/creativity-pretend-play#:~:text=Creativity%20starts%20with%20child%27s%20play&text=When%20children%20engage%20in%20play,no%20limit%20to%20their%20imagination

Given that Game Changers have a propensity for creativity, are they more likely to be the ones who play or do they just play differently? Do Game Changers play with ideas that have the potential to be transformational? We know other proclivities play, what does this look like? Is it the same or different?

We know that Game Changers who are also Implementers bring energy to creative practical problem solving. Could these be the people that Roger von Oech[25] is referring to when he says:

'Necessity may be the mother of invention, but play is certainly the father.'

Bringing creativity and play into the workplace

In a global 2010 IBM study, surveying 1500 CEOs from 60 countries, 33 industries stated that, more than anything, successfully navigating the ever-increasing complexity of the business landscape will require leaders to develop creativity.

This remains relevant when according to Forbes (www.forbes.com;2024) in the 2023 World Economic Forum's Future of Jobs survey, approximately 73% of organisations maintain that the need for creative-thinking skills is increasing in relevance and importance.[26]

Considering the commonality between play and creativity discussed above, does it not stand to reason then that adult play is an essential 'stimulant' for creativity? And if so, how do we create environments in which adults can play?

Let's imagine the value to organisations of understanding the conditions needed to stimulate play and the different ways that people can engage in play.

It seems reasonable to assume that the essential conditions for such an environment include:

---

[25] https://www.brainyquote.com/quotes/roger_von_oech_126393
[26] '70% Of Employers Say Creative Thinking Is Most In-Demand Skill In 2024', forbes.com, https://www.forbes.com/sites/rachelwells/2024/01/28/70-of-employers-say-creative-thinking-is-most-in-demand-skill-in-2024/?sh=75f6a172391d

- Experimentation and creativity is not only allowed, but the accepted culture.
- Where experimentation is a process not prescribed or defined by outcomes.
- 'Failure' is accepted and encouraged as a natural part of learning and essential to the development process. This is consistent with James Dyson's sentiment quoted in Section 1, Chapter 2:
     'The key to success is failure … not other people's failure but how you respond to failure yourself.'
- Where employees feel empowered to take risks without fear of negative consequences if they fail. Where 'failing forward' is a mantra.

And to create these essential conditions organisations need:

- Leadership that
  - communicates the values associated with creativity,
  - nurtures the 'psychological safety' needed to play, experiment, fail, learn and try again,
  - measures and rewards activity related to exploration rather than defined outcomes.

So, making it fun in the office …

I think there is a reason why the gamification market has seen such a substantial growth since its inception around 2003 and according to Cloke, H. (2023)[27] is expected to grow from $9.1 billion in 2020 to as much as $30.7 billion by 2025.

I only have to listen to my otherwise quiet teenage son asserting himself, problem solving and bantering in high-energy interaction with his friends online to appreciate the new way that youth play. This is the current and next generation. The world of work needs to keep up.

---

[27] https://www.growthengineering.co.uk/19-gamification-trends-for-2023-2025-top-stats-facts-examples

What does all of this mean?

If we agree that play is purposeful and has multiple benefits, for adults and children in all environments, how do we harness that, create conducive environments and remove the possible stigmas that suggest that 'play' runs counter to 'work'? How do we unleash our natural proclivities and play more, fill our proverbial cups and become more generative, productive, contributing human beings?

I have opened a 'can of worms'; I hope you sit in the mud and play with them!

Bibliography and References

Brown, Stuart, 'Why Playing is Vital?', Plays-In-Business.com, Play Theorists Resource, harvard.edu

Lundin, S. C., Paul, H., and Christensen, J., *Fish Omnibus: A Remarkable Way to Boost Morale and Improve Results*, Hodder & Stoughton, Great Britain, 2006

Rucker, M., *The Fun Habit: How the Pursuit of Joy and Wonder can Change Your Life*, Bluebird, UK, 2023

Chapter 5

The Power of Your Mind to Optimise Your GCI Profile for Greater Impact, Energy and Success

A practical guide for individuals on how to effectively manage their energy in the workplace.

Jill Whittington and Vanda North

We have made a couple of assumptions about why you are interested in Energy for Impact. You may be a leader, director, manager, facilitator, provider, or an entrepreneur and business owner. Alternatively, you may be someone reading this book from the perspective of curiosity or self-development. Whatever your reason, we hope you'll be inspired from the new learning and wish to translate that into greater focus, motivation, and productive impact.

It is sometimes easy to teach, train, support or facilitate in others but what about YOU? What about your own development? How much time and energy do you give yourself to continuously develop and optimise your impact, and thus your success at work?

Our experience tells us that very often it is difficult to apply new learning in the 'now,' once the book is back on the shelf or the video is over. Despite our best intentions one's enthusiasm and energy can dissipate once back in the frenzy of work.

Very often despite best efforts, recurring unhelpful habits kick in when things get tough, knocking confidence, and thus reverting to old habits. The traditional 'boom or bust' approach so often associated with New Year's resolutions!

And are you too busy to take on anything else?

What if … you had a technique and tools that guarantees results?
What if … it is easy to do?
What if … new learning is embedded as new habit?
What if … it only took 8 minutes a day?

Welcome to a brand new look at how to 'apply' learning from any GCI profile conversations, to create lasting new habits towards optimising energy for positive impact.

Never before have two energy management processes been merged to allow you to direct and focus energy, towards actively developing any new habit that you and/or your team 'choose' to, from any aspect of working with The GC Index.

Welcome to the merger of GC Index with Change in 8

At The Change Maker Group, we have already blended the unique Mind Chi concept with all aspects of managing change and building overall resilience through Change in 8.

Now we are delighted to build on the merger of The GC Index proclivities with our groundbreaking Change in 8 approach as a compelling way to change a habit and acquire the benefits discovered from the results of your GCI profile.

Change in 8

In this chapter we will cover:

1. What has your mind got to do with optimising your Energy for Impact?
2. An introduction to a way to rewire your brain through Change in 8.
3. The role your mind, brain, and energy play in you creating new and lasting habits.
4. An introduction to the easy 4 steps to Change in 8.
5. How to develop ANY of your proclivities and make changes that stick.
6. Two examples of success with Change in 8.
7. Some successfully completed business Change in 8 plans.
8. Return on Investment (ROI) on making the impact you wish.

1. What has your mind got to do with optimising your Energy for Impact?

You may not have given much thought to the relationship between your energy and how you do what you must do. You do know if you are tired, or if some activity reduces your energy, but have you thought about how you might be able to manage that better for your best impact?

Why not stop for a few moments to consider what 'sucks' or 'boosts' your energy?

Please fill in the blocks below:

Suckers

There are certain actions, people or things that even thinking about them, makes you feel your energy drop. They 'suck' the energy from you. **Make a list of those here:**

_____

_____

_____

_____

Boosters

And there are certain actions, people or things that even thinking about them, makes you feel your energy rise. They fuel you with more energy. Make a list of those here:

_____

_____

_____

_____

This is for you, but it equally applies to your family, team or the whole company and can be used to trigger game-changing conversations. If you wish to build understanding and support among your team or group, this simple exercise opens the door to further productive conversations about how to collectively provide more boosters and reduce the suckers.

What about your GCI profile?

Realising that everyone is a little different, look at the five GC Index energy proclivities, each has its own unique energy and combinations, which may trigger specific suckers and boosters. Perhaps think about your own profile, you may wish to add some more.

Now consider what actions or communications from others would suck or boost the energy for each of the five proclivities.

The following are examples of what might be said that would either suck or boost a person's energy:

GC INDEX PROCLIVITY	SUCKERS	BOOSTERS
The Game Changer – Energy for Creating	We can't change now!	Have you any ideas?
The Strategist – Energy for Planning	Let's try it and see what happens!	Would you organise this?
The Implementer – Energy for Doing	You can't do that now!	Can I leave this for you to do?
The Polisher – Energy for Perfecting	There's no time to re-do this!	Let us check this again!
The Play Maker – Energy for Communicating	All this talk is wasting time!	Would you get a group together?

Notice how there is a direct relationship between your energy, how you may respond in any situation, and your ability to make an impact.

Combining The GC Index with a way to direct your mind's energy through a routine called Change in 8, we will show you how to:

- Make a conscious choice towards developing new, lasting habits by blending the energy awareness of your GC profile with Change in 8.
- Support the development of all proclivities and optimise Energy for Impact, and
- Enhance increased resilience, personal growth, and coping strategies for the strain from stress.

It is no accident that this chapter is positioned early in this book because we aim to inspire you to build upon your learning so far to make lasting changes as you progress through this book.

2. An introduction to a way to rewire your brain through Change in 8

Change in 8 is based upon the book *Mind Chi* which was created to help executives overcome the strains of stress and build lasting resilience to any of life's challenges, and it ended up becoming a global sensation. We have now taken the following simple 8-step, 8-minute process and used it to help people nail their goals and transform their habits.

This diagram shows the Mind Chi 8-step/8-minute routine. It is easy to do, requires no additional equipment and can be performed almost anywhere (though not when driving). Do not be misled to think that because it is easy, it is any the less highly effective in its ability to provide you with the way to control yourself in any situation. You hold the reins over your responses, you are no longer a puppet with external situations and people causing you to react.

Here is a map of the 8-steps:

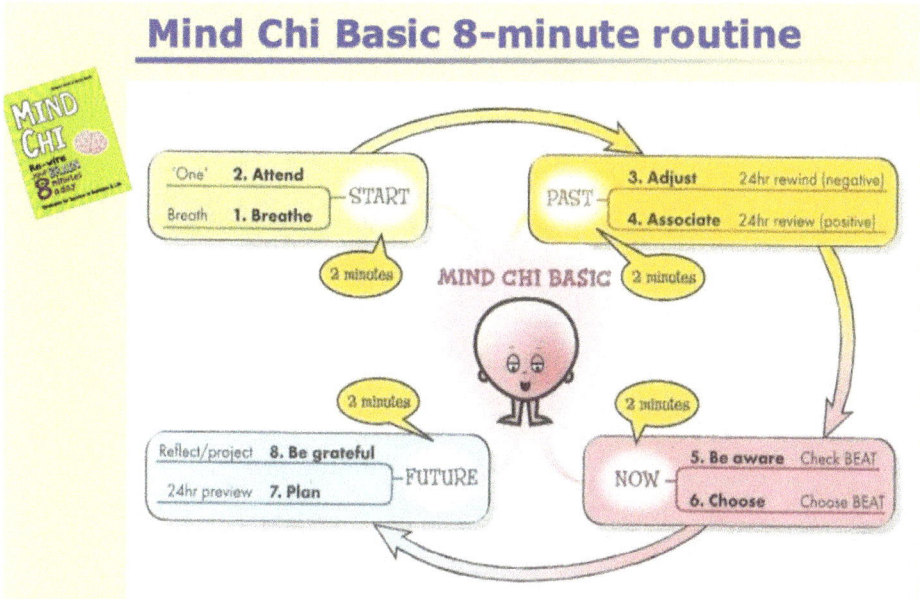

Mind Chi can support you, not just to overcome stress but to take responsibility for utilising the power of your mind to prevent burnout, and routinely function from a place of high resilience and peak performance. If you want to know more, please contact us at
www.TheChangeMakerGroup.com

We will be returning to this in a subsequent book, however, in this chapter, we will focus on applying the fundamentals of Mind Chi through Change in 8 to embed your GC profile learnings and lastingly develop your proclivities.

3. What role do your mind, brain and energy play in you creating new and lasting habits?

Conscious thinking involves complex biological interactions among billions of neurons in the brain.

The brain and the mind work in tandem. It is difficult to separate their function. Generally, it is accepted that the brain refers to the physical, chemical, and electrical functioning. The mind usually refers to abstract cognitive functions. The brain and neurons may be measured and observed, however, as yet, not for the mind. The effects of the mind may be seen in the new neurological wiring of the brain. The relationship is extraordinarily complex, and much is yet to be learned.

The mind changes your brain in temporary and lasting ways by creating new neural pathways – 'neurons which fire together, wire together'.

Your brain has 'plasticity' which means that you can retrain it through conscious and applied thoughts from your mind. You can literally rewire your brain with every thought. There are numerous valid, scientific studies about the power of thought to change the brain.

Our aim is to share a simple, scientifically based, effective daily technique to manage and adopt new learning, to optimise ALL your natural proclivities and mental energy for increased vitality for a powerful impact. We understand that you are aware of your Energy for Impact from your GC profile. This has highlighted some areas that you wish to improve about yourself or goals you wish to achieve. That is where most people fall down. It is great in theory, but HOW to change that habit AND make it stick? Have you experienced this paradox?

Very often, we observe that when individuals work with their GCI profile, they become more aware of how they are managing their energy, they invariably decide to make changes as a natural element of personal development and growth.

This can be in the form of changing a behaviour pattern that is no longer serving them or learning a new skill. Whatever the desired change, it requires reprogramming the brain to create new habits.

Scientifically we know that it takes at least 28 days to start to create new neural pathways. That is why a boom-or-bust approach to any change will never become ingrained as a new habit. How often do New Year's resolutions fail by 1 February?

After 28 days a new pathway has been created; your mind has rewired your brain. However, if you want the new habit to become 'hard wired' then a further 4 to 6 months is required, this means instead of going down the old habit pathway, which is still there especially at times of stress, the natural response is the new habit pathway.

At the heart of any desired change, however, lies choice. A conscious and defined choice to change:

- From a current behavioural state that is now not best use of energy, or
- To develop or learn a new skill which may be job specific, or for personal development and increased impact.

In either case the choice must be informed by a pull to change that is so strong it cannot be ignored, or a negative push so bad that you decide you must act.

Many people find it easy to say what they do not like or want and much harder to focus in on what they do want. Whether you work with a negative push or positive pull it needs to be compelling to have effect.

Change happens best with small steps that are frequently reinforced. Change in 8 exactly follows that model by your daily small awareness and adjustments constantly reinforced. This was Buckminster Fuller's concept of the trim tab, where to turn a large ship, it isn't the rudder that does the work, it is the little trim tab on the edge of the rudder that allows the great ship to shift.

Change in 8 has been developed from the Mind Chi 8 minutes a day routine to build resilience, overcome stress and maximise the use and direction of mental energy.

Mind Chi can be applied to develop new habits through the Change in 8 routine. Integral to this is the creation of a powerful transformative memorable phrase, affirmation or 'meme' defining your choice. This is based on Richard Dawkins research into the power of the meme. The creating of a properly constructed meme repeated at least daily assists the rewiring process. When this is combined with Robert Fritz's Structural Tension, where the tension between your current reality and the desired goal seeks resolution and pulls you along, the lasting effect to be able to change may occur.

4. An introduction to the easy 4 steps to Change in 8

Follow these 4 steps as a guaranteed way to achieve that goal or solve your problem towards greater overall impact.

Fasten your seat belt, you are about to experience innate change through your created plan!

There are only four straightforward steps to make this happen:

1. Decide on a goal or problem that REALLY matters to you
2. Fill in your Change in 8 plan
3. Make your directive, transformative meme and
4. Use just 8 minutes every day for at least 28 days and beyond, until achieved.

Let's go through those step by step – followed by a blank Change in 8 plan for you to complete, or go the www.TheChangeMakerGroup.com to download a fillable plan:

1. **Decide on a goal or problem that REALLY matters to you**
   It is particularly important that you really do want to achieve this. It might be a smaller tweak to start with, or you may wish to dive in with a biggie that you have always wanted to achieve/change. We must emphasise the importance of spending time on this step, repeatedly drilling down into 'why' you are choosing this goal. That way you will embed your volition to make lasting change.

2. **Fill in your Change in 8 plan**
   First the left side, you look at your current reality. What is actually happening in your life because of this problem or needed goal right now? Fill in the space with your current reality, take each letter and really become aware of the negative impacts upon you by trying to recognise three things that occur for each of these four letters, B.E.A.T. This is an acronym for Body, Emotions, Actions and Thoughts. For example:
   Body – What is happening? Sweaty palms; headaches; tense muscles; clenched jaw, etc.

Emotions - How are you feeling? Uncertain; anxious; worried; stressed, etc.

Actions – How are you performing? Fiddling, procrastinating, muti-tasking, etc.

Thoughts – What are you saying to yourself? 'That was a silly thing to say!'; 'I'll never do that'; 'It's so hard to do'; 'I don't know if I can do this', etc. Before you know it, your mind can run away like an untrained puppy with a plethora of unhelpful thoughts!

Really delve into the discomfort your current reality is causing you.

Having defined your current reality, look at the right-hand column and fill in your desired goal or outcome. Complete this, and then compare with what you will experience for your **Body, Emotions, Actions and Thoughts** – fill those in. Make them desirable and ensure that your preferred emotions and thoughts become your best cheerleader. Be really excited about your chosen goal.

3. **Make your transformative, directive meme**

   A meme is a thought or idea that is replicated in your brain. Most of them are current 'fun' things, such as 'Keep calm and carry on', or negative ideas, such as 'Bleach cures Covid'.

   A meme must be constructed carefully for it to work. The first part is 'I choose to …'; not, 'I will' or 'I wish to', as the brain can find a way out of those.

   Then to state positively your desired outcome.

   For example, 'I choose to manage my time efficiently' or 'I choose to delegate effectively and achieve more.' Once you have created it, complete the block that says, 'Transform meme'.

   NB If you find yourself thinking 'I really "should" or "ought" to do something', go back to step 1! It is VITAL that you are making a change that truly matters to you and is a genuine choice and therefore is self-motivating.

4. **Use for just 8 minutes every day for at least 28 days and beyond until achieved.**

   Please see below for the details of how to do the specific 8 steps. Then after 28 days assess where you are in relation to achieving your desired goal.

   This is the length of time to begin to create a new neural pathway, and it is at least 6 months for it to become more 'hard wired' in your brain.

   Here is a blank Change in 8 plan for you to fill in, or visit www.TheChangeMakerGroup.com for a downloadable version:

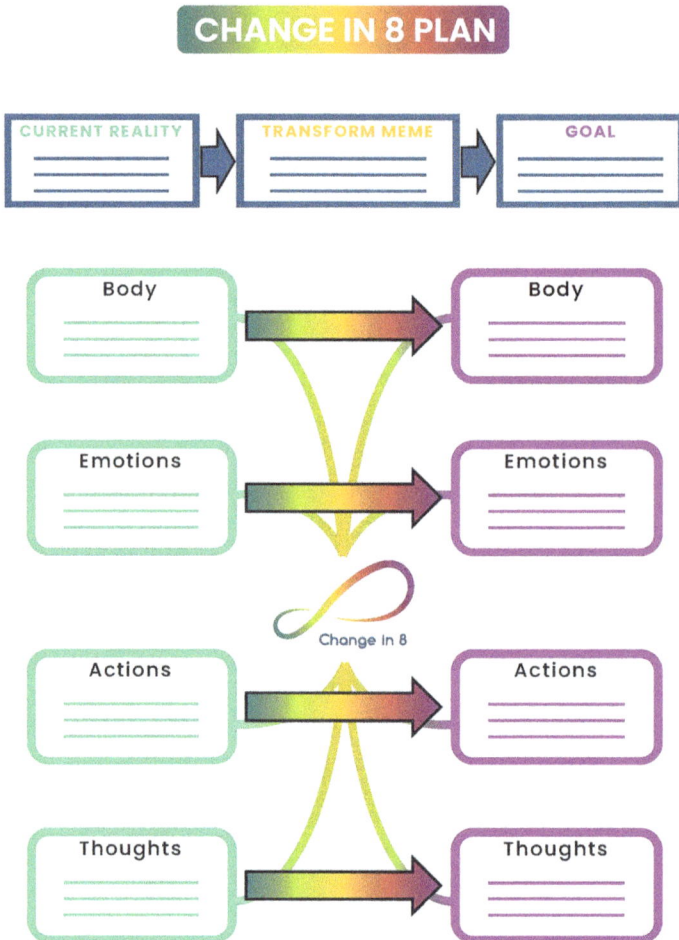

CHANGE IN 8 PLAN

CURRENT REALITY	TRANSFORM MEME	GOAL

Body → **Body**

Emotions → **Emotions**

Change In 8

Actions → **Actions**

Thoughts → **Thoughts**

5. How to develop ANY of your proclivities and make changes that stick

To use the full Change in 8 routine applied towards specific goals perform these simple 8 steps with each of these steps taking just 1 minute.

The full 8 step, 8 minute Change in 8 routine includes:

- **Step 1** – Calming the body with 'square belly' breathing.
- **Step 2** – Focusing the mind by repeating your meme.
- **Step 3** – Looking back over the last 24 hours to see what has not gone so well with your goal attainment to be able to learn what you may choose to do the next time that situation arises. Then only take the learning forward from these and disregard the rest, leaving it in the past, i.e. not dwelling on them!
- **Step 4** – Look back over the past 24 hours to see what did go well and move you towards your desired goal. Use these positive moments to inspire and motivate you to keep going.
- **Step 5** – BEAT – focused on the goal – how is your BEAT now? And if it is not as you'd like it to be …
- **Step 6** – What do you choose your BEAT to be for greater motivation towards your goal, i.e. re-setting yourself in the moment?
- **Step 7** – Using the power of your mind to visualise how you want the next 24 hours to play out, not just what you must do, but how you want to be to be able to be most effective, as if it is a full Technicolor movie. Your actions then will have a much higher chance of playing out as you want them to.
- **Step 8** – Practice gratitude, for all the things that have been achieved or will be going well, which energises and keeps you motivated. Gratitude keeps a sense of proportion and is known to contribute to an overall feeling of greater happiness and more contentment.

You can look back at the diagram of the 8 minute 8 step Mind Chi process in Section 2 to help you.

Now we have shown you how to integrate your Mind Chi and Change in 8 plan, you can progress your meme and create the structural tension towards your goal on a daily basis.

Mind Chi and Change in 8 are based on Cognitive Behavioural Therapy (CBT), positive psychology and the science of happiness; as well as a combined 95 years of testing. That is why it works!

The chosen meme as well as being repeated every day as part of this routine, can also be repeated at any time, especially when recognising a stressful tension. Some people like putting a tune or rhythm to it!

6. Two examples of success with Change in 8

Let's look at a couple of examples from our portfolio of clients:

Example 1

- Female senior manager in a public sector organisation in the UK
- Incessant workload, multiple deadlines, manages a team of six, matrix reporting, micromanagement from bosses with elevated levels of reactive unplanned tasking with constant changes
- Considered in high regard, very competent and a 'safe pair of hands'
- Poor life balance.

GC Index profile:

NB Scores on a GCI profile are in the 1–10 range. Within that range scores from 1–3 reflect low energy; scores in the 4–6 range reflect moderate energy that people can 'lean into' when needed; scores in the 7–10 range reflect strong energy that people may find themselves being 'drawn into'.

This individual was under considerable pressure, highly stressed and verging on 'burnout'.

After discussion and with insight from her GCI profile, we highlighted the fact that her relatively balanced score, tipped in favour of a high Implementer/Strategist, shone a light on the fact that she had a pattern of being pulled in all directions, didn't like to say 'no', wanted to succeed, and to ensure all deadlines were met. Does this sound familiar for you, too?

She concluded that in the short term she wanted to handle stress better and create a more balanced life. After a coaching session really drilling down into why this was important, she decided upon the following Change in 8 plan.

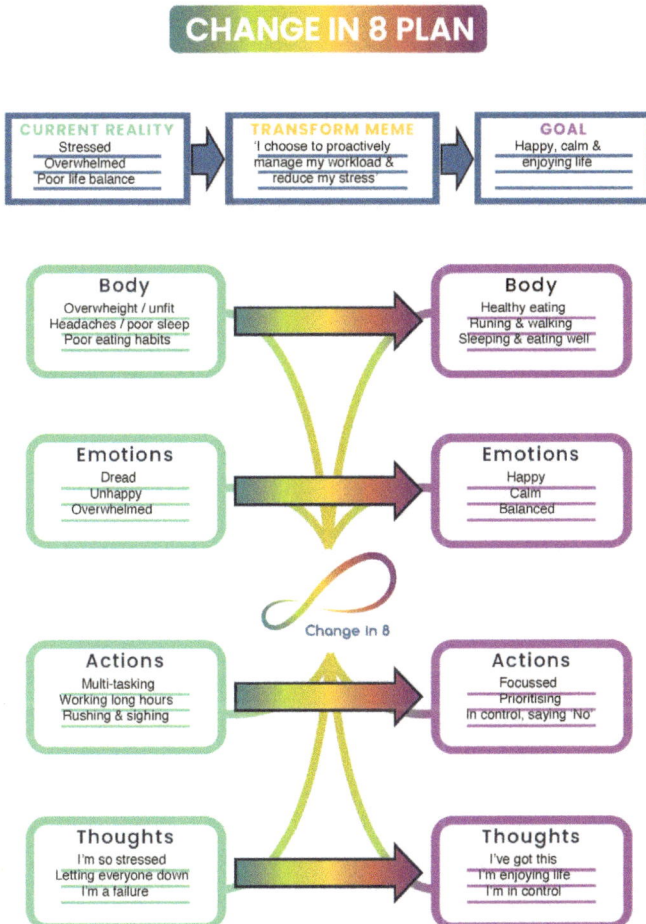

CHANGE IN 8 PLAN

CURRENT REALITY	TRANSFORM MEME	GOAL
Stressed	'I choose to proactively	Happy, calm &
Overwhelmed	manage my workload &	enjoying life
Poor life balance	reduce my stress'	

Body
Overwheight / unfit
Headaches / poor sleep
Poor eating habits

Body
Healthy eating
Runing & walking
Sleeping & eating well

Emotions
Dread
Unhappy
Overwhelmed

Emotions
Happy
Calm
Balanced

Change in 8

Actions
Multi-tasking
Working long hours
Rushing & sighing

Actions
Focussed
Prioritising
In control, saying 'No'

Thoughts
I'm so stressed
Letting everyone down
I'm a failure

Thoughts
I've got this
I'm enjoying life
I'm in control

In so doing, she downloaded everything out of her head. This, in itself, had an immediate stress-relieving effect, stopping the incessant washing machine like churning of unhelpful thought, feelings, and actions.

Then, being the Implementer and Strategist she is, she created a prioritised plan of what she wanted to do, starting with renegotiating her workload.

After a week or so of being led through the full Change in 8 routine she was able to practise it herself daily, as well as supplementing it with some extra BEAT resetting during the day.

Note: Using BEAT to reset is especially effective in stressful moments and/or before a meeting or presentation and between meetings. It can also be used to transition from being in one mode to the next, e.g. end of day before going home.

She also passed some of the tools and tips on to her team which brought about an even greater positive impact to team resilience.

Soon she was assertively pushing back against unreasonable deadlines with options; clearing her inbox.

In this case, there was such a strong negative push that she had no option but to act, since not doing so was severely damaging her well-being.

Example 2

- Female photographer
- Mother of two small children
- Had run a successful, award-winning photography business for 12 years
- Business had plateaued
- Had become overwhelmed with trying to manage her business processes to be able to know how or what she needed to change against new financial pressures due to the recent cost of living paradigm.

GC Index profile:

Without knowing it at the time she started her business, she related with her strong Play Maker/Strategist profile. She recognised this had been the catalyst for doing what she loved. She loves photography and is highly creative with a keen business acumen ... except for the boring stuff of running a business!

She had reached a plateau in her business but did not know what to change or how to change it. She was doing more of the same, working harder and wondering why her business wasn't growing.

Having been on a Business Accelerator programme with one of our business partners, she learned that she had a fear of numbers and had talked herself into thinking she couldn't do them (even though she knew what she was spending and receiving), or where her most profitable business lines were. She did not know which levers to pull or push to change how and where she was attracting business, what was profitable and what was not.

She quickly decided that she was a Game Changer who wants to overcome procrastination! This is the change statement she adopted.

CHANGE IN 8 PLAN

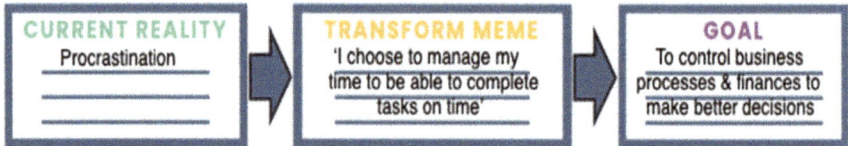

CURRENT REALITY	TRANSFORM MEME	GOAL
Procrastination	'I choose to manage my time to be able to complete tasks on time'	To control business processes & finances to make better decisions

She now LOVES her numbers! So much so, she has gone way beyond the initial learning and has adopted and adapted, using her Game Changer energy to produce a whole suite of financial, business and marketing processes. This has enabled her to make informed decisions.

She now dedicates uninterrupted time on her business once per week. She has reduced one business line, increased another, stopped investment on some items, refocused her marketing, changed her pricing and now has more bookings for the rest of this year and next than ever before!

In doing so she has also created more time for herself, not wasting precious energy procrastinating, has gone back to the gym and keeps weekends solely for family time.

In both scenarios, the individuals have replaced limiting thoughts and beliefs into ones which support and encourage. This is demonstrating change happening with small steps, frequently reinforced.

7. Some successfully completed Change in 8 plans

To kick-start completing your selected Change in 8 plan, goal or problem, we include a few here.

Initially it may prove challenging to become aware of what is really happening and what you really want. Developing your self-awareness is a crucially important skill, another benefit of this Change in 8 approach, informed by your GCI profile.

Change in 8 plan for setting priorities

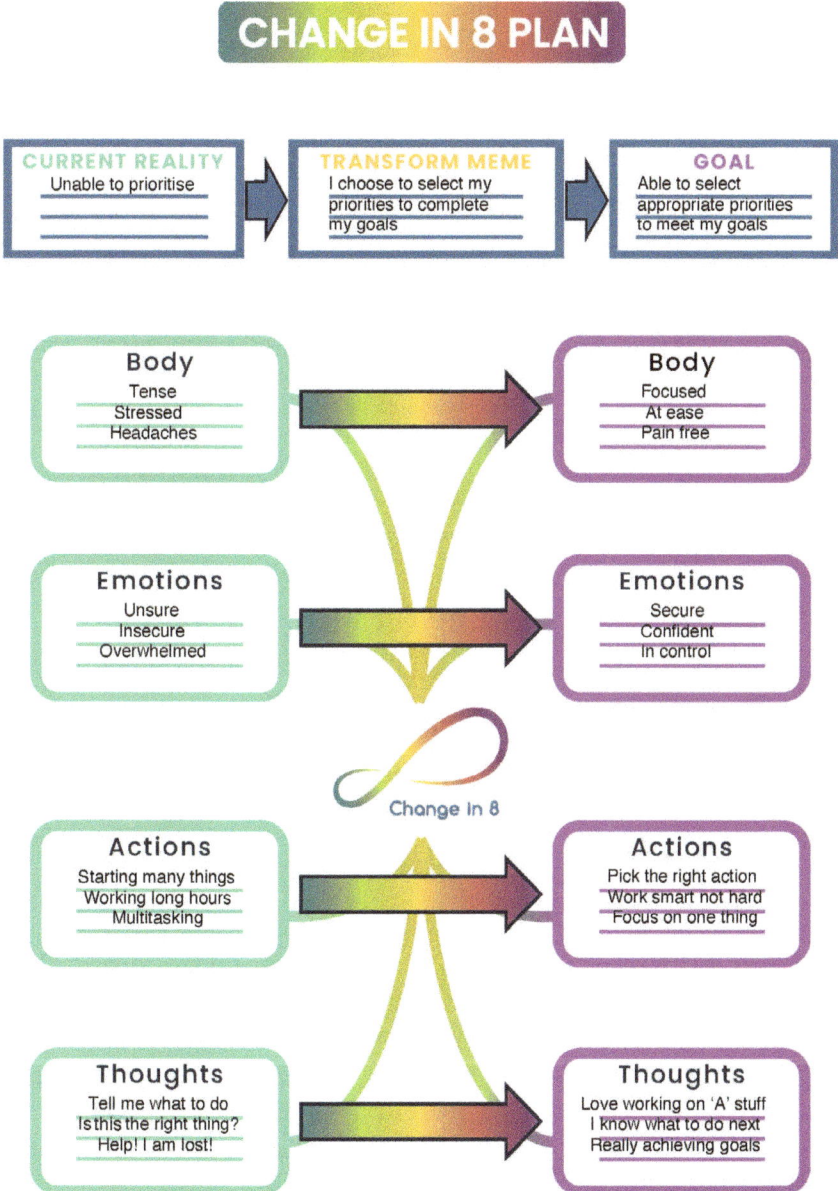

CHANGE IN 8 PLAN

CURRENT REALITY	TRANSFORM MEME	GOAL
Unable to prioritise	I choose to select my priorities to complete my goals	Able to select appropriate priorities to meet my goals

Body
Tense
Stressed
Headaches

Body
Focused
At ease
Pain free

Emotions
Unsure
Insecure
Overwhelmed

Emotions
Secure
Confident
In control

Change In 8

Actions
Starting many things
Working long hours
Multitasking

Actions
Pick the right action
Work smart not hard
Focus on one thing

Thoughts
Tell me what to do
Is this the right thing?
Help! I am lost!

Thoughts
Love working on 'A' stuff
I know what to do next
Really achieving goals

Change in 8 plan for managing stress

CHANGE IN 8 PLAN

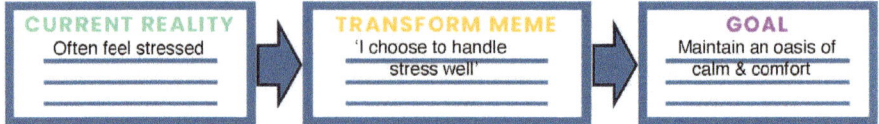

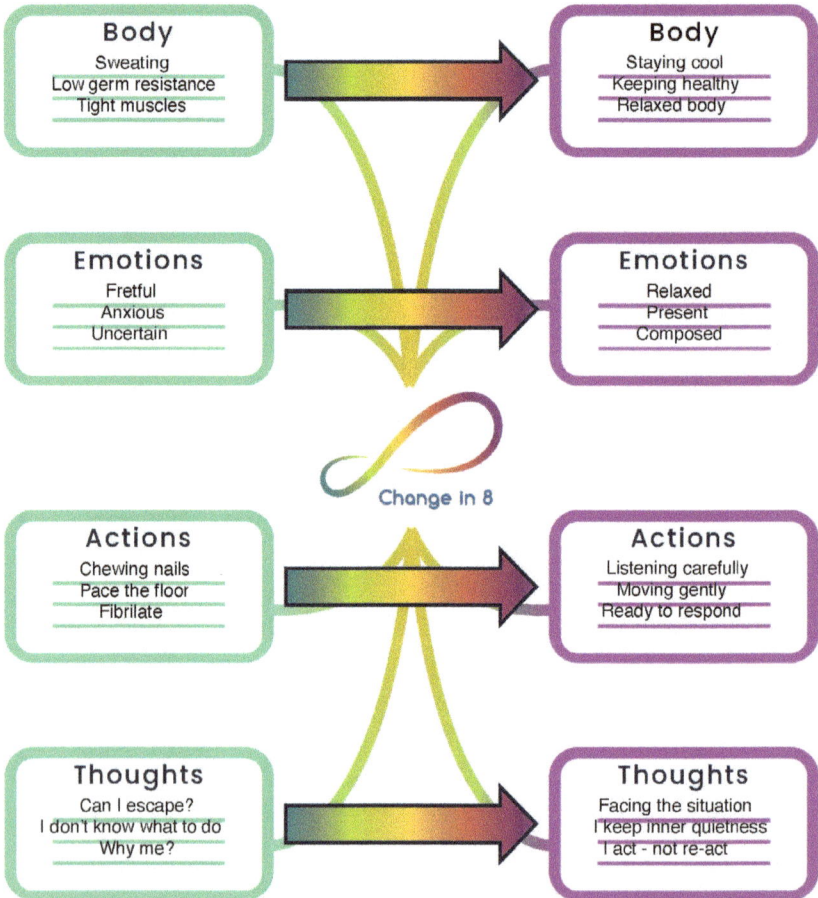

CURRENT REALITY	TRANSFORM MEME	GOAL
Often feel stressed	'I choose to handle stress well'	Maintain an oasis of calm & comfort

Body
Sweating
Low germ resistance
Tight muscles

Body
Staying cool
Keeping healthy
Relaxed body

Emotions
Fretful
Anxious
Uncertain

Emotions
Relaxed
Present
Composed

Change in 8

Actions
Chewing nails
Pace the floor
Fibrilate

Actions
Listening carefully
Moving gently
Ready to respond

Thoughts
Can I escape?
I don't know what to do
Why me?

Thoughts
Facing the situation
I keep inner quietness
I act - not re-act

Change in 8 plan for recalling names and faces

CHANGE IN 8 PLAN

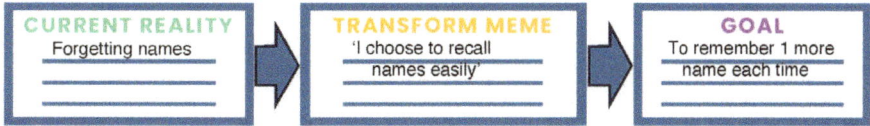

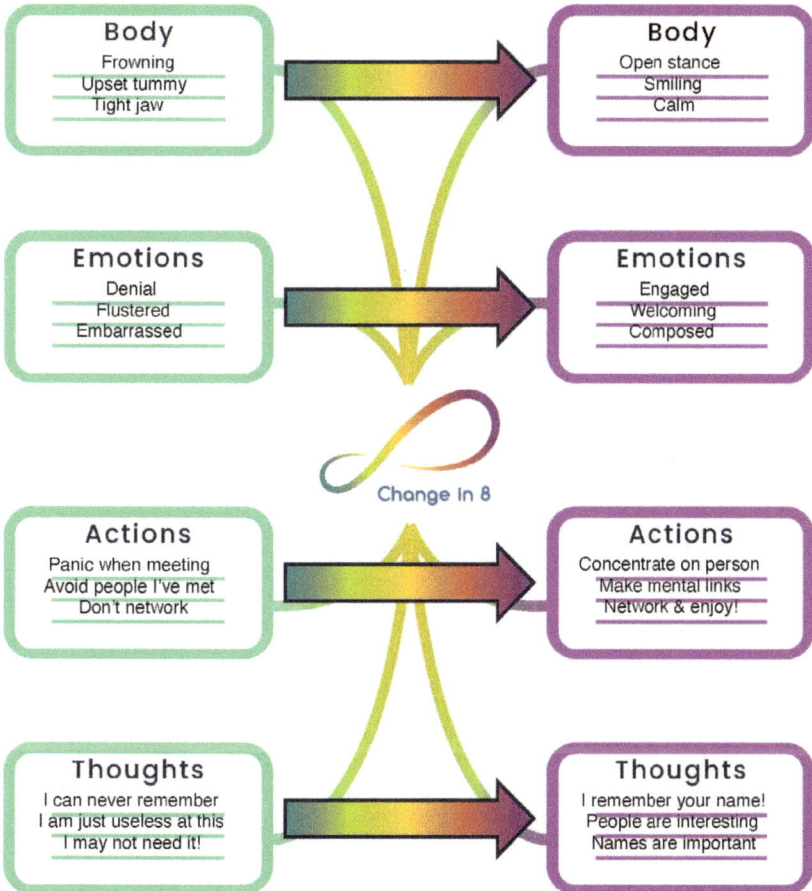

CURRENT REALITY	TRANSFORM MEME	GOAL
Forgetting names	'I choose to recall names easily'	To remember 1 more name each time

Body
Frowning
Upset tummy
Tight jaw

Body
Open stance
Smiling
Calm

Emotions
Denial
Flustered
Embarrassed

Emotions
Engaged
Welcoming
Composed

Change in 8

Actions
Panic when meeting
Avoid people I've met
Don't network

Actions
Concentrate on person
Make mental links
Network & enjoy!

Thoughts
I can never remember
I am just useless at this
I may not need it!

Thoughts
I remember your name!
People are interesting
Names are important

Change in 8 plan for accepting criticism

CHANGE IN 8 PLAN

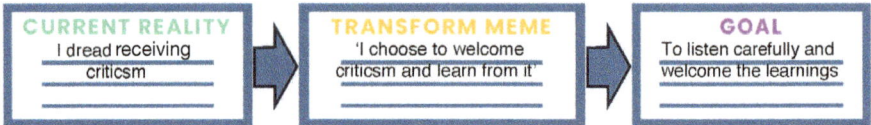

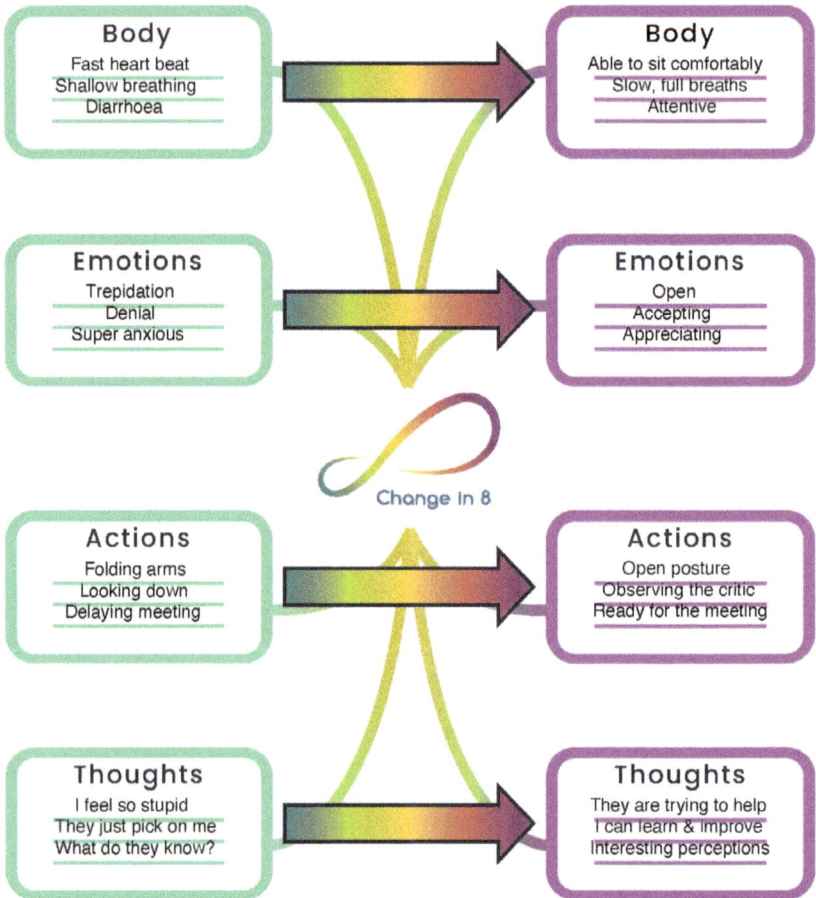

CURRENT REALITY	TRANSFORM MEME	GOAL
I dread receiving criticsm	'I choose to welcome criticsm and learn from it'	To listen carefully and welcome the learnings

Body
Fast heart beat
Shallow breathing
Diarrhoea

Body
Able to sit comfortably
Slow, full breaths
Attentive

Emotions
Trepidation
Denial
Super anxious

Emotions
Open
Accepting
Appreciating

Change in 8

Actions
Folding arms
Looking down
Delaying meeting

Actions
Open posture
Observing the critic
Ready for the meeting

Thoughts
I feel so stupid
They just pick on me
What do they know?

Thoughts
They are trying to help
I can learn & improve
Interesting perceptions

Change in 8 plan for increasing creativity

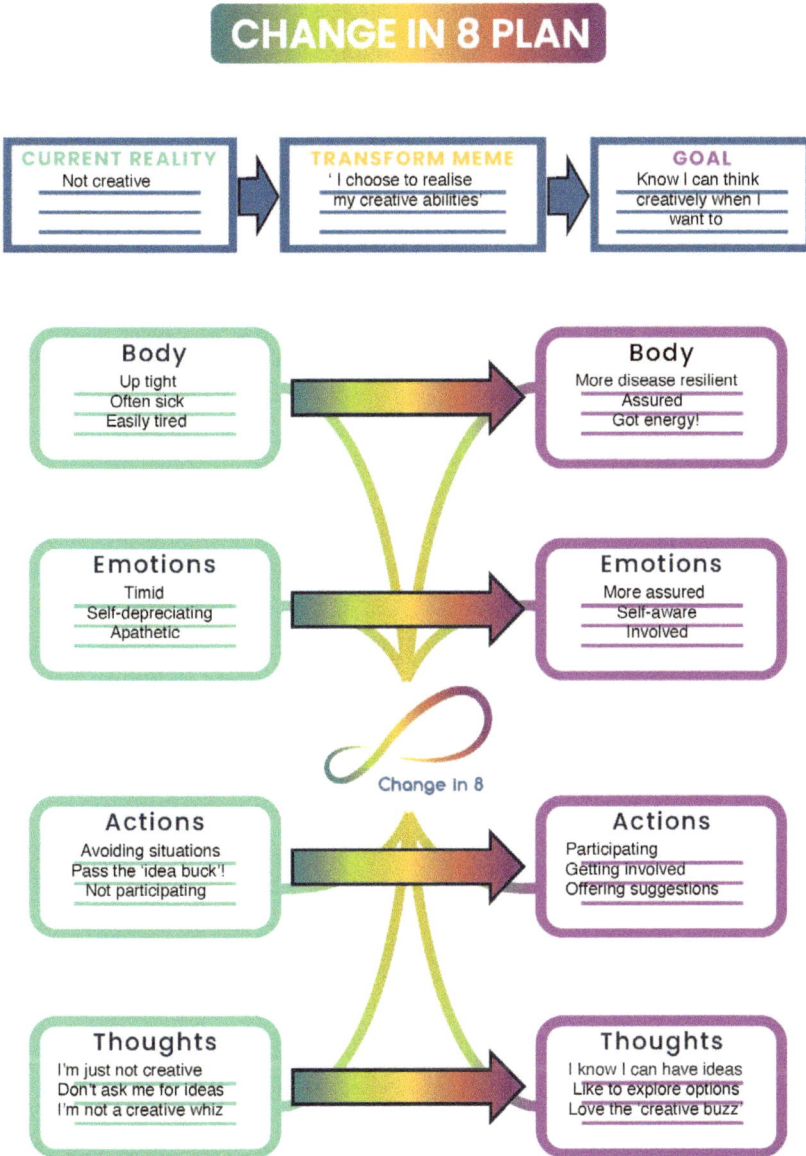

CHANGE IN 8 PLAN

CURRENT REALITY	TRANSFORM MEME	GOAL
Not creative	' I choose to realise my creative abilities'	Know I can think creatively when I want to

Body
Up tight
Often sick
Easily tired

Body
More disease resilient
Assured
Got energy!

Emotions
Timid
Self-depreciating
Apathetic

Emotions
More assured
Self-aware
Involved

Change in 8

Actions
Avoiding situations
Pass the 'idea buck'!
Not participating

Actions
Participating
Getting involved
Offering suggestions

Thoughts
I'm just not creative
Don't ask me for ideas
I'm not a creative whiz

Thoughts
I know I can have ideas
Like to explore options
Love the 'creative buzz'

We have some 45 other completed Change in 8 plans, which may be viewed at www.TheChangeMakerGroup.com_

Please share your Change in 8 plans with us, you may also help someone else to change a habit.

8. ROI on making the impact you wish

What difference it would make to you, if you could improve one area that would have a positive business result for you? What if, you adopted a new habit to help you work with greater ease, efficiency, and impact, knowing that habit would stay?!

It is the most satisfying and empowering feeling when you know that you are really in control of yourself, regardless of what is occurring around you. It is you who has the power to take control and choose how you will respond to any situation.

Now imagine if your whole team knew about The GC Index and Change in 8, with some working in their preferred energy place and some not. The difference being that you are all now aware of your options and choices that you can make not just individually but collectively. You will be able to apply new learning in the 'now' and optimise your investment in ANY training or new learning.

Organisations frequently feel that they may not be receiving good practical value from the training courses attended. You may be inspired in the moment but return to your work responsibilities and even the best intentions often fade away. For the first time we are sharing a way to change that. Yes, it does take some time – a whole 8 minutes a day – and it does take a commitment to follow the 8 steps of Change in 8 every day.

Think of how quickly 8 minutes passes over a coffee break, or an enjoyable discussion. That is all you are asking of yourself.

Now expand your thinking to imagine how a focused team might achieve their individual and team goals, the synergy of such constructive collaboration whilst supporting each other and seeing the benefits. Whilst you are imagining, how about an entire company doing the same? Talk about a competitive edge!

In summary, managing your energy is a vital indicator of your being able to truly take new learning on board for lasting positive change and lead yourself through any situation.

We therefore urge you to take control of that vital resource. Fostering your precious mental energy enables you to make conscious choices to become all the person you wish to be and live the life you choose. It all starts with YOU!

We invite you to bear this in mind, and potentially apply this Energy for Impact learning as you progress with the subsequent chapters in this book.

Chapter 6

The Entrepreneurial Couple

An inspiring story of one couple's journey from despair to joy …
with the help of The GC Index.

John and Natalie Franklin-Hackett

Do opposites attract? And what happens when a relationship is tested? How is energy lost during a period of challenge and regained from a major life change that can result? And how can couples work together as a successful team to navigate all this?

Relationships are interesting things. It's said that 'opposites attract', and my wife and I have always been opposites. While I enjoy setting 'big, fat, hairy' goals and making sense of how to achieve them, she enjoys getting tasks done. She lives for tangible achievement, I live for ideas and, dare I admit, more than a touch of 'navel-gazing'.

Were you to watch each of us work, isolate us from one another and see how we prefer to do things, I'd be willing to bet that you'd have little difficulty identifying that we go about our business in totally different ways.

This difference in the ways in which we channel our energy is reflected in our GC Index profiles (see Figs. 1 and 2 below).

Natalie has a high-energy Implementer profile, with a touch of Polisher energy in the mix. My profile features a healthy dose of Game Changer energy, followed by Strategist and Polisher energy. I share next to nothing of Natalie's Implementer energy, and she shares little of my Game Changer proclivity.

Figure 1: Natalie's GC Index profile

Figure 2: John's GC Index profile

In terms of our energy to make an impact, we are truly opposites.

At home, our differing energies play out clearly and in ways consistent with our GC Index profiles. I am often the one who comes up with ideas about projects we could carry out in the house, places to visit or life goals to achieve. Natalie is usually the one who takes the initiative to get things done. While I can regularly be found thinking, dreaming and analysing, she is usually found attending to tasks, ticking things off lists and working out what to do next.

You may think after reading this that I do the thinking and Natalie does the doing. And to some extent, this is true. In reality though, there is rather more nuance than that. There are times when Natalie comes up with interesting, albeit practical, ideas, or is more inclined to take a risk than I am. Conversely, there are occasions where I can be very task-focused. What seems to be true though, is that we largely 'stay in our lanes' and we've learned over time to give each other the space to express our energies and stay true to what motivates us.

This is not to say that we don't clash. While we have been lucky to share a harmonious relationship, there are times when, inevitably, we become frustrated with each other. What's interesting is that conflict often arises when our differing energies are not aligned towards the same purpose or motivation. In these situations, we can become irritated with each other:

Natalie may tire of my 'big picture' focus or tendency to over-analyse, while I may become intolerant of her relentless task focus. My willingness to hold back from doing something while I try to establish whether acting on it makes sense in the bigger picture can be highly frustrating to Natalie. Her whirlwind of implementing and dislike of standing back and considering the 'why', 'what' and 'how' can exhaust me when I don't see a strong 'why' behind the effort.

It would be tempting in these situations to point the finger at who is right and who is wrong. But it turns out that most of the time we're both right. In reality, the problem to be solved is usually whose energies will make the most useful impact at a specific time.

Fortunately, in most cases, our understanding of each other's energies allows us to identify the source of conflict and find a suitable resolution. Commonly, all it takes is for us to remind ourselves to give each other space and respect. I sometimes think that getting the best balance in this way is one of the ongoing challenges and successes of our relationship.

To illustrate how this energy dynamic has played out, I'd like to tell you about one of the biggest challenges in our relationship and how our GC Index profiles helped us to overcome it. And it's all about purpose and meaning in life, via a huge change in career and lifestyle.

As in most areas of life, our energies were strongly reflected in our earlier career choices, as well as our satisfaction with them. In fact, in this respect we were entirely different from each other.

Natalie knew what she wanted to do from her early teens. She wanted to be a teacher.

This she achieved immediately after leaving university, following which she 'climbed the ranks' to become an assistant headteacher in a very large and challenging inner-city primary school. Her career was a great match for her energies. Teaching is all about tasks: delivering learning, marking work, planning lessons. She loved the clarity of purpose that came from carrying out a clearly defined role. She was fortunate to work with head teachers who set clear priorities, which made it simple for her to understand what she had to achieve, what success looked like and when she'd achieved it.

She spent her entire career in one school, which she loved, as it gave her a clear sense of what she needed to do to make a difference. She knew the children, understood their needs and how best to help them learn. She could see the difference she made on a daily basis and this then fuelled her energies to keep going, keep implementing and stay energised.

I've met very few people who truly love their work and who get up each day full of enthusiasm for what they're about to spend the day doing. Natalie was one of these people. She truly loved her job. It's true to say that in some respects, her job was her life.

And for the best part of 18 years, the alignment between her Implementer/Polisher energies and her career couldn't have been better.

My career path was less straightforward and comparatively chaotic. On leaving university, I felt a desire to explore entrepreneurial ideas, do something creative, find a direction through experimentation. Perhaps, in keeping with many others, that's not what I ended up doing.

For one reason or another, I found myself working as a project administrator at a small charity and not having a particularly fulfilling time doing it. I had the skills required but I struggled to find the energy to stay on top of administrative tasks, often leaving things incomplete until the last moment and then being dissatisfied with the result. Sensing that this wasn't the recipe for a great life, I attempted to move up to more challenging roles, eventually finding myself as a business analyst in a local authority. This seemed to fit better, as I enjoyed the process of analysing a service, finding out the facts and coming up with recommendations for how things could be improved; the role, to some extent, fed my Polisher energy. However, when I began to notice that my recommendations were either not approved of or not implemented, the familiar loss of energy came to the surface once again. So, I tried my hand at corporate project management – too formulaic; then service management – too administrative, until I finally fell into the role of customer services development manager. This role required me to both manage customer services functions whilst also making changes and improvements. It seemed like a nice sandpit to play in. Except, once again, I found my creativity stifled by corporate processes and risk aversion.

I remember one such example: I had been reading about some fascinating science that had shown that smells in buildings could have a measurable effect on human behaviour. As I was in charge of a one-stop shop in a town hall where we were often visited by agitated and emotional customers, I saw an opportunity to use fragrances to create a more welcoming, relaxing mood that would help to calm customers down and create a more positive environment. After researching the required equipment and costs, I presented a proposal to management. Despite the very low costs involved, the proposal was rejected on the basis that an influential councillor thought it was 'mumbo-jumbo'.

And so, it was goodbye to yet another idea and hello to more swearing and shaking of fists on my part.

This inability to bring many of my ideas to reality became increasingly frustrating and I found myself sinking into apathy and cynicism.

So finally, and perhaps, inevitably, out into the land of self-employment I ventured, becoming an external consultant and adviser. I was free to work with lots of organisations, make recommendations and not have to worry about whether they would be implemented or not. I could move on to something else and gain new creative energy that way.

This proved to be a 'baptism of fire'. On one hand, I had lots of 'sandpits to play in', where I could make good use of my Game Changer energy and be paid for doing so. On the other, I had to find these sandpits in the first place and often convince people who didn't share my energies that they should let me play in them. It turned out that while I was good at the former, I wasn't so good at the latter. This was often due to the fact that the individuals who held the purse strings in potential client organisations were most likely more Implementer-biased and were therefore less receptive to my Game Changer-led sales pitch than I'd have liked.

The irony here was that I needed Natalie's energies to fill in my gaps; but more on that later.

So, after nearly 10 years of this, I was on the cusp of building my business into something more than a solo performance. My 'big picture thinking' looked to have paid off with the advent of two potentially game-changing partnership opportunities. Once these were live, lots of leads would be coming my way and, therefore, I needed a team of associates to help me deliver the work. Now this was a 'big fat hairy goal' that I could get excited about!

During this period, Natalie provided unwavering emotional support and a fair degree of patience as I landed a new role or project, became loudly dissatisfied and then moved on to something else. I've wondered if this was easier for her because she was so fulfilled in her own career. Because her own energies were recognised, rewarded and utilised, she had space to better support me as I struggled to find the same fulfilment for myself.

So, for the first 15 years of our relationship, Natalie was the satisfied Implementer who loved her career and managed our home, and I was the dissatisfied Game Changer, looking to express my creativity, land a big idea and struggling to find a fulfilling career.

As ever, opposites.

Which brings us neatly to the cataclysmic events of 2020.

At the start of 2020, as for many, we had hopes and aspirations for the year. Except this year was different. For one, both of us were approaching our forties, which certainly made us evaluate where we'd been in life and where we were going. But at the same time, both of us had career aspirations that were on their way to being realised during the year. Natalie was exploring a potential opportunity to move on from the school she'd worked at for 15 years into a new role under a previous head teacher, who'd moved on some years earlier.

For me, from a business perspective 2020 was 'the big one'. I had spent much of 2019 working tirelessly to set up two partnerships, one in the recruitment sector and one in the public sector. The master plan was this:

by having partnerships with member organisations in two key industries, I would have access to thousands of potential clients and two influential organisations promoting and helping to sell my consulting services. It was probably in keeping with my Game Changer energies to find a left-field approach to expanding a consultancy business as opposed to growing organically. I'd always struggled with the process of securing individual projects and clients and felt that a 'top-down' systemic approach would deliver better results, more quickly. I suspect I was compensating for my weakness in the sales process by finding teams of individuals with a more task and relationship focused energy. But nonetheless, as we neared the start of the new financial year in April 2020, I was sufficiently confident in the potential of this to start recruiting associates. With all the leads coming in, I would need support. Lots of it.

It's hard to overstate how obsessed I was at seeing this vision become a reality. My career as a self-employed consultant had been less satisfactory than I'd have liked and I really felt as though I had finally found a way to make a big impact. It seemed I was about to unleash a system, through these partnerships, that would allow me to deliver game-changing results in two key industries. The website was in place, I was building a team and press releases were being prepared. I'd visualised what success was going to look like. I was hungry, even desperate perhaps, for seeing this success become a reality.

My achievement in getting these partnerships in place gave me a sense of pride, as well as confidence that I could make exciting things happen as an entrepreneur.

In hindsight, it was a classic example of my Game Changer/Strategist energy working overtime to drive me forward in pursuit of a big vision. It was a feeling of 'potency' – an ability to express one's energy freely in an effective manner.

During the second week of March 2020, I was in London training a team of 10 account managers at one of the member organisations to sell our services. We weren't sure whether to shake hands, as there was a flu virus of some sort featuring prominently in the media, but I paid little attention to that. Training these people, who were in regular contact with 11,000 professionals in their industry, to sell my services was the prelude to my 'big picture vision' becoming a reality. It was tremendously exciting and as far as I was concerned, nothing was getting in the way of making it happen.

At the same time, Natalie was navigating some changes in her work environment. During 2019, a new head teacher had taken over at her school. His style was very different from his predecessor's, with whom Natalie had enjoyed a healthy working relationship. He seemed less concerned about detail and process and had a lot of ideas about how the school could do things differently.

As 2020 rolled in, Natalie began to feel some dissatisfaction with her job, possibly for the first time in her career. The new head teacher was merrily tearing up processes and procedures in the school, some of which she'd implemented herself. It was becoming more difficult to understand the 'why', 'what' and 'how' in her role, as despite having thrown a 'wrecking ball' at these things, her new boss was unable to articulate exactly what would take priority in their place. As we came to the start of March, she was beginning to lose some confidence in what she was doing.

Nevertheless, the potential of an opportunity to move to a new role under her previous head teacher loomed on the horizon. It was just a matter of having a few conversations to firm things up which meant that the situation at her present school, while concerning, was not necessarily a serious issue for Natalie. She had a list of tasks to carry out that would create a path to continue her hitherto satisfying career somewhere else. So, from her perspective as an Implementer, all she had to do was implement them and everything would be fine.

So here we were in March 2020. I was seemingly 'on a roll' as my 'big business vision' began to come together, and Natalie was becoming less satisfied and less certain in her role as an assistant head teacher. After years of me being the frustrated individual looking for a more satisfying career and Natalie being the contented, dedicated professional, had we switched places?

As events would have it, it didn't matter. Because then everything went crazy.

On 23 March 2020, the then UK Prime Minister Boris Johnson announced lockdown in response to the Covid-19 pandemic. I can vividly recall watching my email inbox in the following hours, recoiling in horror as both of the partnerships I'd been working so hard to secure, both of which were on the cusp of going live, were immediately put on ice. Then, I saw my entire business diary wiped out for the foreseeable future. Everything withdrawn or cancelled. All my paid work and potential work, gone. I was suddenly in a position where I had no business, no income and no sense of when or if things would change.

As someone with a Game Changer-biased GC Index profile, this was a devastating blow. The great benefit of this energy is the enjoyment of developing original and creative ideas and the intense obsession with seeing them come to fruition. For me, watching my business and my goals being wiped out by such a dramatic set of external events was the equivalent of watching one's house burn down in front of their eyes. It was my ideas being 'shot down' in front of me. It was deeply distressing.

I had some history in this area which made this situation even more traumatic. When I was 23, I had attempted to buy a redundant building from my old school – a fantastic modern building with a drama studio, recording studio and great facilities. I was obsessed with it. After a long battle with the local authority I'd finally secured the money from a third party to buy the building and get going, only for political shenanigans to stop us from proceeding. I eventually saw the building destroyed in an arson attack after sitting derelict for several years.

So, because I was obsessed with getting these business partnerships 'over the line', because I saw them as the means of achieving my goal of creating a successful consultancy practice, I cared intensely about their success. Just as with the earlier project, failure was therefore an incredibly personal blow. It was my energies working against me once again. Losing all of my existing paid work as well meant that I felt my strategy for providing my share of the income into the household had failed. Therefore, I was a failure.

Conversely, for Natalie the start of lockdown was somewhat less problematic. Although, like me and many others she was concerned about the future and the effect on our financial and personal health, she reacted to the news by getting busy. She developed a schedule for our week so we'd have a sense of what to do each day. She enjoyed getting on with jobs in the house that she'd previously not had time to accomplish.

Her Implementer energy came to the fore helping her to feel potent in her world in contrast to my feelings of impotence.

As a teacher, she had to navigate considerable change as lessons initially switched to remote learning and then, arrangements for in-school provision chopped and changed as the government lurched from one set of rules to another. She found each change was initially jarring, but once she knew the parameters for working, she would quickly internalise them and get on with the business of delivery. This again, showed her strong Implementer energy working at its best. So long as she knew what she had to do and what outcomes were expected, she was 'good to go'.

The concern she had felt about her new head teacher's style temporarily abated, as the school focused on delivering the government's guidelines, leaving no room for anything but operational delivery. In hindsight, she effectively built a protective environment for herself, concentrating on implementing what was possible in the here-and-now, without worrying about the future.

My first reaction to lockdown, once the initial shock had lessened, and in keeping with my GC Index energies, was to come up with ideas for how to adapt my business to suit the situation. Maybe I could sell my services in a different way? Perhaps companies needed more help than ever now their staff were furloughed and working practices had changed so dramatically? Could this be a spur to even greater success? It was a classic example of what Kübler-Ross described as the 'bargaining' stage of the grief cycle[28] (see Figure 3 below). I was kidding myself, trying to use my Game Changer energy to find a way through. And, in keeping with her model, I slowly began to realise that there was no room for bargaining. I was on the bench at the side of the field and I wasn't going to be getting back on the pitch for some time, if ever.

---

[28] E. Kübler-Ross and D. Kessler, *On Grief and Grieving: Finding the Meaning of Grief Through the Five Stages of Loss,* Scribner, New York, 2014.

Kübler-Ross Grief Cycle

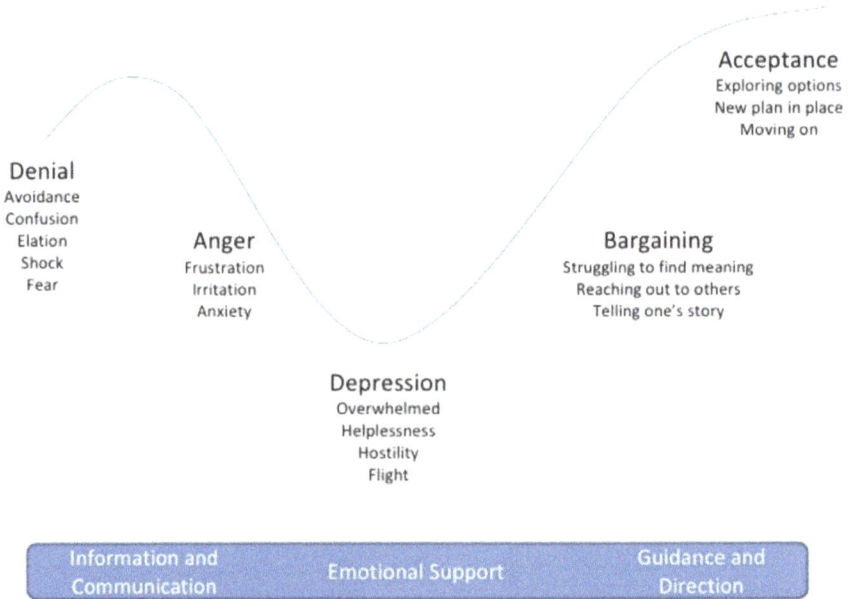

Acceptance
Exploring options
New plan in place
Moving on

Denial
Avoidance
Confusion
Elation
Shock
Fear

Anger
Frustration
Irritation
Anxiety

Bargaining
Struggling to find meaning
Reaching out to others
Telling one's story

Depression
Overwhelmed
Helplessness
Hostility
Flight

Information and Communication	Emotional Support	Guidance and Direction

Figure 3: Kübler-Ross Grief Cycle

So, as the months in lockdown rolled by, the impact of the loss of my business began to affect my health, both physical and mental. I lost a large amount of weight, experienced fatigue, skin issues and digestive problems. In terms of mental health, I found my creativity stifled, my self-confidence collapsed, and I began to sink into depression. Forgive me for saying it, but on the worst days I became interested in the height of bridges!

From a GC Index perspective, all of this was predictable. My strongest proclivity is Game Changer, which means I thrive on original thinking, setting big goals and nurturing them to fruition with considerable obsession and emotional investment. The shock of lockdown was telling me that my ideas were now unrealistic, my goals unachievable and my emotional investment was wasted. Lockdown and the uncertainty around the future at the time was telling me that I had no means of understanding the situation, no way of forming a plan to get out of it and no certainty about what may happen in the future. This was also depleting my Strategist energy. The feeling that my energies were wholly unsuited to the situation at the time was a key cause of my emotional and physical ill health.

So, it took Natalie, still in a relatively good energy space, to fill in my gaps. This she did in the form of a distraction. In order to get me out of my head and into an environment that might be therapeutic, she hit on the idea of taking me to an alpaca farm. As ridiculous as it may sound, this small act would prove to be life-changing.

Natalie had visited the alpaca farm once before with our niece, so she knew what to expect, what activities would take place and how enjoyable the outing could be. It was classic Implementer energy – 'here's something we can do right now, and I know it will work because I know how to do it and have done it before. So let's go.'

What she was doing was taking me away from my natural energy space, obsessive imagination, and putting me in a task space. This simple, pragmatic and task-based approach is typical of the way in which Natalie 'grounds' me when my energies are working against me.

And so it was that in July 2020, I came face to face with an alpaca for the first time. Initially, I didn't know what to make of them. A bizarre mix of deer, camel, sheep and goodness knows what else. I found them fascinating.

So, after an hour in the sun walking alpacas around a small, ramshackle farm in Warwickshire, both of us had fallen in love with these cute camelids. And I felt better than I had in months.

For the rest of the year then, every time Natalie felt I was sinking into the pits of despair, she would book a visit to the alpaca farm. Strangely, this usually seemed to be in keeping with the Covid restrictions. But no matter, it was a great way of getting out and distracting ourselves from the worries at home.

By December, I'd seen barely a sniff of any consultancy work since lockdown was announced. Attempts to rescue the two partnerships had failed and it was increasingly obvious that when the pandemic was over, it was unlikely that I would be able to put my business back to where it was. The thought that this may be true filled me with horror and as Christmas approached, I sank further into depression. This was exacerbated by the fact that as a Game Changer I had no other goal or vision to re-energise me. I was still emotionally attached to what I'd lost. To reference the Kübler-Ross Grief Cycle again, I was a million miles from acceptance, let alone integration.

At Christmas 2020, government guidance once again dealt many people another bitter blow as they found themselves unable to legally see their families. This included us, as a planned visit to meet up with my parents and siblings in the Black Country was cancelled; particularly sad as we hadn't seen some of them since January. Natalie once again booked us in for an alpaca experience and on Boxing Day 2020, we found ourselves back at the little farm in Warwickshire.

As we left after another lovely experience, I lingered at the entrance to the farm, watching people happily walking their alpacas around this tumble-down, slightly shabby but charming place. I thought about the events of the past few months, still in disbelief that it had happened at all. I noted that I wasn't particularly keen to go home, as I'd had such a relaxing time plodding around with the alpacas.

Then, the Game Changer/Strategist energy kicked in. I thought about what we'd paid for our experience, counted how many people were there and how many more were arriving and did the sums in my head. This was a neat little business, but not only that, it was the easiest sales pitch since bread came sliced. Who doesn't want to get out and do something fun in a beautiful countryside setting? It was certainly a world away from the corporate world where I'd been doing business before Covid-19 came on the scene. Consultancy is not the easiest service to sell at the best of times, but this was very different. I could see how this shabby little farm was making money; and making a lot of people very happy too. For the first time in months, the Game Changer/Strategist energies were working again. I was making sense of the place from a business perspective, and that was sparking some exciting ideas.

That little spark of excitement at a new possibility shot through me.

As we got into the car, I turned to Natalie and said, 'Do you think we could run an alpaca farm like this?' She thought for a moment and replied, 'Yes, I think we could. We have the skills and we're both good with animals.' Hearing this, I then said, somewhat nervously, 'Would you like to?' Natalie immediately replied, 'Yes. Yes, I think I would.'

As 2020 rolled into 2021, the government eased restrictions and started rolling out the vaccination programme. Things were a long way from 'normal' and would remain so for some time to come, but the lifting of restrictions allowed schools to return to something approaching business as usual. Natalie therefore found herself back at school full-time, in her role as assistant headteacher, much to her delight. This, she thought, would be relatively easy. She loved her job, she enjoyed being a busy Implementer in a challenging environment and it was good to be properly back in the driving seat. All she needed was a little direction from the head teacher so she could get on with leading her teams to deliver for the children. Easy Implementer comfort zone stuff – 'show me what I need to do, and I'll get on with it'.

And this is where the wheels fell off for Natalie. The new head teacher, as I explained earlier, was in the business of change and disruption. Having been prevented from getting his hands excessively dirty by the onset of the pandemic and lockdown restrictions, he now decided that this was the perfect time to put his 'stamp' on the school. I liken this stamp to the giant foot that appears at the end of the opening titles to the UK's *Monty Python's Flying Circus* television series from the 1970s, squashing everything below it with a resounding 'splat!' He thus began a ruthless process of ripping out process and procedure across the school, whilst providing no coherent direction as to what the alternative approach might be. He also preferred an autocratic, manipulative leadership style. He disliked giving feedback and would only do so if he had something negative to say. And he was certainly not prepared to receive any feedback whatsoever.

Within months, the mood amongst staff at the school had sunk as they realised that they lacked strong leadership and that standards were slipping. Morale was dreadful and staff began to leave.

The head teacher's behaviour deprived Natalie of the two things she needed to fully express her Implementer energies: clear direction and positive validation for the outcomes she achieves. Suddenly, for the first time in 18 years, she found herself getting in the car to head home at the end of the day not knowing what she'd achieved, whether it was any good, and what she needed to do tomorrow. She was deeply concerned that the school was not delivering for the children and as someone who was emotionally attached to their workplace and their role, she took it very personally. She was an Implementer without purpose, who had no gauge from which to determine whether she'd achieved anything. Effectively, she was becoming an Implementer who wasn't being allowed to implement.

This was totally alien to a person who had always enjoyed a seamless match between their job and their energies. And as a result, coming as it did after many years of a happy career, this was an enormous shock for Natalie. She'd entered the first stage of the Kübler-Ross Grief Cycle and was about to take a trip through its various stages, just as I was doing.

She initially found herself becoming incredibly angry at the head teacher for stopping her doing what she loved in the way she preferred to do it. She began to believe that she was a 'failure', that she was not competent in her role. Her inability to maintain the high pace of delivery that she'd become accustomed to was deeply de-energising for her. She felt blocked at every turn by the head teacher.

From a GC Index perspective, two of Natalie's energies were being suppressed. Clearly, she could no longer express her Implementer energy with the same enthusiasm and freedom she had before. Her score of 10 here, the highest possible, only magnified the resulting trauma. A situation that would have been merely problematic for individuals with a lower scoring Implementer-led profile was completely disabling for Natalie, the strength of her proclivity making the negative expression of it far more extreme. Her secondary Polisher proclivity seemed to worsen the negative effects of the situation. Her need to do things well, to hit high standards as well as 'getting the job done' emerged as a tendency to self-punish. Not only was she de-energised from being unable to fully implement, but she was disabled by a belief that, as a result, she wasn't 'good enough'.

In short, she couldn't fully implement and when she could, she couldn't do so to her own self-imposed high standards. Depression inevitably set in.

This situation was the same as my own, just 12 months earlier, albeit resulting from the suppression of a different set of energies. The GC Index science was incredibly helpful in understanding what was going on for each of us when we found ourselves struggling. We can think of proclivities in two ways. In situations where a proclivity is utilised, recognised and rewarded and appropriate, it can emerge as a 'superpower': individuals feel potent, they have higher self-esteem, and they make a positive impact. But in situations where a proclivity is suppressed, undermined, disabled or simply inappropriate, it can emerge as a 'disabler'. Individuals feel impotent, they lose self-esteem and they become less ineffective. They may shut down altogether or even become disruptive and/or destructive.

For Natalie, things finally came to a head in early 2022 when an Ofsted inspection heavily criticised her school, in particular, areas she had personally managed. In keeping with the manner in which her proclivities were working against her, she once again took the criticism personally. We've seen some high profile and very distressing case studies in the media of senior education leaders experiencing catastrophic mental health issues as a result of the very same set of circumstances. And in much the same way, it was clear how severely Natalie's self-confidence had declined when, one morning on the way to work, she was tempted to steer her car into the centre barrier on the motorway.

At this time, our roles reversed once again, as I took it upon myself to help and support Natalie. I did this by encouraging her to see the 'bigger picture' behind the situation. I helped her to understand that she wasn't to blame for the problems at her school, encouraging her to reflect on all the things she'd achieved over the years. I also encouraged her to think about the opportunities that the situation offered, even though it was challenging, it could be a springboard to move on to newer, better things.

You will no doubt have realised that I was using my Game Changer/Strategist proclivities to 'fill in the gaps' for Natalie, in the same way she used her Implementer proclivity to do so for me when I struggled. By taking her away from her natural task focus and providing context and meaning, I was able to help her appreciate how she might regain her energy in a new environment in the future. From here, she could work out the steps towards achieving that herself, thus reasserting and redirecting her Implementer energy in a more positive direction.

So, by this point, both of us had experienced a physical and mental health collapse due to a traumatic experience that had suppressed our energies. And we'd both used our energies to support the other in moving forward positively by regaining their energy.

So, what did we do next?

In early 2021, as things were becoming more difficult in Natalie's role, we discussed the possibility of a new direction. We were in our early forties and there was a sense of time marching on. I was still uncertain as to whether I would be able to rebuild my consultancy business and was feeling utterly burned out with the whole thing. With Natalie feeling disenfranchised with teaching for the first time, we were both in a bad place. Would it be easier to plan a new path, leave our old life behind and do something different?

After all, at this point, with everything going on in the world, what did we have to lose?

The potential new direction was obvious to both of us. Following the inspiration we'd felt at the alpaca farm we visited, we wanted to move to the countryside and set up our own farm-based visitor attraction. This was a big ask. Firstly, neither of us was from a farming background, nor had we ever lived in the countryside. Secondly, we didn't have any money to start anything. We'd been operating without 50% of our household income for the best part of 12 months and, like many, were amassing debt trying to stay afloat during the pandemic. And finally, could we actually work together? Being life partners was one thing, but business partners as well?

However, this new life held appeal for both of us from an energy perspective. For Natalie, the idea of a life spent performing husbandry tasks on a farm, looking after animals, teaching groups of people facts about them, appealed to her Implementer energies. She would have plenty of tasks to get stuck into, but she would also have control over how and when they were completed. For me, the opportunity to start again with a new business idea and build something unique with wide appeal got the creative Game Changer juices flowing. The need to understand how best to do it and under what structure was ideal Strategist territory.

This set the template early on – I would focus my energies on vision, direction and marketing, while Natalie would focus her energies on delivery, administration and husbandry.

It took me then, with my Game Changer and Strategist energies to start the process. I began thinking about what we needed to do to get underway. I felt it would be a five-year undertaking to gain knowledge, build a credible business plan, establish networks, improve our financial position after the impact of the pandemic and finally approach a bank for a commercial mortgage to buy a farm.

Firstly, we both agreed to target Shropshire, as the county was an ideal place to base a visitor attraction due to its proximity to the West Midlands conurbation. A bit of research had established there was a gap in the market for an alpaca-based attraction in the south-east of the county. Because my confidence in my ability to run and grow a business was completely gone following the events of 2020, I suggested we enrolled in some business start-up mentoring. Natalie was strongly in favour, as she felt this would help her understand how to run and manage a business from a task-based perspective, something that would be important to giving her confidence to fully engage her Implementer energies. For my part, I was looking for guidance on strategy, primarily to re-engage my Strategist energies, which had been suppressed by the uncertainty of the previous 12 months.

So, with this in mind, I signed us up with an organisation called Good2Great, based in Bridgnorth, Shropshire. In summer 2021, we began attending their start-up course and were assigned a mentor.

While following the start-up course we spent a lot of time carrying out research. I tended to focus my attention on identifying successful farm-based tourist attractions and looking at their branding, marketing, product offer and pricing. Classic 'high-level' Strategist territory. Natalie focused on the details of animal care, farm operations and accounting. Excellent topics to direct Implementer energy towards. We would often compare notes, although we found that if one of us spent too long talking from their energy perspective, the other would lose interest. We quickly realised there was a sweet spot where our energies met in the middle and if we focused our time there, we came up with solutions to problems incredibly quickly. This helped to prevent arguments! In essence, I would 'set the scene', Natalie would identify what tasks needed to be completed in the short and medium term and I would then contextualise what was more or less important in achieving the plan and long-term vision. We usually found ourselves agreeing with each other by the time the conversation was over.

In the first couple of months, I received an education in how to manage my own energies better to help Natalie engage in the process. One afternoon, I sat in our old garden with her, daydreaming about our mythical farm and what an amazing place it would be. I imagined it filled with animals and people, all having a great time. I imagined a cafe, a gift shop, a function room. I pictured the money coming in from all the bookings. It was going to be the best farm in the world ... in my head anyway. I turned to Natalie and played back my daydream, asking her, 'Isn't it going to be amazing?' Her reply consisted of little more than a muted, 'Yes, I suppose.' Getting anxious, I asked her, 'Aren't you up for this any more?' Her reply, 'Of course I am. It's just that I can't share in your daydream because I don't know what it is I need to do right now to get us there.'

I then realised that I needed to use more task-focused language to appeal to Natalie's Implementer energies. This was confirmed when, the following day after reflecting, I asked her if she'd like to look into what merchandise we could sell in a gift shop. She was so enthusiastic about this that she appeared a couple of hours later with a comprehensive list of products and prices to talk over.

When we set out on our journey I was adamant that we would have to raise a lot of money to acquire a farm via a mortgage. I suspect Natalie was more open-minded than I was, although we would both admit to a complete lack of understanding of how things work in the countryside at that point! No matter, the perceived need to own a site was a major headache. We could see how we could run an attraction, how we'd market it and how we'd make it a success. But we were very concerned that we'd never raise the money to actually have a farm from which to run a business in the first place.

Our mentor on the start-up course was skilled at coaching us through issues like this. I noted that he changed his style depending upon whether he was talking to Natalie or me. Good coaching technique! I suspect he was matching our energies as he'd talk operationally with Natalie but indulge me in the big picture stuff. One day in late summer 2021, he suggested that we talk to an important figure in Shropshire who happened to be a partner in a large firm of estate agents, on the basis that he'd help us understand how best to acquire a farm. As this was a big picture conversation, it fell to me to talk to him.

He started our conversation with an existential question 'Why do you want to buy a farm?' I found myself slightly irritated by this – most likely because as a Game Changer, I was now obsessed with the idea of owning a farm and as a Strategist, I'd spent a lot of time thinking through the pros and cons. Why was he challenging me? After what was probably a lengthy and overly detailed reply, he said to me, 'You don't want to do that.' Now I was definitely annoyed! I asked him why not. He replied, 'Because you don't need to. You can rent one.'

What neither Natalie nor I understood is that much of rural Shropshire is owned by large family estates and the National Trust. This means that farms rarely come onto the market for sale and when they do, they often have eye-watering price tags. The estates have lots of farms on them and many of them are at risk of becoming void properties as the tenants die off and hand them back to the estate. This means there are opportunities for new tenants to come in and breathe life back into the properties.

Such an arrangement was exactly what this gentleman was proposing to me, but I didn't want to hear it. It was a case of 'not my idea', an example of my Game Changer energies working against me, and 'not in my plan', which was the shadow side of my Strategist energies.

I took the idea back to Natalie, who shared some of my scepticism, but was keener to consider it. She could see, from a pragmatic perspective, how it might be achieved. However, I pooh-poohed it completely and went back to writing the most robust business plan the world has seen so we could raise the money from a bank to buy somewhere as planned. I've wondered since if this is the same impulse that led me to spend so much time building two partnerships to enable the growth of my consultancy business. I suspect that my Game Changer energy sometimes blinds me to the obvious, as I go for the more audacious big fat hairy goals instead of seeking a more pragmatic route. When I worked by myself in the consultancy business, I had no one to restrain me from this overindul-gence of energy. However, with the new business we were planning, I had Natalie to bring me back to Earth. She suggested I speak to a few more people for a second opinion. Very pragmatic, very task based.

Thus, as summer led into autumn, I spoke with a financial adviser and another local estate agent. Both advised us to find a family estate and to rent a farm from them. I ignored both.

Finally, the owner of Good2Great, the start-up mentoring organisation, asked to speak with us. He repeated the advice about renting and told us that he knew the person who ran an estate in South Shropshire and that if we wanted, he could put us in touch with her. At this point, not even I could afford to continue to be stubborn. Both of us agreed; we had to meet this person and find out what opportunities might lie in wait.

It was a windy, cold autumnal evening in October 2021 when we made the long journey to a rambling old rectory in a tiny village, a few miles up the road from Ironbridge, to meet the chief executive and co-owner of the estate in Shropshire. After a very convivial chat over tea and biscuits, she suggested that she could find somewhere on the estate for us, but that an existing tenant kept alpacas and, on account of decency, she wouldn't want to put us in competition with him or him in competition with us.

Feeling slightly deflated by this news we were reassured by her offer to put us in touch with him as 'he might be able to give you some advice about the alpacas'. Her parting words 'If it's meant to be we'll hopefully speak again some time.'

We were still a long way from making our idea a reality but at least we now had another contact for the future and the possibility of another research opportunity with the alpaca-owning tenant. So, on an even colder and very gloomy December evening we made our way to Caughley Farm in Broseley, Shropshire, to meet him.

Once again, Natalie went into this meeting with a pragmatic approach. From her perspective, we were there to fact-find and things would pan out however they were meant to. I, of course, was looking to confirm my vision of what a farm might look like. I had a fixed picture in my head, so it was something of a shock when we arrived at Caughley Farm (pronounced 'Carf-lee') for the first time.

Firstly, the farm is accessed via 1½ miles of rough track. On the day we visited, this track was in a deplorable condition, with some sections being more in keeping with a highly challenging off-road driving course. This created many 'squeaky bottom' moments as our Lexus, entirely unsuited to such terrain, navigated the ruts and bumps. I was less than impressed.

Secondly, as we pulled into the farmyard we were taken aback by the state of the place. It looked like somewhere you might visit and never return from. The entire farmyard was strewn with litter, discarded pieces of equipment and various forms of the nasty brown stuff. A fire burned in front of the farmhouse and there was evidence of multiple other previous fires in several places. A primitive washing line had been fashioned from bailer twine, strung from a bracket on the farmhouse and tied at the other end to a telegraph pole. The various undergarments that had previously escaped this feeble construction were hanging from the branches of the trees that ran along the entrance to the courtyard. Two fearsome looking dogs stared at us from behind a gate under an archway between a pair of barns.

And finally, there was the pièce de résistance: a steel funnel on legs that was dripping with blood, the result of it having been used to 'dispatch' many turkeys which the farm's occupant was rearing to sell to people for their Christmas dinners.

It's fair to say we were both a little uneasy about our visit.

However, our host was affable enough and on meeting his alpacas, we found they were surprisingly attractive and seemed to be well natured. After a conversation about the 'whys' and 'wherefores' of alpaca farming, we asked him what his future plans for the farm were.

To our surprise, he revealed that his plan was to leave and move to a remote island near Scotland. Not really what we expected to hear. Furthermore, if we liked, we could buy some or all of his alpacas and maybe talk to the estate about taking over the farm when he left.

As a Game Changer, my energy was immediately piqued by this revelation. One of the strengths of the energy is a high appetite for risk and opportunity. And I could clearly see the door of opportunity opening in front of us. My Strategist energy was less convinced. This ramshackle place, which at the time seemed to be in the middle of nowhere, did not in any way represent a successful visitor attraction. From a pragmatic perspective, it was nothing like what we thought we had planned.

Natalie's Implementer energy kicked into gear straight away. From her perspective, here was a tangible opportunity to get the task of moving to the countryside underway. She could see what we needed to do and how it could be done. Even though it was a leap of faith from our present lifestyle, she knew that this was an easy way of getting hold of a property suitable for alpaca farming. The tenant had shared with us the value of the rent he was paying, and while this had me yodeling with nerves, Natalie had already worked out that the amount was the equivalent of our mortgage payment, one car loan that we were already paying and a few little indulgences. If we could sell our house and make some cutbacks, we could just about get away with it.

So, with night falling we set off back to Warwickshire. On the journey home, Natalie was full of energy, making verbal lists of tasks we needed to undertake in the next couple of days. I was a bundle of nerves, wrestling between the two extremes of my Game Changer and Strategist energy. The creative energy in me said 'this is the one'. The pragmatic side said 'this place needs a lot of work, and it may be quite a challenge'. The shadow side of both said 'what if it all goes hideously wrong?' It was a strange feeling. I felt very conflicted.

Natalie and I spoke extensively about Caughley Farm for several days after our visit, weighing up the pros and cons of taking it over when the existing tenant left and trying to visualise ourselves living at the farm. It was such a stark contrast to the neat new-build estate on which we lived. Could we make it work?

Our eventual conclusion was simple; this was too good an opportunity to turn down. And anyway, we were both pretty unhappy with our life at that time. It had been a tempestuous 18 months, and we'd come close to losing everything. So, what was left to lose? We had to try.

The deal was sweetened further for us when the estate, having learned of the tenant's island escape plan and our interest in buying his alpacas, offered us the use of a 14-acre field for six months, rent free if we bought them, so 'you can see if you think you can make it work'.

So, in February 2022, Natalie and I signed some paperwork and became alpaca owners for the first time. We put our house on the market shortly afterwards and after one week it was sold subject to contract. Things were suddenly getting VERY interesting ...

Here we were with a 14-acre field that we didn't own, that we weren't paying any rent for and which we only had the use of for six months, plus nine alpacas and absolutely no experience of owning livestock or running a tourist attraction. We didn't even have running water, electricity or any facilities at the site, which was around a quarter of a mile down the lane from the main body of Caughley Farm. We were still living over 1½ hours away, in a house that was sold subject to contract and with, as yet, nowhere to go once it came time to move out. I was still struggling to revive my consultancy business, so we continued to exist on Natalie's income alone, which came from a job that was progressively ruining her health. We were unfit, tired and feeling very middle aged.

It was from this point on that the combination of our individual energies became a recipe for success. Realising that we had to double down and make this situation work, we set about creating a business that could grow into the farm attraction we wanted to develop. Firstly, the name, which came about in a brainstorming conversation with my dad, who to his credit suggested a pun on our surname 'Franklin-Hackett'. So, our new business was quickly christened 'Frankly Alpacas'.

Next, we had to develop a website, a social media presence and set up a booking system and means of taking money. As these tasks seemed to fit naturally with our energies, I took the first two – website and social media – and Natalie took the last two – booking system and payment system. Within a month, both were ready to go.

Getting the site ready for visitors was another example of our energies working in harmony. While I thought about the layout and the signage, Natalie sorted out the practicalities, such as animal housing, hand washing for visitors and parking.

Finally, albeit in an extremely basic and rough-around-the-edges manner, Frankly Alpacas opened for business on 1 April 2022.

In those early days, we offered just two visitor experiences. The first was a simple guided meet and greet with the alpacas, which allowed visitors to get hands-on and personal with them in a beautiful setting. The second was the same offer but followed by a picnic in the company of the herd.

We knew within a month that we had a potential success on our hands. Despite our clunky set-up, visitors loved the alpacas and were full of praise for the tours we led. We began to notice that Natalie and I had slightly different styles when running experiences. I would be more humorous and quirky in my delivery, while Natalie would be more factual and educational. Once again, this was a clear reflection of our energies. My Game Changer bias meant that I preferred a creative approach, while her Implementer focus meant that she would lean towards a task-based delivery style. Both, of course, worked equally well.

After three months, we had taken a few thousand pounds in bookings. Hardly retirement money, but it was a tantalising glimpse of the potential revenues that may be possible if we could scale up.

July came around and with it, another unexpected twist. The tenant at Caughley Farm was leaving earlier than expected and, as a result, this meant that we would need to sign the tenancy for the entire farm by the end of August. Our house sale was progressing very slowly and there were no guarantees that it would go through in time, which would leave us paying a mortgage and a significant amount in rent at the same time. We simply couldn't afford it.

In the end, we realised that we had no real choice. We had to make it work, there was simply no other option. Bailing out of the deal would leave us worse off financially than we started. So, we did everything we could to progress the house sale and called in a few favours to help us if we couldn't manage financially while everything went through.

As it turned out, our house sale went through in the nick of time and at the start of September 2022, we became the new tenants of Caughley Farm in Broseley, Shropshire.

Our life since then has been a real roller-coaster ride and we can scarcely believe it all happened. In the two and a half years since we started Frankly Alpacas in April 2022, we have had over 4000 visitors to the farm. We've expanded our range of animals to include the smallest sheep in the world; the smallest cows in Europe; ducks and chickens; other rare breed sheep and small animals, which is why we changed our name to Frankly Farm Tours at the start of 2024. We've launched a programme of animal education for schools and visited over 25 schools in our first year of running it. We've attended parties, village fetes, festivals and corporate events with our animals. We've seen births and deaths and watched the seasons come and go. We've built a huge wedding-spec marquee and watched it be destroyed two days after Boxing Day having been battered by six named storms. We've transformed the previously ramshackle and dirty farmyard and turned it into a welcoming and attractive destination to visit. In early 2024 we created a function room space out of a barn where the previous tenant kept his turkeys and started building a cafe in another former barn. Tripadvisor have presented us with their Traveler's Choice award for 2023 and 2024 on the strength of reviews left by over 150 of our visitors.

It's been remarkable. If you'd have told me that all of this would happen on the evening of 23 March 2020, as I was watching my business burn down in front of my eyes, I would never have believed you.

Throughout the journey, Natalie and I have been sustained by our individual energies and the sheer joy of combining them to solve problems. While we do have moments of tension where one or both of us overplay our strengths, we both agree that our success in making this enormous change in our lives has come about as a result of our ability to be potent in making the impact that comes naturally to us.

As well as friends and partners in life, we've become successful business partners.

Life continues to have its 'ups and downs' and I would be lying if I didn't admit that we've had some very challenging days since we started our new life in the country. But the feeling of potency, the sense of being able to fully exploit our individual energies and the joy of working together to make an impact continues to be joyous. It has highlighted how much latent potential we both had, which was not fully utilised in our old lives. We've found ourselves wondering 'why didn't we work together before?'

It turns out that to be truly potent in our work lives, we needed each other.

Chapter 7

Energy for Sales

A practical understanding of the sales dynamic through the lens of The GC Index.

Mark Savage

Introduction

Having been involved in B2B Sales for over 20 years, I have witnessed and learned a lot of good, bad and frankly indifferent sales techniques. Not just as a salesperson myself, but as someone who has been sold to in the corporate and small business worlds.

I have personally made sales ranging from the thousands of pounds to the millions of pounds. I have also lost my fair share of sales in that exact same brackets! When you win a sale, you naturally feel elated, proud and you celebrate. But when you lose a sale, you feel rejected, and when the dust has settled, you start to reflect and ask 'why?'

As I write this chapter reflecting on my many years of sales, I have found there to be three core layers to successful selling:

Firstly, understanding the prospective client's needs, wants and 'pain-points'.

Secondly, reassuring the prospective client that they are achieving 'best value'.

And finally, and today I consider this the most crucial of all, ensuring that there is a good energy connection between the salesperson and the prospect/client.

The first two layers are well-trodden paths in sales, namely:

1. Unless a salesperson understands the key outcomes their client is looking for – by deeply understanding their needs, wants and pain-points – they are highly unlikely to sell anything.
2. Once a client is convinced the seller's service or product does address the outcomes they require, they will then, of course, enter a procurement phase of the sales process, focusing on best value. Please note 'best value' does not mean cheapest price!

The 'Energy for Sales' chapter in this book focuses on the third layer – establishing a good energy connection between the salesperson and the prospect/client.

From the prospect or client's perspective, I would propose to you that a good energy connection incorporates liking, trusting and respecting their salesperson.

If there is an energy disconnect between buyer and seller, it will generally result in a breakdown in the professional relationship which impacts trust and, ultimately, impacts the sale!

Establishing that positive energy connection is a critical outcome in any sales dynamic.

The GC Index

The GC Index identifies how people have Energy for Impact in the world in general and, for this chapter, in the world of sales.

Many salespeople and buyers will have a lead proclivity of either Game Changer, Strategist, Play Maker, Polisher or Implementer, and tapping into the energy of this lead proclivity is often critical for establishing that energy connection between buyer and seller.

From your buyer's perspective, tapping into the following energy is critical if a successful sale is to be closed:

- **The Game Changer**: they will be energised by creative possibilities and original ideas that have the potential to underpin transformational change within an organisation. They are likely to be seen as risk-takers and will be particularly engaged by genuine invention.
- **The Strategist**: they like to make sense of big ideas and data, often looking for patterns and trends in that data as a basis of prediction and the basis of planning. They will be energised by the 'big picture'; the context of their client's business and what they are seeking to achieve in broad terms.
- **The Play Maker**: they are all about people and inclusion. They feel particularly responsible for teams collaborating and reaching consensus. Their energy comes from building a shared view and everyone working together.
- **The Polisher**: they are particularly focused on progress, and this progress will fuel continuous improvement, innovation and the pursuit of excellence. They are particularly energised by excellence and continually improving solutions, products, processes and procedures.
- **The Implementer**: they have a keen focus on productivity and practicality. They make ideas happen and love to deliver; indeed, they have a practical, operational focus on delivery. As such, they are energised by the delivery of projects and programmes.

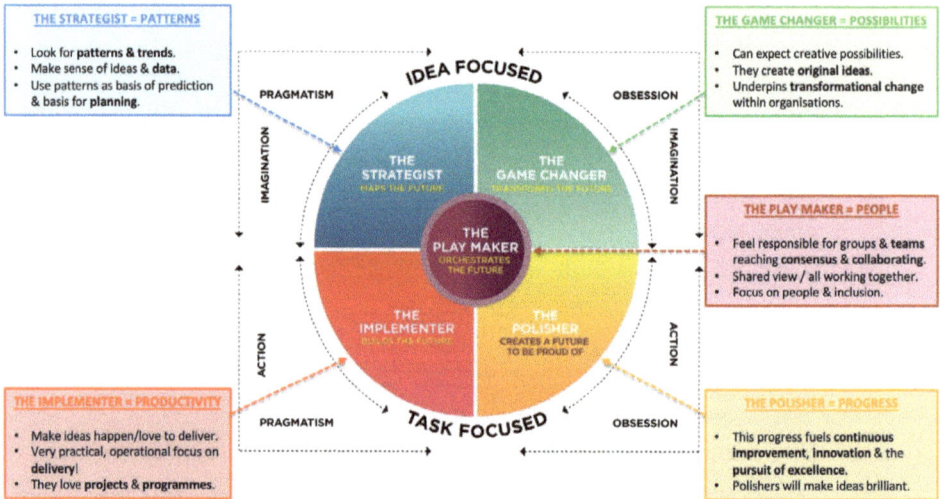

THE STRATEGIST = PATTERNS
- Look for **patterns & trends**.
- Make sense of **ideas & data**.
- Use patterns as basis of prediction & basis for **planning**.

THE GAME CHANGER = POSSIBILITIES
- Can expect creative possibilities.
- They create **original ideas**.
- Underpins **transformational change** within organisations.

THE PLAY MAKER = PEOPLE
- Feel responsible for groups & **teams** reaching **consensus & collaborating**.
- Shared view / all working together.
- Focus on people & inclusion.

THE IMPLEMENTER = PRODUCTIVITY
- Make ideas happen/love to deliver.
- Very practical, operational focus on delivery!
- They love **projects & programmes**.

THE POLISHER = PROGRESS
- This progress fuels **continuous improvement, innovation** & the pursuit of excellence.
- Polishers will make ideas brilliant.

IDEA FOCUSED · PRAGMATISM · OBSESSION · IMAGINATION · TASK FOCUSED · ACTION

THE STRATEGIST · THE GAME CHANGER · THE PLAY MAKER · THE IMPLEMENTER · THE POLISHER

Tapping into the energy connection

Every salesperson has their own natural energy which is especially aligned to their lead and secondary proclivities, their two highest GC Index scores, otherwise known as their impact profile.

From an energy connection perspective, for a salesperson to successfully make the sale they need to firstly establish what the lead energy is of their buyer and then connect to that energy!

There are two ways of establishing what the lead energy of the prospective buyer is: either ask their buyer if they would like to complete The GC Index themselves (the straightforward option) or, listen out very carefully for key signals at the very start of the sales process.

If you are listening out for key signals, carefully consider the following:

- Is your buyer focused on ideas and possibilities that have the potential to change the landscape of their world? Do they talk passionately about invention or transformational change? Do they reference 'safe to fail' cultures that encourage experimentation in innovation and creativity? If so, they may be a lead **Game Changer**.

- Is your buyer focused on the 'big picture'? Are they data-centric? Do they reference their own strategic context, the importance of having a robust strategic plan and focus on core commercials or financials? If so, they may be a lead **Strategist**.
- Is your buyer focused on the wider team? Are they considering your product or solution in the context of how it will aid collaboration and consensus across their team or wider organisation? Do they emphasise the importance of relationships and the importance of needing genuine team players? If so, they may be a lead **Play Maker**.
- Is your buyer focused on 'delivery' and getting things done? Are they very focused on your own implementation methodology and are they seeking robust client endorsements and references from you? If so, they may be a lead **Implementer**.
- Is your buyer focused on how your products or solutions will facilitate continuous improvement, innovation or the pursuit of continuous improvement within their organisation? Are they emphasising a 'high standard' in delivery? Do they have a keen focus on 'learning and development'? If so, they may be a lead **Polisher**.

Case studies

As part of my research into establishing the respective energy connections between the salesperson and their prospective buyer, I used The GC Index to profile four senior sales professionals, all with different lead proclivities.

The results and their respective approaches to how they successfully sold as individuals proved to be incredibly insightful.

The below four case studies outline these approaches.

Case study 1: Ruth Minhall, Game Changer/Strategist

Q: *Tell me a little bit about you and your company?*

'I celebrated a big birthday earlier this year and in that time, I have explored all sorts of opportunities. I was lucky to have parents who encouraged different activities and I've pretty much tried everything you can possibly imagine. From skydiving and extreme sports, to rugby, horse riding, ballet and music, I have embraced risk and creativity whilst enjoying travel and experiencing the globe.

'I have been lucky enough to harness my music and be able to work creatively in the studio and with live performance as a singer and songwriter. This path has allowed me the privilege of working with some of the most incredible musicians in the industry.

'My organisation is Tuition Extra Group. I started the business 10 years ago, literally with me sitting in a small office on my own. Today I have a team of 160 … and growing! We offer a bespoke education service which provides one-to-one and small group tutoring, home schooling support, alternative and SEN provision and professional training. Our work particularly resonates with neurodiverse young-sters and those who struggle to access mainstream schooling due to their profile.

'We look at individual interests and requirements and shape our education programmes in a bespoke way to respond to each student's requirements. We understand that meeting the needs of our youngsters, particularly those with complex needs or neuro-diversity, is life changing. Many of these young people, for whatever reason, have not managed to progress in school or engage successfully with education. We are a lifeline.

'We have three sites: a therapeutic site which deals with vocational skills and animal therapy; our lead Tuition Extra site, providing an operational base and a tutoring area for tutors to work with students on a one-to-one basis; and finally, Haven Nook School, which provides an independent special school set up for neurodiverse youngsters, predominantly with a profile of anxiety, ADHD and autism.'

Q: *Looking at your own GC Index profile, what do you see?*

'I see a Game Changer/Strategist predominantly. Somebody who has got big ideas but who is also engaged by data and commercials and will think through a plan. I like to see the bigger picture and sit above everything – I think this really shows through in my profile.

'Whilst I enjoy working in a team, I certainly do not need a team around me. I am quite happy to do stuff on my own. I have had to learn to finish what I start and that is not always an easy thing with my Game Changer/Strategist profile.

'Whilst I love new ideas and new projects, I can find it tedious having to see something through to the end because it just becomes boring.'

Q: Tell me about your selling style?

'Again, this is something that I have really had to practise and focus on. I am direct when I sell. Very, very, very direct. I enjoy working tactically and I prepare with care to understand the person and context I am selling to. This enables me to tailor any pitch to requirements and needs that are specific to them.

'When I am doing business, my thought process is targeted and whilst working directly with a potential client, my messaging is clear and time efficient. Before I walk into a meeting, I will prepare and rehearse my key points of focus. I always have an absolute understanding of what I want to achieve from the meeting based on what my potential client needs, what is going to tick their box, what is going to "rock their boat". I'll do it quickly and directly.

'Because I have a chaotic mindset and a constant flow of ideas, I find myself consciously leaning into my Strategist proclivity to provide a self-structure. Indeed, when I sell, I always do my research and gather all the necessary data before I pitch. I know that if I am entering a meeting and I want to achieve a specific outcome, it requires specific preparation. That's the key to my success.'

Q: Are there any GC Index profile types you'll struggle to sell to, and why?

'Probably a Play Maker/Polisher, because my experience is that they procrastinate and want to ask everybody else in their team for their opinion, as opposed to making their own decision in the moment. They struggle to be decisive about the delivery of ideas and overthink a point of completion. This irritates me and I lack patience due to overcomplication or unnecessary delay!'

Q: Are there any GC Index profile types you enjoy selling to, and why?

'Naturally I enjoy selling to fellow Game Changers, but particularly Strategists, especially those who are energised by possibilities but also those with strategic energy who understand where I am coming from. Selling to somebody who not only gets the idea but can also see strategically how it could work, and the value in whatever I am selling, is my "sweet spot".

'The people I have successfully sold to in the past have tended to be board level decision makers, those typically with Strategist energy. The leaders that I've worked with in the past, particularly in the FTSE 100 field, were not only strategic and decisive, but interestingly, not collaborative. They would see the commercial value and trust their own knowledge and expertise. Bottom line, you have to know what people want before you walk in the room and then carefully tailor your sales pitch!'

Case study 2: Chris Dawson, Strategist/Polisher

Q: *Tell me a little bit about you and your company?*

'I'm something like 35 years into a career that started in a technical role, and I've stayed close to technology throughout my career. What I like doing is taking all the complexity of technology and packaging it into something that solves a problem and is easy to consume. I've always worked in services in one form or another and spent time as a project manager where I was taking a lot of process complexity and turning it into an added-value client deliverable.

'My company, Longwall, was founded to do exactly this sort of thing. We are a team of expert and extraordinary people who share a passion for delivering impactful business outcomes and outstanding service. Our purpose is to secure organisations so they can confidently do what they do best. We aspire to become the leading cyber security specialists, delivering innovative and preventative strategies to protect organisations, their communities and data.

'This starts at the outset with advisory consulting to assess current state and help to shape a comprehensive cyber security strategy for our client. Recognising that budget rarely exists to do everything at once, we then work with the client on a roadmap to prioritise invest-ments in time and technology that deliver measurable outcomes in line with the strategic business objectives. We offer a complete port-folio of managed services, from round-the-clock threat detection and response, risk and exposure management, and ongoing advis-ory consulting to ensure continual evolution of the client's strategy and cyber resilience.'

Q: *Looking at your own GC Index profile, what do you see?*

'My profile shows me as having two strong proclivities, one as a Strategist and one as a Polisher. I'm relatively balanced in the other areas, but there are clear spikes in these two.

'Initially, this seemed quite surprising to me, but I also recognised that those are two very strong traits in the way that I work and the way that I act, both in my working life and in my private life as well.

'I'm a bit of a dreamer. I'm often daydreaming about things that are over the horizon, so the Strategist/Game Changer part of my profile should be no surprise. But I'm also very easily drawn into the detail of problem solving and I enjoy and naturally fall into that mode of trying to continually refine and improve. Be it a spreadsheet at work, or a DIY project at home, I can get drawn into giving that my entire focus to the exclusion of all else: my Polisher focus.

'I suppose the initial surprise when I had my profile review was that I assumed that I would be a strong Implementer because a lot of my career has been spent in implementation type roles. But what I've come to recognise since doing The GC Index is that I can and do implement, but what tends to happen in any implementation situation is that I make a start, come up with a grand plan, but then I'm distracted because I see a way of improving the next part of the plan in the future. So, I am action focused but probably more through a continuous improvement lens than a core implementation lens.'

Q: *Tell me about your selling style?*

'The cliche is consultative selling, but I am naturally consultative in the way that I sell.

'And, again, I can see the two strongest proclivities coming to play here. I'm very good at identifying the big picture, and with the use of core data specifically helping my clients see the problem that they're going to solve with our solution.

'And one of the reasons I think I'm often successful is that I'm also good when it comes to the detail of the proposal that answers the questions that the client hasn't thought of yet.

'And so, by doing all this very proactively and laying the proposal out in a very clear, polished way, with a clear "big picture", the proposal often sails through and is accepted much more readily than it might be otherwise.'

Q: *Are there any profile types you'll struggle to sell to, and why?*

'Anybody that's not really getting the big picture is a starting point! And as a Strategist, I feel I naturally work best with other Strategists.

'So, somebody that's not really getting the big picture, or is too focused on pleasing everybody or, too focused on the latest, greatest game-changing innovation, then I probably won't satisfy them in quite the same way. Likewise, I won't necessarily understand what their motivation is in quite the same way as I will naturally with a Strategist.

'Aside from this, selling to a Polisher is a bit of a nightmare because they want so much detail and, you know, they're never satisfied with what you present.'

Q: *Are there any profile types you enjoy selling to, and why?*

'Well, probably the same answer, that I enjoy selling to people that are clear about the problem they're trying to solve.

'I also think my polishing capability kind of suits everybody because the people who aren't Strategists are helped by having a clearly, laid out proposal. And I've often felt that this was quite a "big win" in lots of cases. So, I think I enjoy most selling to people that get it and know what they want, and why they want it!'

Case study 3: Tertius Rust, Play Maker/Game Changer

Q: *Tell me a little bit about you and your company?*

'I am a chartered civil engineer with a master's in water engineering and an MBA in innovation management. Although never diagnosed,

I am fairly certain I have some form of dyslexia, so one might say I have familiarity and appreciation for neurodiversity.

'I have worked in the water sector for more than 14 years and have always loved the physical, economical, and social aspect of water. I grew up on a farm in Africa where water scarcity challenges were more than just a seasonal occurrence, so I've got this deep-founded ambition to protect water and ensure water accessibility.

'My company, The Innovation Consulting Company, has been set up to support leaders in traditional companies to build an innovation ecosystem that is more risk-averse. We partner with these organisations to initially provide an "innovation as a service" model where we bring the capability and resources to enhance the maturity of any organisation innovation journey.'

Q: *Looking at your own GC Index profile, what do you see?*

'Well, I'm a 10 Play Maker and very balanced and can lean into anything really but Play Maker Game Changer is my leadership profile.

'My profile helps me to think about my direct community: Who are they? Where do they fit in? When did I last talk to them? And just by keeping up to date with people was critical for me because I don't like to do anything on my own; in fact, I will not do something unless I do have partners or support. I see myself as a conductor, so I can't make music without an orchestra, and what I found was that because of my Play Maker/Game Changer profile, the instruments I was planning to use didn't exist and I was in essence trying to be an orchestra of something new.

'To get the company up and running, which I did on my own, I found I had to lean into my Game Changer/Strategist energies and temporarily forget about my Play Maker, as I needed to get that momentum and traction first off. Then, as soon as people started understanding the instruments I was talking about, I hired people to do the doing, allowing me to step back into my Play Maker role, which is now more focused on business-development.'

Q: *Tell me about your selling style?*

'Firstly, I hate the word "selling"! I think partnerships and collaboration is a capability, and it's a skill, and if you use "selling" it means that someone is winning. In my mind, if you're trying to introduce value via a relationship or a partnership, then the capability of that is more about finding common ground. For me it's all about curiosity, the long term, so my view is I don't need your work, I need your relationship because we're going to be working together for the next 30 to 40 years, so I'm way more interested in building a long-term relationship!

'After an introduction to someone, I will say, if we are good enough, and we have the skills to partner, then I feel we should have something that we can mutually get value from. Even if it's just a connection here, a connection there, my selling style is more out of a position of curiosity and long-term relationship building.'

Q: *Are there any profile types you'll struggle to sell to, and why?*

'For me, a Strategist/Polisher or Polisher/Strategist profile seems to be difficult to sell to, but only if they are very confident and have a lot of experience. I tend to feel that these profiles would only partner if they absolutely have too. They would rather miss a partnering opportunity than risk making a collaboration attempt that fails to deliver and waste time and money. Also, these profiles are normally very detail focused and feel they have a good understanding of what is missing and what should be done for them to achieve their goals, so they don't see the need for other support. If they wanted your services they would have asked, so selling means they don't think they need it. So, it's a very difficult starting position.'

Q: *Are there any profile types you enjoy selling to, and why?*

'I really enjoy collaborating with Game Changer/Strategists, especially in my industry when the opportunity requires a little bit of imagination, then there's a bit of a jump, a leap of faith. So, the risk appetite needs to be a bit higher when you engage with what we are doing.

'Also Game Changer/Implementers, I do find them being able to say, "this is great", but then actually pushing it forward and practically anchoring it into the organisation, and they cut through red tape and bureaucracy to make it happen.

'I don't necessarily like working with Play Makers, because I find they tend to send you on wild goose chases all over the place, and once you've met everyone you still don't have anything to do!

'Finally, with the Implementer/Strategist, where the value that you're selling is very clear to your clients, then an Implementer is the best person to sell it to.'

Case study 4: Bernhard Pussel, Implementer/Strategist

Q: *Tell me a little bit about you and your company?*

'As a seasoned sales executive with a detailed understanding of technical builds, business case implementation and people management, I am very comfortable operating throughout the entire business development life cycle.

'I'm currently the Chief Sales Officer and Deputy CEO of Riedel Networks and have been responsible for all Riedel Networks sales since October 2017. Prior to joining Riedel, I held senior positions in international telecommunications companies such as Truphone and Colt Technology Services having originally cut my teeth in sales as an account manager at IBM.

'My technical background is underpinned by an electrical engineering and communications engineering degree from the Stuttgart University of Cooperative Education.

'Riedel Networks is a global operating network provider based in Butzbach, Germany, focused on customised networks for enterprises and the broadcast sector. As part of the Riedel Communication Group, we have access to a corporate structure of over 1000 colleagues, at over 30 locations in Europe, Australia, Asia and America. Oh yes, and our head office is literally based in a castle!'

Q: *Looking at your own GC Index profile, what do you see?*

'My GC Index leadership style is an Implementer/Strategist, but also with a dominant Game Changer inclination. As an individual, I absolutely need to be challenged with problems and I then apply ideas and data to solving these problems, ultimately leading to my drive of getting things done! I recognise that this is in effect a blend of my Game Changer, Strategist and Implementer dominant proclivities.

'I also pride myself on being very pragmatic as an individual and this also plays through strongly in my leadership style as an Implementer/Strategist. The "big picture" – particularly understanding the "why?" of action – is critical for me to bring the energy and focus to deliver operational objectives.

'In summary, I would say I'm at my best when I'm able to see and clearly articulate direction, change and action within a strategic context that takes account of commercial, operational and people needs. This is when I am most successful as a sales professional.'

Q: Tell me about your selling style?

'A lot of my selling comes on the back of big, corporate RFPs, and my first task is always to read and properly digest the RFP.

'Having done this, my approach is typically:

1. Come up with a unique idea that will differentiate us from the competition.
2. Gather the data that supports our big idea; and then
3. Present a robust project plan which in turn reassures the prospect/client that we are a safe pair of hands, and we will deliver for them!

'Indeed, blending that big idea and tried-and-tested implementation is always a fine balancing act, but underpinned by robust data and a strategic plan we more than often prevail.'

Q: Are there any profile types you'll struggle to sell to, and why?

'I wouldn't say there are any profile types I would struggle to sell to because I always intensely listen first and then adapt my selling style according to my client's position.

'That said, clients who have the need to collaborate and seek agreement from absolutely everyone before communicating a decision is a natural frustration to me!'

Q: Are there any profile types you enjoy selling to, and why?

'I particularly enjoy selling to Strategist/Implementers, or those knowledgeable clients who are very clear on the types of suppliers that might suit their needs.

'Clients who strategically understand "why" they need a particular supplier or solution, and then have a very clear idea of the "what", "when" and "who" when it comes to implementation is my ideal scenario. But my dream scenario is when they are also asking for original ideas as part of the planning phase!

'Looking back on my career, I have tended to have most sales success with senior leaders who have both a "big picture" outlook, blended with an urgent need to deliver bottom line success to their business.'

Top tips for establishing the energy connection with your client

In my experience, and with the benefit of selling underpinned with data from The GC Index, these are my top three tips for selling to each of the five proclivity types:

Selling to *Game Changers:*

1. Show Game Changers ideas and possibilities that have the potential to change the landscape of their world. And be enthusiastic and obsessive in this process if that too is your nature!
2. Game Changers will live in a world of possibilities which might seem unrealistic or intangible to many. Be seen as their transformational 'partner in crime' and someone they are comfortable in reaching out to express their ideas in a safe and supportive way.
3. Game Changers work best in 'safe to fail' cultures that encourages experimentation in innovation and creativity. Offer to host a 'brainstorming' workshop to facilitate this process.

Selling to *Strategists:*

1. Demonstrate to Strategists that you understand their world. They are engaged by the 'bigger picture' and thus will be energised by ideas, data, patterns and trends that predict the future.
2. Ask considered questions that demonstrate your willingness to understand their strategic context. A Strategist will only ever buy from you if they can clearly see how your solution or product fits into their own strategic context.
3. You need to demonstrate that you can help them achieve their strategic objectives. A Strategist will need to see objectives within a commercial context, so articulating solutions that can help them achieve their strategic goals is key to selling to a Strategist.

Selling to Play Makers:

1. A Play Maker must feel there is genuine collaboration and feel you are a genuine team player. A Play Maker's energy comes from a team of people collaborating and reaching consensus. They are more likely to buy from you if you get along well with them and you can help with the overall team dynamic.

2. You will have already invested in building a relationship with the Play Maker before you try and sell to them. A Play Maker invests in relationships – they want people to be the best they can be. They don't like to dominate, control and command people. They believe in shared endeavour with teamwork.

3. Your proposal will afford the Play Maker a central, coordinating role. Play Makers pride themselves on people being able to approach them, and a central, coordinating role will help people relate to them and receive motivating advice. They consider themselves natural leaders who prefer to enable rather than delegate.

Selling to Implementers:

1. You need to have demonstrated clear expectations and objectives. Your solution or product must help an Implementer get the job done. If it doesn't aid them with their delivery agenda, they are highly unlikely to buy.

2. You must show an Implementer that you have the skills to deliver. Track record and experience is crucial to an Implementer, and they will only buy from you if you have convinced them of your credentials to deliver.

3. You demonstrate that you have a reputation for getting things done! Implementers will also require cast-iron guarantees and check that you have robust client references and endorsements. They will want to know you are a 'safe pair of hands' and that they can rely on you to get things done.

Selling to *Polishers:*

1. You need to have demonstrated your credibility and high standards early. A sales proposal which focuses on continuous improvement, innovation and the pursuit of excellence is likely to strike a strong chord with a Polisher.

2. You must demonstrate that you will do what you say you are going to do. At the heart of Polishers is a fear of not being good enough and a fear of being let down. Demonstrate that they can rely on you to do what you say what they are going to do. Don't over-promise and under-deliver!

3. You give them the opportunity to critique and build upon your proposal. Polishers are likely to spend time checking things over to make sure they are of a high standard. They like to feel they are continually making progress, learning and developing. Help them do this.

In summary

Establishing an energy connection between the salesperson and a prospective buyer is the most critical of the three layers of sales!

Yes, you must understand the key outcomes your prospective client is looking for – by understanding their needs, wants and 'pain-points'. And yes, your prospective client must believe they are obtaining 'best value' from you.

But if there is an energy disconnect between the salesperson and the prospective buyer, this will likely result in a breakdown in the professional relationship which impacts trust ... which ultimately will negatively impact your sale!

Section 3:

Collective Energy for Impact: Teams at Their Most Effective

Chapter 8

Energy for Impact in Teams

In this chapter, the focus is upon how talented individuals can make a collective impact in teams.

Nathan Ott

Understanding the role of impact in team dynamics

When a football manager assembles a team for match day, the immediate focus isn't on individual personality traits like extroversion, introversion, empathy and so on. The primary question is: What impact is needed from the players individually and collectively, to secure a win?

While understanding personality and behavioural traits may be valuable for individual self-awareness, development and communication, the most critical factor for the team on match day is the direct impact each player can have upon the game. This emphasis on impact is vital for any team striving to achieve its objectives, whether in sports, business, or education.

At a fundamental level, people want to feel potent as individuals and within teams; they want to know that their contributions are meaningful. This desire spans all types of teams: from professional sports teams and corporate leadership teams to school project teams. When someone contributes in a way that energises them, that they can excel at, and are valued by their teammates, they feel potent and have the basis for thriving, not just surviving. Anyone who has had this experience will seek to replicate it.

This recognition of, and alignment of energy and impact is key to transforming a team from merely performing to high performing, and, ultimately, to becoming game-changing.

An illustrative analogy is that of a rowing eight. Even if the team consists of the fittest rowers in the most advanced boat, victory isn't guaranteed unless every member is 'pulling together', making the right impact at the right time towards a common goal. The collective impact of the team is the defining factor of success.

Unleashing Energy for Impact: a strategic framework

Imagine a team as a complex ecosystem, with each member contributing a unique blend of skills, perspectives, and energy. When harnessed effectively, this Energy for Impact becomes the driving force behind the team's performance. The GC Index offers a framework that helps teams map and understand the diverse sources of energy within their dynamic, providing a pathway to optimise their collective impact.

Understanding the mix of energies within a team is the first step toward maximising its potential. As you would have read in previous chapters The GC Index categorises these energies into distinct proclivities, each with their own distinct Energy for Impact: Game Changers, Strategists, Polishers, Implementers, and Play Makers – each bringing a unique contribution to the table. By recognising and aligning these energies, teams can achieve a synergy where the whole is greater than the sum of the parts.

When should a team use The GC Index?

The GC Index equips teams with the language and data needed to collectively achieve their objectives whether that is in business, education or sports. After a team assessment, members become aware of how their individual and collective Energy for Impact can help or hinder the team in achieving its objectives and identify areas requiring focus to drive better team impact. The GC Index is unique in its ability to mirror the language of a fundamental decision cycle – a cycle teams and organisations navigate countless times each day.

Teams continually make decisions revolving around questions like:

- Do we need to do something different? (Game Changer)
- Do we have a clear direction? (Strategist)
- What are the things we must get done? (Implementer)
- What are the things we must improve? (Polisher)
- Are we getting the best out of everyone? (Play Maker)

The GC Index excels at swiftly aligning people to the impact required within any project, process, or key initiative. Teams can achieve this alignment through a quick 1- to 2-hour exercise highlighted later in this chapter which can be incorporated into any team meeting, workshop or any other team get-together.

Starting with The GC Index: a strategic advantage

Barbara Lancaster from Parallel Planet once said, 'If you don't use The GC Index at the start of any team intervention, you will be starting in the middle of the movie.' This sentiment resonates strongly within the GC community because The GC Index provides an upfront framework, language, and data for teams to have robust, positive, and non-personal conversations about what they need to do to succeed.

Leadership teams aiming to be high-performing are increasingly turning to GCologists to leverage The GC Index. According to Dr John Mervyn-Smith who has coached leadership teams for over 30 years, high-performing teams are characterised by 'quality debates that support quality decisions, which in turn support the execution of agreed objectives within agreed parameters.'

The GC Index helps leadership teams assess and develop their capabilities for quality debates, decisions, and execution. By starting with The GC Index, teams can stay focused and ask the questions that drive them forward, such as:

- What helps and what hinders the team when it comes to quality debates, sound decisions, and effective execution?
- How does this profile help or hinder us in achieving our objectives?
- What activities is this team most likely to prioritise or overlook?
- What does this data reveal about our team culture?
- Which types of conversations are most likely to dominate in this team?

By asking these questions, teams can make informed, quality decisions and set the stage for success from the very beginning. The GC Index enables teams to have the necessary insights and data to support their ongoing development and achievement of their goals.

Practical application: Initiative Impact Mapping

To effectively utilise The GC Index, teams can employ a structured two-step process known as Initiative Impact Mapping. This process is designed to help teams align their energies with their key initiatives, ensuring that the right impact is made at the right time.

Step 1: discussion and prioritisation

The team, either in small groups or collectively, discusses the key initiative they need to undertake and prioritises The GC Index proclivities needed at each phase or stage. This step encourages open dialogue and a clear focus on what needs to be done and the energy for impact required to achieve it. Teams are provided with a list of example questions to facilitate this discussion, driving a clear and focused approach to the initiative. These are shown below in Figure 1.

AN EXAMPLE QUESTION FRAMEWORK FOR THE TEAM TO EXPLORE

THE TEAM CAN BUILD UPON THESE QUESTIONS OR ASK ITS OWN QUESTIONS RELATIVE TO THE TEAM'S OWN CONTEXT.

STRATEGIST	'Does this Team see the future challenges for the organisation?' 'Can we see how other organisational initiatives/objectives may fit into our plans?' 'Is everyone aligned and clear of what they need to deliver?'
GAME CHANGER	'Do we need to exploit new opportunities?' 'Do we need to do some things radically different?' 'Do we need to differentiate ourselves from the competition?'
PLAY MAKER	'Are we getting the best out of everyone in the team?' 'Have we engaged our key stakeholders properly?' 'Are we leveraging other people across the business to our advantage?'
IMPLEMENTER	'Do we have the capability to deliver our objectives?' 'Do we have a team that is energised by delivering tangible results?' 'Are we doing the right tasks at the right time for maximum impact?'
POLISHER	'Do we spend the time we need to learn from success and failure?' 'Are there any areas we must improve/not compromise on?' 'Do we over deliver to the detriment of having a fit for purpose solution?'

Figure 1: Example questions for driving a clear and focused approach to team performance

Step 2: alignment with GC Index data

Once the team has aligned on the necessary impact for their key initiatives, they compare this with their GC Index data. This comparison helps the team make informed decisions about the best approach for successfully delivering their initiatives. It is remarkable how quickly teams can utilise their GC Index data to guide their decisions, often arriving at solutions in 1 to 2 hours that might otherwise take days or weeks.

This impact-focused framework not only streamlines decision making but also helps depersonalise any tensions within the team. By focusing on the impact rather than personal differences, teams can engage in robust, depersonalised dialogues that best achieve agreed objectives.

Below is an example of how a team can break down what Energy for Impact is needed for each of their key initiatives and compare what is needed with their individual GC impact profiles. In this instance the initiatives range from creating a new volume recruitment process, planning an SAP upgrade through to organising an office move.

For example, if we take the volume recruitment process initiative (see Figure 2), you can see from the top line: 'New Volume Recruitment Process', that the team agreed that there needed to be a strong initial focus on doing things radically different and exploring possibilities (Game Changer).

However, from their individual and collective GC impact profiles you can see that Game Changer is their lowest proclivity by a significant margin. The conversation for the team then was: 'if we agree we need to do something radically different, how are we going to find the energy and make the space to do this?'

The options that they explored included:

- For people to move into that Game Changer space albeit they know it isn't their natural inclination or,
- Look outside the team for people with higher Game Changer proclivities to help the team through the first stage of the initiative.

As you can see, the team has a strong Strategist proclivity so once they are given new radical ideas and thinking they are more energised to take those possibilities and structure a clear way forward and prioritise what needs to be done (Strategist). The team decided to play to this energy and seek to harvest Game Changer ideas from outside the team.

1) NEW VOLUME RECRUITMENT PROCESS

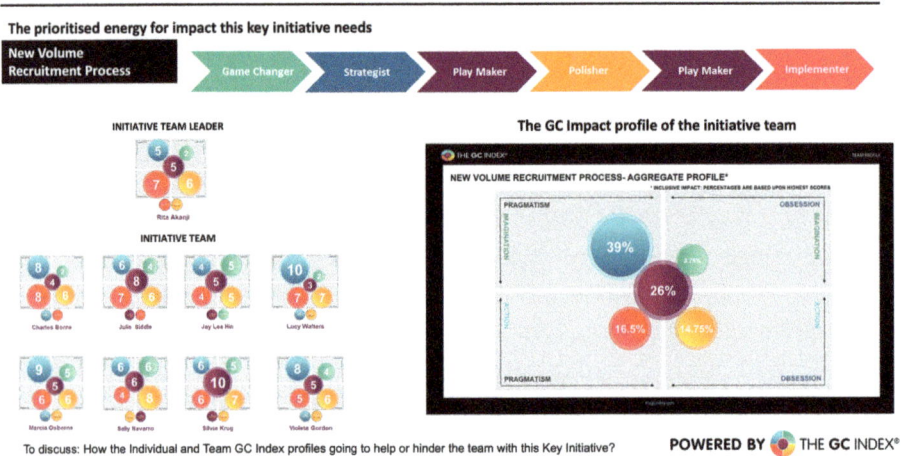

Figure 2: A team managing a volume recruitment process

The broader benefits of The GC Index and teams

By adopting this simple two-step exercise, teams can make decisions in 1 to 2 hours that might otherwise take days or weeks. Some of the benefits include:

- Aligning project teams with the work needed: ensuring that each team member is contributing in the most effective way.
- Ensuring team alignment with objectives: making sure that everyone is working towards the same goals.
- Matching the right people to the right roles at the right time: identifying who can make the most significant impact in each role.
- Defining and mapping the impact needed at any process stage: providing clarity on what needs to be achieved at each step of a project.
- Creating a common language of impact across cross-functional

teams: facilitating communication and collaboration between different departments.

- Driving impactful inter-team collaboration: encouraging teams to work together more effectively.
- Recruiting new members based on the impact they can bring: focusing on the potential impact of new hires, rather than just their skills or experience.
- Aligning activities to energy for impact and improving team well-being: ensuring that the team's activities are energising and impactful, leading to better morale and productivity.

Below, I present two case studies that bring this approach to life; you will be able to see how it works in action.

Case study 1: a large technology company's sales team

A leading technology company faced a significant challenge as it sought to balance the promotion of its existing, revenue-generating technologies with the introduction of new, groundbreaking products. The sales team was divided between those who excelled at selling the traditional technology, which constituted 80% of the company's revenue, and those who were more enthusiastic about the new offerings.

Using The GC Index, the company was able to analyse the energy profiles of its sales team members. Those who preferred selling traditional products exhibited a stronger Strategist, Implementer, and Polisher profile, valuing tried-and-tested methods and showing reluctance towards the new, untested technologies. See Figure 3 below for an aggregate picture of this group's – Team A – GC Index profiles.

On the other hand, the salespeople who were more excited about the new technology had a Game Changer, Strategist, and Play Maker profile, being more open to the exciting future possibilities the new technology could bring. See Figure 4 below for an aggregate picture of this group's – Team B – GC Index profiles.

Armed with this data, the company reorganised its sales team into two focused groups: one dedicated to the traditional technology – Team A –

and the other to the new offerings – Team B. Additionally, the company paired individuals from both groups when engaging with clients, ensuring that customers received comprehensive insights into both the existing and new technologies. This approach not only increased sales across both product lines but also improved team morale and engagement.

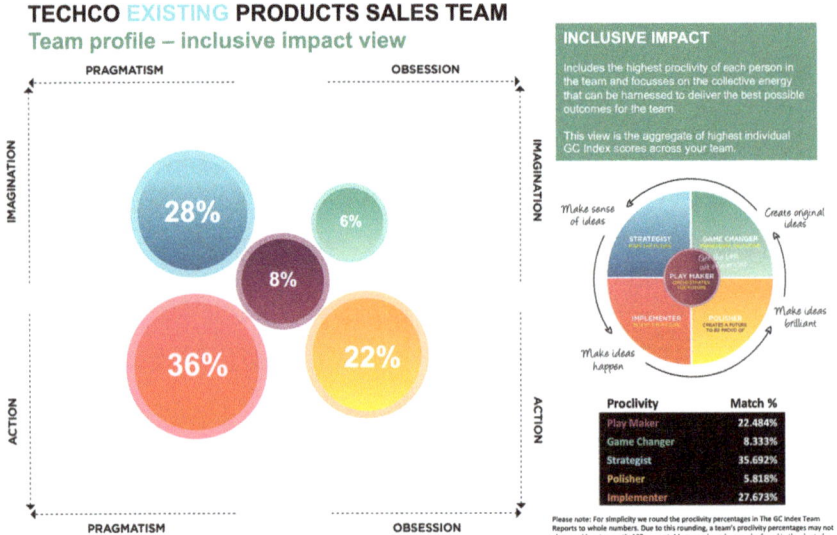

Figure 3: An aggregate picture of Team A's GC Index profiles

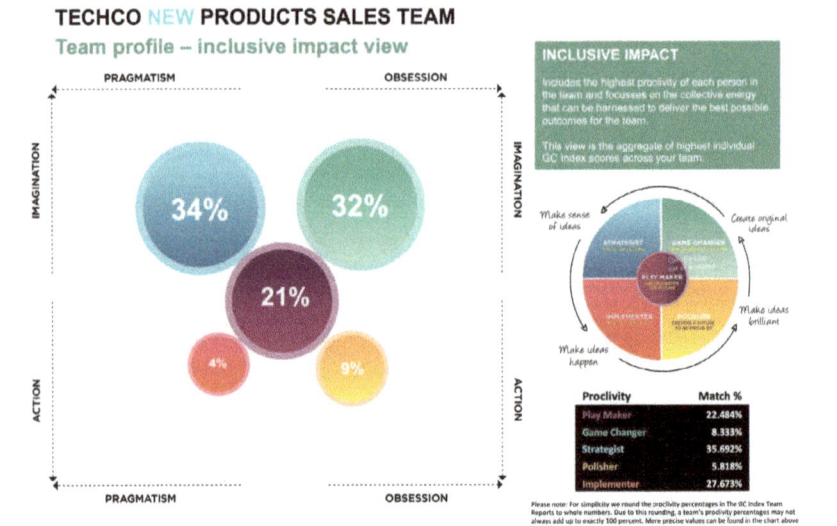

Figure 4: An aggregate picture of Team B's GC Index profiles

Case study 2: a global banking institution's technology team

A global bank's technology team faced challenges after implementing a new global procurement system. While the system had initially been successful, it soon began experiencing bugs and customer complaints. At the same time, the team was eager to move on to a new version of the system, excited by the possibilities it could offer.

The GC Index revealed that the leadership team driving the push for the new version had strong Game Changer and Strategist profiles, focusing on future possibilities rather than addressing existing issues. This energy had permeated the entire team, leading to a lack of focus on fixing the current system's problems.

With this insight from The GC Index team data, the bank reorganised its technology team. A subgroup with Implementer, Polisher, and Strategist profiles was tasked with addressing the bugs and complaints, ensuring the current system was operating optimally. Meanwhile, the Game Changer and Strategist leaders continued to explore the potential of the new version, but with a greater understanding of the importance of the Implementer and Polisher energy needed by the team to maintain and enhance the existing system until the upgrade was ready.

This balanced approach allowed the bank to improve customer satisfaction with the current system while also preparing for a smooth transition to the new version.

Inter-team impact and the power of energy for impactful collaboration

In the ever-evolving landscape of modern organisations, the success of a team is not solely dependent on its internal dynamics but also on its ability to collaborate effectively with other teams. This concept, known as inter-team impact, is crucial for ensuring seamless communication, mutual understanding, and shared objectives across different functions within a business. The GC Index provides a powerful framework for understanding and optimising the energy within and between teams, allowing organisations to break down silos and foster a more collaborative environment.

The challenge of inter-team collaboration

In many organisations, the boundaries between teams can often become sources of tension. For instance, sales teams might feel that the delivery or product development teams are not responsive enough to customer needs, while delivery teams might view sales as overly optimistic and disconnected from the practical realities of what can be delivered. These tensions are not unique to any one industry; they are a common occurrence in any environment where different teams must work together to achieve a common goal.

One typical example is the interaction between a sales team, focused on closing deals and driving revenue, and a delivery team, responsible for implementing the promised solutions.

A case in point is a client marketing team for a leading national telecommunications company energised by Game Changer and Strategist proclivities, who were very forward looking and enthusiastic about pushing the boundaries of what is possible. In contrast, the product development team, with a stronger Implementer and Polisher profile, were more cautious, focusing on ensuring that what is promised is feasible and delivered to a high standard.

Bridging the gap: the role of The GC Index

The GC Index then, offers a structured approach to understanding these different energies and how they can be aligned to reduce friction and enhance collaboration. By mapping the energy profiles of different teams, organisations can identify where potential conflicts might arise and take proactive steps to address them.

Case study 3: global telecoms communications company

For example, in the case of a telecommunications company, The GC Index revealed a significant gap between the marketing team's visionary approach and the product development team's pragmatic focus. This insight allowed the company to facilitate more constructive conversations between the teams, leading to better alignment and improved outcomes.

The GC Index framework encourages teams to appreciate the value each group brings to the table. In the telecommunications example, the marketing team was encouraged to continue pushing the envelope with clients, but with a greater understanding of the practical constraints faced by the product development team. Similarly, the product development team learned to value the marketing team's role in driving leading edge thinking, differentiation and competitiveness in the market. By fostering this mutual respect and understanding, the organisation was able to reduce inter-team tensions and significantly improve overall performance.

Inter-team impact is a critical factor in the success of any organisation. By understanding the different Energy for Impact profiles within and between teams, organisations can foster better collaboration, reduce tensions, and ensure that all teams are working towards common goals. The GC Index provides a practical and effective tool for achieving this, allowing teams to align their energies and focus on delivering the best possible outcomes.

In a world where collaboration across teams is increasingly essential, those organisations that can harness the power of inter-team impact will not only survive but thrive, driving innovation, improving performance, and achieving long-term success. The GC Index is not just a tool for improving individual team performance; it is a framework for transforming the way entire organisations work together, creating a culture of mutual respect, understanding, and shared achievement.

Conclusion: the essential role of Energy for Impact

In the fast-paced and ever-evolving landscape of team dynamics, understanding and optimising Energy for Impact is crucial. The GC Index provides a comprehensive framework for teams to identify, harness, and amplify the unique energies within their midst. By embracing the diverse strengths of Game Changers, Strategists, Polishers, Implementers, and Play Makers, teams can create a powerful synergy that propels them toward unparalleled success.

As teams navigate future challenges, those armed with a deep understanding of their energy dynamics, coupled with The GC Index framework, will not only survive but thrive, leaving an indelible mark on the landscape of high-performance teamwork.

Chapter 9

Energy for Impact in Projects and Processes

The concept of Energy for Impact helps us to understand how individual energies align with various tasks and stages within a project, and can provide profound insights into why some projects succeed while others fail.

Simon Etherington

Introduction: the role of energy in project success

Energy for Impact refers to the intrinsic motivation and enthusiasm individuals have for specific types of work. This concept underscores the fact that people are naturally drawn to certain tasks while being repelled by others. Recognising these preferences is essential for ensuring that projects are managed effectively and reach their desired outcomes.

In any group activity, from business projects to school assignments, the distribution of energy significantly influences performance. Individuals may exhibit high energy levels for tasks they enjoy and low energy levels for tasks they find unappealing. This variance can directly impact the success or failure of a project. It's reasonable to assume that, in any setting, when an individual is engaged by a task, they are more likely to apply themselves to that task and developing the skills needed to achieve that task.

Effective project management hinges on understanding these dynamics and leveraging them appropriately. It involves recognising that energy is not a static resource but a dynamic force that can be harnessed to drive productivity, innovation, engagement and satisfaction. Therefore, aligning individual energies with project needs becomes a crucial strategy for achieving desired results.

Introducing The GC Index framework

Every organisation engages in five high-level activities to achieve anything.

THE GC INDEX LANGUAGE OF THE ORGANISATION

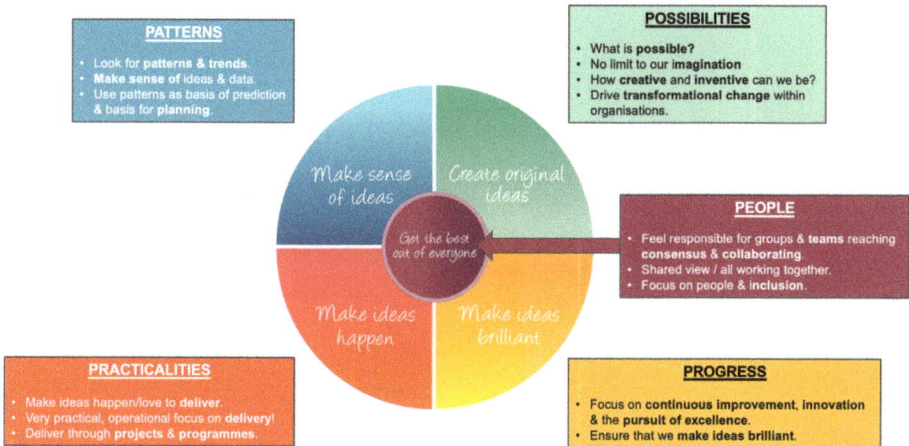

PATTERNS
- Look for **patterns & trends**.
- **Make sense** of ideas & data.
- Use patterns as basis of prediction & basis for **planning**.

POSSIBILITIES
- What is **possible?**
- No limit to our **imagination**
- How **creative** and **inventive** can we be?
- Drive **transformational change** within organisations.

PEOPLE
- Feel responsible for groups & **teams** reaching **consensus & collaborating**.
- Shared view / all working together.
- Focus on people & **inclusion**.

PRACTICALITIES
- Make ideas happen/love to **deliver**.
- Very practical, operational focus on **delivery!**
- Deliver through **projects & programmes**.

PROGRESS
- Focus on **continuous improvement, innovation** & the **pursuit of excellence**.
- Ensure that we **make ideas brilliant**.

Make sense of ideas — *Create original ideas* — *Get the best out of everyone* — *Make ideas happen* — *Make ideas brilliant*

The GC Index framework then, categorises individuals based on their proclivities: the ways in which people channel energy to have an impact in their world in each of these five activities.

Understanding these individual differences then provides a structured way to understand and harness these dynamics within a project. The framework identifies five key proclivities and when each are at their best, this is what we see:

1. Game Changer: energised by exploring new, original ways of doing things.
2. Strategist: focused on making sense of things and understanding the problem before starting.
3. Implementer: prefers to take action and get things done effectively.
4. Polisher: concentrates on incremental improvements and refining existing ideas and solutions.
5. Play Maker: ensures that people work together effectively and that stakeholder interests are managed.

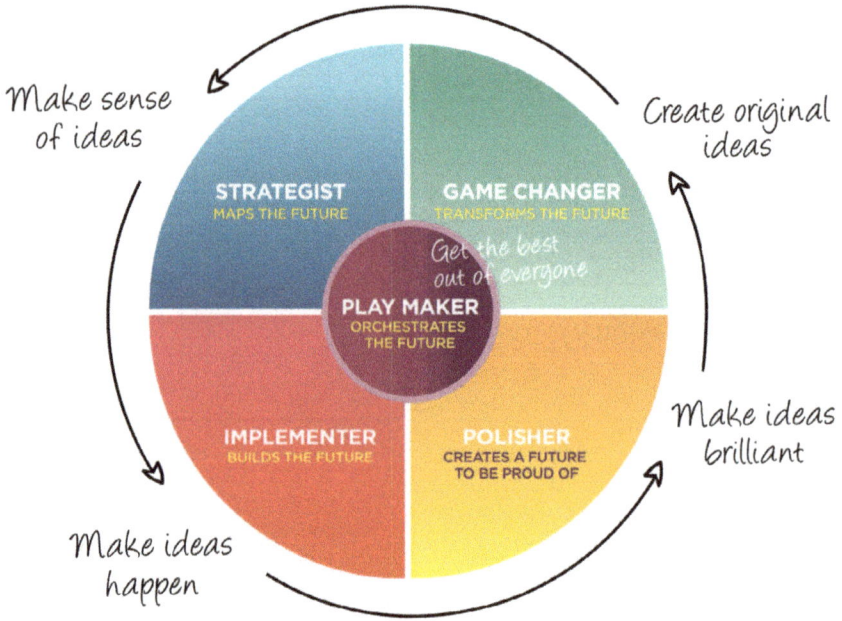

Make sense of ideas

Create original ideas

Make ideas brilliant

Make ideas happen

STRATEGIST
MAPS THE FUTURE

GAME CHANGER
TRANSFORMS THE FUTURE

Get the best out of everyone

PLAY MAKER
ORCHESTRATES THE FUTURE

IMPLEMENTER
BUILDS THE FUTURE

POLISHER
CREATES A FUTURE TO BE PROUD OF

Each proclivity plays a vital role at different stages of a project. For instance, Game Changers are crucial during the ideation phase, while Implementers are engaged by execution. Our experience suggests that understanding and leveraging these proclivities can significantly enhance project outcomes.

Energy requirements across project phases

Projects typically undergo several phases, each requiring different types of energy. For example, the initial phase may demand high levels of Game Changer energy to foster innovation and creativity. As the project progresses, the need for Strategist and Implementer energies becomes evident to ensure that ideas have strategic relevance and are practical and executable. In later stages, Polisher energy becomes essential to refine and perfect the project outcomes, building a platform for future 'best practice'.

An absence of certain proclivities in a team or a lack of alignment between the energies of team members and the needs of the project, can lead to failure. Ensuring that the right energies are applied at the right times is crucial for maintaining momentum and achieving success. The challenge lies in dynamically adjusting team compositions and responsibilities to match these evolving needs.

The following case study serves to illustrate how these approaches work in practice.

Case study 1: telecommunications provider

A global telecommunications provider's R&D division, known as the Moon Shot, serves as a practical example of the importance of Energy for Impact. This division excelled at creating minimal viable products (MVPs), with high energy levels observed during the initial stages of development. However, as projects moved from MVP1 to MVP2 and beyond, maintaining motivation and energy became challenging.

I have presented the team's aggregate GC Index profile below in Figure 1. The percentage scores are based upon individuals' highest individual scores, so 28% of individuals had a highest score for Game Changer; 28% a highest score for Implementer; 24% a highest score for Play Maker and so on.

The team, then, had strong Game Changer, Play Maker and Implementer energies but lacked Polisher energy. Teams like this, typically, have energy for coming together (Play Maker) for creative (Game Changer), practical (Implementer) problem solving.

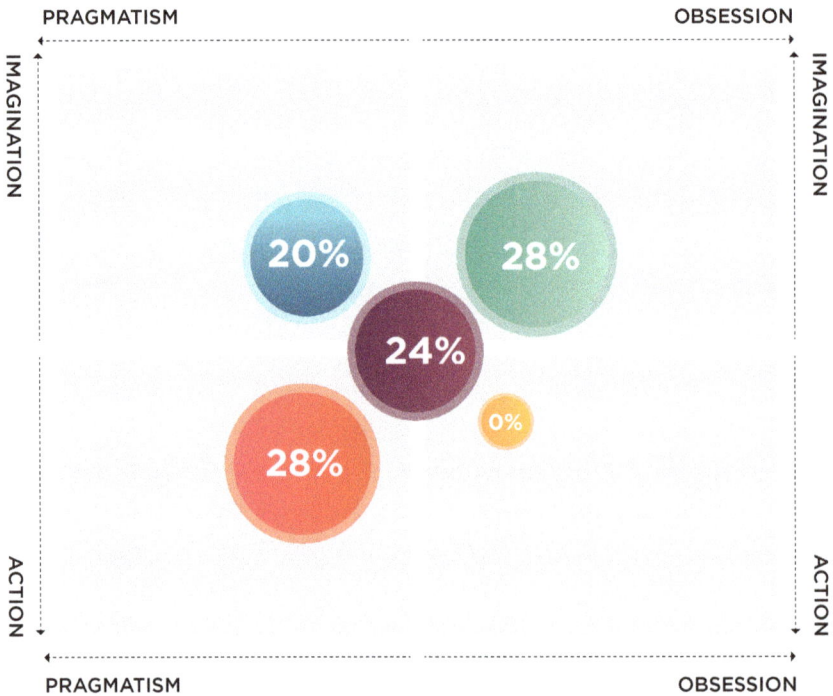

Figure 1: Moon Shot aggregate GC Index profile

You will note that no one in the team had a highest score for Polisher: those individuals that bring energy to continuous improvements of ideas, solutions and outputs.

This gap explained why the team struggled with later stages of development: they were more engaged by the next problem to solve rather than developing the solutions that they had already created.

By understanding and addressing such an imbalance, the organisation can adjust its team composition or bring in individuals with the necessary Polisher energy to sustain project momentum.

Moon Shot's experience highlights the importance of continuous energy assessment and adjustment throughout a project's life cycle. This proactive approach ensures that the right mix of energies is always available to meet the demands of each phase. I consider these below.

Strategic planning and energy alignment

Projects typically start with effective strategic planning and this also benefits from considering Energy for Impact. For instance, a team tasked with developing a three-year strategy plan needed to rethink their approach. Traditionally, they conducted planning in 'silos', involving the same people and producing similar results.

By recognising the need for diverse proclivities, the team decided to incorporate more Play Maker and Game Changer energy into their planning process. They involved different stakeholders to ensure a broad range of perspectives and dedicated time to exploring new ideas and possibilities. This shift allowed them to develop a more innovative and comprehensive strategy.

Game Changers/Play Makers will bring energy to including and involving all team members in 'finding their voice' when it comes to generating, exploring and agreeing upon new ideas and possibilities.

Strategic planning is often seen as a purely analytical exercise, but incorporating Energy for Impact introduces a vital human element. It acknowledges that the effectiveness of a strategy depends not just on its technical soundness but also on the energy and enthusiasm of those who will create it and implement it.

Flexibility across methodologies

Projects often seek to take on a planned, linear and step-by-step approach to getting things done. But we know that real life is rarely that ordered and the concept of Energy for Impact allows for versatility and can be integrated into various project management methodologies, such as agile, lean, and design thinking that, for their success, require teams to be versatile and 'fast on their feet'. Given this, at any point in the life cycle of a project, it helps determine the right person for the right task based not only on the skills and experience that they can bring but also on their intrinsic energy for the activity.

For example, during a transformational change process, understanding individual energies helps ensure that everyone contributes effectively.

People with strong Play Maker proclivities might lead stakeholder engagement efforts, while those with Game Changer proclivities focus on generating new ideas.

Agile methodologies, with their emphasis on iterative development and adaptability, are particularly well suited to leveraging Energy for Impact. Agile teams can be structured to include a balance of energies, ensuring that each sprint benefits from the right mix of creativity (Game Changer), planning (Strategist), execution (Implementer), and refinement (Polisher).

Lean methodologies, focused on efficiency and waste reduction, also benefit from understanding Energy for Impact. By aligning tasks with individuals' energies, lean teams can achieve higher levels of productivity and morale, leading to better overall outcomes.

Enhancing innovation and change

Energy for Impact also plays a pivotal role in driving innovation and change. Organisations often encourage employees to be innovative, but this directive can be vague and unhelpful. By using The GC Index framework, organisations can identify how each person contributes to innovation based on their energy profile.

For instance, a company like Nike, with a mantra of continuous innovation, can use this approach to show employees how their unique energies contribute to the overall innovation process. This understanding fosters a more inclusive and effective culture of innovation.

Innovation is not a one-size-fits-all activity. It requires a blend of different energies to move from ideation to implementation to refinement. By recognising and harnessing these diverse energies, organisations can create a more robust and dynamic innovation ecosystem.

Overcoming challenges and resistance

Projects and processes often encounter resistance and challenges that can derail progress. Understanding Energy for Impact can help leaders anticipate and address these issues more effectively. Resistance often arises when individuals are asked to engage in tasks that do not align with their natural energies, leading to disengagement and frustration.

By recognising these mismatches early, leaders can make adjustments to roles and responsibilities, ensuring that each team member is working in a capacity that aligns with their energy. This proactive approach minimises resistance and enhances overall project momentum.

For instance, if a team member with strong Polisher energy is struggling with the creative demands of the ideation phase, they can be reassigned to a role that better suits their strengths, while someone with a Game Changer proclivity takes on the creative tasks. This flexibility ensures that all team members are contributing effectively and that the project continues to move forward smoothly.

In broad terms this is how we can use The GC Index to understand resistance to change:

- Game Changers resist change when they think that they can offer an even better way of doing things.
- Strategists resist change when the purpose for change is not clear. Strategists need to feel purposeful if they are to engage in change: 'why are we doing this?'
- Implementers resist change if they feel that the change won't work: 'we've tried that before and it didn't work then ...'
- Polishers resist change if they think that it has not been thought through and could lead to embarrassment, failure; not the ideal outcome: 'we could do better than this'.
- Play Makers resist change if they feel that it is not in the best interests of people: 'how does this change benefit our people?'

The human element in project management

My comments above on resistance to change highlight that project management cannot just be viewed through the lens of processes, tools, and methodologies: the human element is equally important.

Understanding Energy for Impact brings this human element to the forefront, emphasising the need to consider individuals' motivations, preferences, and intrinsic energies.

Effective project management requires a balance between technical expertise and human understanding. By incorporating Energy for Impact into project planning and execution, leaders can create a more holistic approach that addresses both the practical and personal aspects of project work.

This holistic approach not only enhances project outcomes but is also likely to improve employee satisfaction and retention. When individuals feel that their energies are recognised and valued, they are more likely, we would argue, to be engaged, motivated, and committed to their work.

Practical applications and tools

Implementing the concept of Energy for Impact in real-world projects involves several practical steps and tools. The GC Index framework provides a structured approach for assessing and understanding individual proclivities, but it must be integrated into the broader project management process.

One practical tool is the 'Energy Mapping' exercise, where team members' energies are mapped against the requirements of different project phases. This visual representation helps identify gaps and imbalances, allowing leaders to make informed decisions about team composition and role assignments.

Another useful tool is the 'Energy Alignment' workshop, where team members discuss their energies and proclivities openly. These workshops foster a deeper understanding of each other's strengths and challenges, promoting a culture of collaboration and mutual support.

Regular energy assessments can also be conducted throughout the project life cycle to ensure that the team remains aligned and motivated. These assessments provide valuable insights into how energies are shifting and where adjustments might be needed.

Building high-performing teams

When teams take seriously the need to align individual and collective Energy for Impact to a task or series of tasks, they create the potential to build high-performing teams involving more than just assembling a group of skilled individuals.

It requires a strategic understanding of how different energies can be combined to maximise impact. The GC Index framework provides a valuable tool for constructing teams that are not only capable but also energised and motivated.

High-performing teams are characterised by their ability to work collaboratively and adapt to changing circumstances. By aligning team members' proclivities with their roles and responsibilities, leaders can ensure that each individual is working at their highest level of engagement and effectiveness.

For example, a team tasked with launching a new product might include Game Changers to drive innovation, Strategists to develop a coherent plan, Implementers to execute the plan efficiently, Polishers to refine the product, and Play Makers to manage team dynamics and stakeholder relationships. This balanced approach ensures that all aspects of the project are covered and that the team remains motivated throughout the process.

Case study 2: tech start-up innovation

A tech start-up focused on developing 'cutting-edge' software solutions provides another example of how Energy for Impact can drive project success. The start-up was struggling to move beyond the initial idea phase. Despite having a talented team, progress was slow, and morale was low.

I have presented the team's aggregate GC Index Profile below. You will note that the team was heavily skewed towards Game Changer and Strategist proclivities, with very little Implementer or Polisher energy: 40% of the team had a highest individual score for Strategist and 27% a highest individual score for Game Changer. This was a team with much more energy for ideas than it had for Implementer and/or Polisher action.

This imbalance explained why the team was excellent at generating ideas but struggled with execution and refinement.

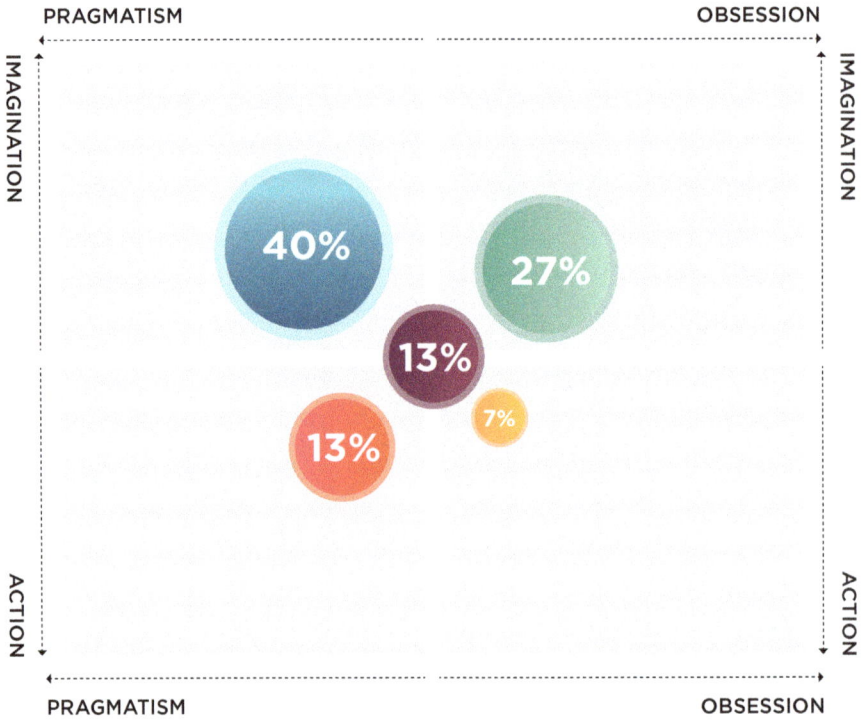

Figure 2: Tech start-up aggregate GC Index profile

By bringing in individuals with strong Implementer and Polisher proclivities, the start-up was able to create a more balanced team. The new
team composition led to a significant increase in productivity and progress, with ideas moving from concept to reality much more effectively and
efficiently.

This case study highlights the importance of continuously assessing and
adjusting team energies to match project needs. It also demonstrates the
transformative impact that the right energy alignment can have on project
outcomes.

Sustaining energy over time

As the example above illustrates, sustaining Energy for Impact over the
duration of a project or process is a key challenge. Projects often start

with high energy levels, but sustaining this energy requires ongoing effort and attention.

Regular check-ins and energy assessments help maintain alignment and motivation. Leaders can use these check-ins to gauge team members' energy levels, address any emerging issues, and make necessary adjustments to roles and responsibilities.

Creating a supportive and inclusive team culture also plays a vital role in sustaining energy. When team members feel valued and supported, they are more likely to remain engaged and motivated. Celebrating successes, providing opportunities for professional growth, and fostering a positive work environment all contribute to sustaining energy over time.

Conclusions

Understanding and leveraging Energy for Impact is crucial for the success of projects and processes. By aligning individual energies with project needs, organisations can enhance productivity, improve project outcomes, and boost employee satisfaction. The GC Index framework provides a valuable tool for identifying and harnessing these energies, ensuring that the right people are involved at the right stages of a project.

As we continue to explore the dynamics of energy in project management, it becomes clear that the success of any project hinges not just on skills and experience but also on the intrinsic energies that individuals bring to the table. By embracing this holistic approach, organisations can achieve greater efficiency, innovation, and success in their endeavours.

By integrating the concept of Energy for Impact into project management practices, leaders can create more dynamic, resilient, and high-performing teams. This approach not only enhances project outcomes but also fosters a more engaged and motivated workforce, ultimately driving organisational success and growth.

Chapter 10

Keeping the Band Together

At the heart of this exploration is the view that great art
'connects' with people and to do so, those making that art must
feel connected to each other.

John Frost

The arts definitely have something important to say to the world at this moment in our history. I am happy to make this bold statement because I believe it to be true.

In his book *21 Lessons for the 21st Century* Yuval Noah Harari said:

'We (humans) are left with the task of creating an updated story for the world.'

I am attracted to the notion of reimaging contained in this statement. And, if we are to reimagine our future, then I believe that, together, the arts, The GC Index and leadership, connecting people on so many levels as they do, will have a critical role to play in how that updated story unfolds.

But what's that got to do with rock bands?

When I thought about the title of this chapter, 'Keeping the Band Together', it provoked a number of thoughts and feelings; and, as usual, for me at least, this led to a question.

What do I mean by band?

At one level, of course, I mean rock bands generically as well as my experience of the band that I play in: Rebel and the Banned. So, the band in this sense can be looked at from a team perspective. However, we might also think of the GCI proclivities themselves as a band of different energies; the interest there might be how does that (GCI) band work and interact within the individual as a leader or as a team member. And we can also think of a system, either local or global, as a band with different energies impacting on the look, feel and perhaps focus of that system.

So, however we define the band, the GCI proclivities interact with each other and provide one of the lenses through which we can understand what is happening and importantly why it is happening in that way. The band is, of course, more than just its energies and raw abilities. Thriving as an individual, as a musical group or even as a global system is also dependent on the skills and leadership with which we deploy our energies.

So, the focus of this chapter using the context of the arts, is how we create bands and teams that make beautiful music by understanding how The GC Index and leadership work together to create the platform for success.

So, let's turn first to bands and specifically the elements of a successful rock band. What might we observe? Perhaps unsurprisingly it looks quite similar to any team in any organisation.

The vocalist, guitarist, bassist and drummer all have defined roles and responsibilities on stage. For example, the lead vocalist is responsible for delivering the lyrics and engaging with the audience. The guitarists provide the band's melodic and harmonic foundation. Bass and drum drive the timing and rhythm that really anchor the band. The roles are critical and interdependent.

However, there is more to a band's roles and responsibility than just those attached to performance. The performance could be defined as the expression of the art but that is the culmination of a lot of other elements critical to the success of the band; essentially how they work together and the culture that they create within the band.

Collaboration is critical. For example, in the songwriting process which is often a collaborative effort of melodies, lyrics and arrangements.

This is, of course, supported by safe spaces for **communication** and enriching conversations. Making space for creative input and **feedback** is often based on the quality of the communication. Ensuring that each band member feels psychologically safe, empowered and trusted to bring their unique perspective and influences, contributing to the band's overall sound. This ensures that everyone feels valued, and that the music reflects the band's collective vision.

Leadership and how decisions are made is also key to a band's success. Bands sometimes have charismatic front people, for example Jagger and Mercury. However, in many successful bands, leadership is shared, with different members taking charge in areas where they excel, whether it's songwriting, production, or managing the band's business affairs.

Like any team, rock bands have conflicts, whether it's creative differences or personal issues. How these **conflicts are managed and resolved** can determine the band's longevity and success. So, compromise and negotiation have to be a part of the creative process, and successful bands will generally have the skills and mindset to appreciate what everyone brings and find a middle ground where all members feel valued and satisfied with the decisions made.

A sense of **shared purpose** will often be the hallmark of a great rock band. It could be creating groundbreaking music, achieving commercial success, or impacting on social justice issues. Whatever it is, a unified purpose drives their efforts and often supports the consistency of their artistic direction.

Mutual trust and support are found in all great teams. Band members often support each other in their personal and professional growth. Whether it's encouraging a fellow member through a tough time or pushing each other to improve musically, mutual trust and support is crucial.

The music industry is a crowded space and it's forever changing. So, bands that survive and thrive over the years often do so by **adapting to changes** in the industry, shifting trends, and personal circumstances

Collective achievement and accountability happen when bands feel connected to each other. Everyone contributes to the band's triumphs and deals with setbacks together. In the same way each member is accountable to the group, ensuring that they perform their best and contribute positively to the band's team dynamics and the quality of the **interpersonal relationships.**

So, this chapter is at one level a story about music and musicians. And it is also my story as a member of a band; someone who was only comfortable to refer to themselves a musician relatively recently. It's a story of how I have opened up a new chapter in my life, how I got here; and how I nearly didn't get here! And some of the stuff in between, including nearly losing it all.

However, it is also story of leadership, my leadership, the band's leadership and how leadership facilitates the power of The GC Index for bands and other teams.

The story includes my learning and observations; it will pose questions based on those observations not all of which I will attempt to answer. Some questions are best left for reflection and further thought as you draw your own conclusions.

I hope it also provokes further questions that may be a catalyst for your own curiosity whether or not you are familiar with the arts. And, of course, the chapter will also draw on my knowledge of The GC Index as a way of framing some of my learning and observations. This is my profile:

My strongest proclivities are Strategist and Implementer.

In this way I hope that this chapter will, in some way, also enhance my understanding of The GC Index and hopefully your own.

So, what about the music?

I haven't always been in a band, albeit I loved music from a very early age. I was born in 1961 when the Beatles were still primarily a covers band. As I grew up, I became aware of my parents' record collection including Beatles 45s as they became known for their own music. My parents were not musicians, but music was a noticeable part of their life, so I was very aware of music in my surroundings.

A brief flirtation with the guitar at a young age gained me some music school grades but not what I would call a devotion to the instrument! My love of music on the other hand continued to grow as I attended many gigs in my hometown of Wolverhampton.

These were the days when tours were long, and bands played smaller venues than the stadiums of today. It was therefore a much more intimate experience to see a band. This love of music was enhanced at Lancaster University, which also attracted significant names at the time; back in the early 1980s universities were very much on the tour list of bands such as U2 and Dire Straits.

Many of my friends at school and university were either into music, or formed their own bands. One friend even progressed in to a senior role in the music industry which he still holds as I write this. And yet, even with all that enthusiasm, I wasn't a musician, except in my dreams! That said, I know that I was always conscious of holding the question – could I do that? That never left me. Some of my friends took that further and made their dreams a reality – but, at that time, not me.

My interest in music has continued throughout my life and I am now also a trustee of the Bewdley Arts Festival a multi-arts festival based in my town on the river Severn in Worcestershire. The activity of the festival also offers young musicians a chance to develop their skills through performances supported by the event. It is amazing to see their confidence grow through this opportunity, not just as musicians but as people.

So, why did I sit on the sidelines and not take the plunge as some of my friends did? I can make excuses about other distractions and there were some, but, in the end, I think that it came down to a lack of self-belief fuelled by my personal fears.

Research shows that some of the reasons cited for not realising an ambition to play on stage are:

Fear of judgement: being worried about being judged by the audience or fear that you will make mistakes and not meet their expectations.

Lack of experience: a lack of experience performing in front of others, the unfamiliarity of the situation can lead to anxiety.

Perfectionism: the desire to perform perfectly which can create immense pressure and lead to fear of making even minor mistakes.

Self-doubt: doubts about abilities or feeling that you are not good enough to perform in front of an audience.

Physical symptoms: stage fright can manifest as physical symptoms such as shaking, sweating, or a racing heart, which can be distressing and make you feel even more anxious.

I can certainly associate with a number of these!

For me there was a lot of negative self-talk going on. 'What if I make a mistake or freeze?' and 'what if people laugh at me?' are two that were often present.

It is said that one of the strategies that we can adopt to handle fear is to embrace it. Understand where it is coming from and try small changes; breaking the fear down into smaller parts and dealing with those small parts in the first instance.

If I think about my own journey from the dream of playing in a band to actually doing it, I can relate to this idea. It started with a jam! Most music does, but in my case that jamming session with friends was a safe space to make mistakes and learn from other more experienced players not just technique but also the reality of playing music.

Musically, everyone starts in the same place and everyone, even the most experienced player, make mistakes. Mistakes are a part of the learning process. I have a low Polisher score in my GC Index profile. So, for me in GC Index terms the idea of making a mistake was not an obsession with perfection that was driving the fear of failure; it was more the insecurity that I felt from a fear of being embarrassed. I was, if anything, overthinking it; trying to understand the process and working out what was good enough to unfreeze the fear, to counter the negative self-talk and just play. But then again, as a Strategist/Implementer perhaps they were the lenses through which I was processing the problem! In hindsight, there were perhaps less dots to join up than I thought there were.

Our fears often exaggerate. As I built up the picture of what was possible (and good enough), I could literally feel my confidence growing. Susan Jeffers is right, sometimes we just need to feel the fear and do it anyway![29]

And when I was able to connect to my fear in this way then it was easier for me to address where my lack of confidence was coming from.

> *'Left unrecognized and unaddressed ... self-limiting belief patterns can confine a potentially confident and self-actualized person to a lifetime of insecurity.'*
>
> Thomas Rutledge, *Psychology Today*, US edition, July 2023

In the same article Rutledge talks about the core beliefs of confidence as:

- Knowing that outcomes cannot be controlled and that what matters is effort, persistence, preparation, and goals.
- Seeing success as an ongoing process and appreciating that setbacks are a necessary part of the process.
- Believing that success is inevitable if we can stick with it and adapt.

[29] Susan Jeffers, *Feel the Fear and Do It Anyway*, Harvest Publications, 2003.

- Seeing failure as temporary, a positive source of feedback and a learning opportunity.
- Seeing anxiety, fear and doubts as a healthy sign that we are testing ourselves rather than as a sign of impending failure.
- Not taking rejection of failure personally.

Pretty much all of the musicians that I have met would be able to relate to some or all of the above. For me personally, I really connect to the notion of 'seeing anxiety, fear and doubts as a healthy sign that we are testing ourselves'. And the belief that 'failure is both temporary and a positive source of feedback'. I see this all the time in the way that bands, mine and others, work together in the creative process of making music.

So, what if we could connect to our fears in a different and empowering way? What else might be available to us? What might we be able to reach for? Who else might also benefit if we handle our fears in a more empowering way?

Another characteristic of the Strategist/Implementer is pragmatism. And it feels as if that pragmatic energy has underpinned my journey of growing my confidence and capability as a musician. A good example of this was the liberation, and it did feel like a sense of freedom, that came with the knowledge that all musicians, new and experienced, make mistakes whether in rehearsal or live.

This really helped me to connect with the process of creating and making music and the possibility of collaborating with others to do this. Imperfection is literally part of the creative process in this context. Easier said than done perhaps. Embracing imperfection can be a challenge! But having an amazing group of supportive people around you always helps! And, as a musician, I have always been fortunate enough to have such people around me.

Of course, sometimes life throws a curved ball at you. And this part of the story is where my self-leadership crosses over with my ambition to be a musician.

On 15 November 2022, I had a cardiac arrest.

I was fortunate enough to be in a place that had both a defibrillator and trained first responders. They saved my life before the emergency services arrived. I am one of only 7% who survive cardiac arrests. Most people are in the wrong place when it happens, a place where those two essential ingredients are not available. And so, by the time the paramedics arrive, it is often too late.

I believe that this is relevant to this story because of the connection that it gave me to myself and what was important to me. I remember quite soon after the cardiac arrest asking myself, 'what might emerge from this?' Of the many things that did emerge, my connection to the desire to play music became stronger and the fear (that was stopping me) was certainly put into perspective. I remember asking myself, 'what are you waiting for?' Had things turned out differently, I might never have played in a band, never had the opportunity to reframe those fears, anxieties and doubts, and do something that has been transformative for me and my life in many ways. The band is a metaphor for how I now want to live my life.

So, my question falling out of this experience was this: if we believe in the idea of creating 'an updated story' for ourselves and others, how can we possibly do this without embracing the unknown and the inevitable imperfection that sits in the space of not knowing as we learn and grow? And also, what might be the cost to us and those around us of being led by our fears?

I think that these questions highlight the role of leadership in navigating not just life but also the lenses through which we look at life and how we show up as people. And one of those lenses, of course, is The GC Index.

In GC Index terms I believe that leadership is a catalyst that really helps to bring the dynamic nature of The GC Index and its power to life. It is in that sense a factor that can really ignite the energies that are available within yourself and within your team. I would further argue that without leadership we, and the teams we work in, are limiting the scope of our potential.

Leadership has many definitions but central to many of these definitions is a focus of leadership being about people, winning the 'hearts and minds' of people in pursuit of a defined common purpose.

I see The GC Index proclivities as a band of energies and just like a musical band the different energies can both support or conflict with each other and, of course, obviously do! But it is in the exploration of the diversity of The GC Index energies with an open and curious mind that we can ignite its possibilities and create extraordinary cultures in which teams and individuals thrive.

I have been working in leadership development since 1994 as a facilitator and professional executive coach. I came to the conclusion quite recently that what I have done for most, if not all, of that time is help others to curate their conversations; conversations with themselves (their internal dialogue), conversations in the team and sometimes conversations within the larger organisation and system. The quality of the conversations that we have I believe has a significant impact of the possibilities that we can imagine in any situation. And leadership tends to be a lens that I use a lot when looking at situations and how people are interacting with the situation; the conversations that they are having. It is an occupational hazard in that sense! And this was the case with The GC Index. I am interested in the energies and how they manifest themselves of course, but also the context in which the energies are working, and the impact of leadership on the energies in that context.

I think it's helpful to think about leadership in a number of dimensions:

Self-leadership: how we lead ourselves in any situation and stay empowered psychologically. This implies a degree of self-awareness and self-management that is often associated with our emotional intelligence and how we maintain an empowered mindset through the ups and downs of leadership.

Team leadership: the impact of our leadership on the team; maybe the team we are leading or in a team that we a member of. Leadership in a high-performing team can come from any team member and not necessarily always from the nominal leader.

Organisational and systemic leadership: how we are leading within the context of the organisation or system in which our leadership is taking place and the impact that they have on our leadership.

If these different dimensions of leadership are relevant and pertinent to any given situation, then the skills that leaders have to work within these dimensions, alongside The GC Index, will be key factors in their impact and the outcomes they achieve.

Exploring this further, the inspiration for my beliefs about leadership came from a belief that at this time we also need to be reimagining leadership. The need for global change has never been more urgent whether you look at this from a political, organisational or social perspective; at the same time, we also need to hold what the great scientist Richard Feynman referred to as the 'satisfactory philosophy of not knowing'.

And yet, this notion of embracing doubt as he articulated it as something to be welcomed rather than feared, seems to pose a significant challenge to leadership. Perhaps this is because it is counter-intuitive to leaders who are part of a system that values certainty. Nevertheless, that is where we are; a place of not knowing. A place where we must reimagine our future and our response to the challenges that we face, rather than relying on the thinking and the ways of being that created the challenges in the first place.

Reimagining requires us to have conversations in which we can enter a space of not knowing in a creative and open way. One path that we might follow is to explore reimagination by looking at situations through what I call leadership lenses; this can help us to question and explore our perception of reality and find new possibilities.

So, what if we looked at situations using these five lenses?

- Consciousness
- Connection
- Curiosity
- Collaboration
- Compassion

What additional impact might we have from using these lenses in conjunction with The GC Index energies?

I believe leadership starts with leading ourselves. Our ability to lead other people is based ability to understand and lead ourselves first. Therefore, the quality of the conversation that we have with ourselves and with those around us is significant in terms of our leadership impact. That also means understanding how we can work with The GC Index as a leadership development tool, understanding the proclivities to positively impact on our conversations. So, let's look at the lenses in more detail.

Consciousness

Consciousness gives us the potential at least to access our skills. Consciousness creates awareness of what we are experiencing in the moment; it is being present and aware of how we are feeling, our focus. It creates an understanding of the questions that make up our internal dialogue and the choices we are making as a result; those that are empowering and those that are disempowering.

Knowing our GC Index profile helps us to become conscious of how we are processing what is happening and from that we might ask, what are the assumptions and beliefs that I am holding about this situation? How are other people with different GC Index profiles seeing the situation? How might their beliefs and assumptions be influenced by their profile?

In my band consciousness is critical. Being aware of what underpins creative differences and how we might approach them, as well as how we are individually behaving in the situation is important, as is the ability to give each other feedback.

Connection

Connection enables us to find a sense of meaning in our lives; where our values are aligned with the contribution and the service we are providing to society. Connecting with ourselves creates the possibility at least of connecting with others. In a band this may manifest itself in discussions about creative direction or why we are choosing to be in a band at this time. In my band we, and therefore the music, are inspired by issues of social and climate justice. It is a factor that connects us all.

So, the action to use music to highlight these issues was a connecting factor as much as the playing of the music itself, which of course we also love.

Connection is critical in The GC Index when we look at how the different proclivities are interdependent and support each other to achieve the goal. From a leadership perspective using the lens of what connects us can help us to really explore the diverse knowledge and perspective that each of the proclivities offers.

Curiosity

> *'Two roads diverged in a wood, and I –*
> *I took the one less travelled by,*
> *And that has made all the difference.'*
> Robert Frost, 'The Road Not Taken'

Curiosity is where we challenge what is, by asking, 'what if?' Curiosity is the catalyst for reimagining; the foundation of our innovation, creativity and our ability to manage differences. It is our motivation to take the road less travelled. Creating the 'updated story' will require a consciousness, that questions from a place of curiosity not judgement; one that can be present with uncertainty and tension while a solution is emerging; one that embraces and explores new options to find a just and equitable solution.

In our band curiosity informs our lyrics and the melody, but also the process of composing. The process often starts with a riff a musical version of the 'what if' question. The riff asks a creative question of the band members even while the future is just an empty space at this point. What can you add to this as the bass player, drummer, singer or guitarist?

An example of this was our guitarist in rehearsal saying, 'Let's just have some fun,' and we started a jam based on a few chords. It was mid-December and the riff led to the idea, what if we wrote a Christmas song based on the themes of sustainability and climate change. To cut a long story short, we had the basis of the song in 20 minutes. And the foundation of that was being able to hold the lens of curiosity to the suggestion and let this challenge our existing processes and ways of working. Curiosity helps our band of proclivities to get the best out of each other.

In GC Index terms curiosity supports connection and possibility. Genuinely being present to listen to the perspective of other energies is not always easy. It can challenge beliefs and assumptions and even highlight biases. But it is perhaps from the consciousness of this discomfort that we can find new solutions and routes. Open the possibility for ourselves of taking the road 'less travelled'.

Collaboration

Collaboration is where we co-create. When we collaborate effectively it produces innovative and beautiful options, that embrace cognitive diversity and bring different ideas and perspectives together to, as Matthew Syed has said, 'recombine ideas'.

Collaboration happens when we are present for each other in psychologically safe spaces, where we can ask and explore the question 'what's the conversation that needs to happen here?' When we explore this question with authenticity, curiosity, and most importantly without fear, we thrive and grow. For my band collaboration in safe spaces is critical part of the creative process and the release of energies. So being aware of and letting go of our natural energies can be important particularly if they are dominating the creative process.

For example, in a band the imagination and obsession of the Game Changer can be really powerful in the development of original ideas for new songs. And in the case of my own band, our songwriter is incredibly imaginative with his lyrics. The rest of the band supports this by feeding him lyrics, usually just one line will fire his imagination and start the process.

A collaborative mindset perhaps starts with curiosity and is an essential component of creating great music by using all the collective strengths brought by The GC Index proclivities. It is perhaps how we make our individual talents dance. This will, of course, mean that we have to manage conflict well, perhaps using our curiosity to let go of an assumption or even a belief about the best way forward; maybe managing the fear within ourselves of the uncertainty that this course might invoke. It will almost certainly involve compromise and a belief in the idea that we create, can create, something extraordinary by really leaning into the lens of collaboration.

Compassion

Compassion supports and enables and facilitates the other lenses. The Dalai Lama has said, 'Love and compassion are necessities, not luxuries. Without them humanity cannot survive.' Compassion enables us to find the resources within ourselves to collaborate with others to create together and to navigate through our own biases and the complexities of division and judgement. In a band context this is important.

Knowing each other from a GC Index perspective as well as just spending time with each other and getting to know the person that sits behind the musician is incredibly powerful. Compassion in that sense could be called the glue that helps to bind our energies and potential together.

When as a band we are preparing for gigs all the proclivities come to the fore. For some members of the band a gig is fun and while preparation in terms of rehearsal is critical, they love the fun of playing and so will take the pragmatic view of the Implementer. For others, the gig is a work of art so we can never do too much rehearsal in preparation. Shades of the Polisher perhaps! For others still the gig is also part of the ongoing development of the band's brand, a marketing channel to our help us create our audience.

The point is there are many different proclivities and energies at play in the different aspects of playing in a band and the understanding that comes from compassion is a lens that really helps us to navigate through this and, from our perspective at least, make great music.

The leadership lenses together with The GC Index proclivities can be a powerful cocktail of possibilities for bands and other teams. But how does that work in reality?

To start answering that question I want to talk about David Bowie. I have always been attracted to Bowie as a musician. There was something about his ability to lead musically and socially, standing up for his values, that has always stood out to me. I am instinctively drawn to curious people, people whose life appears to be founded on exploration and pushing at boundaries. And for me, Bowie was one of those people in life and even after his passing. I am still learning from Bowie.

The language and structure of The GC Index provides a framework to help me unpick this fascination and it's also a great insight into the way that Bowie led his life and created amazing musical bands.

So, how does David Bowie, one of the most influential musicians and cultural figures of the 20th and early 21st century, exemplify the roles identified in The GC Index? I believe that his impact can be seen through all The GC Index roles. These are my thoughts:

Game Changer

- Innovation and visionary ideas: Bowie was a quintessential Game Changer. Throughout his career, he consistently pushed the boundaries of music, fashion, and performance art. His ability to reinvent himself – whether as Ziggy Stardust, the Thin White Duke, or other personas – demonstrates a relentless drive for innovation. He often introduced groundbreaking concepts and challenged the status quo, making him a visionary in multiple artistic fields.
- Influence on culture: Bowie's work didn't just reflect the times; it often shaped them. Bowie's influence extended beyond music, impacting fashion, visual art, and even social norms. This transformative effect on culture aligns perfectly with the Game Changer role.

Strategist

- Long-term vision: while Bowie was primarily a Game Changer, he also displayed traits of a Strategist. He had a keen sense of where he wanted his career to go and how to navigate the music indus-try's changing landscape. His ability to foresee trends and adapt his style accordingly (e.g. shifting from glam rock to soul, electronic, and industrial sounds) suggests a strategic approach to maintaining relevance.

- Cohesive themes: albums often had overarching themes or concepts (e.g. *The Rise and Fall of Ziggy Stardust*, *Heroes*), showing his ability to structure his creative output within a larger framework, which is a key characteristic of a Strategist.

Polisher

- Attention to detail: Bowie was known for his meticulous attention to detail in both his music and visual presentations. Whether it was the sonic texture of an album or the intricate design of a stage costume, he demonstrated the traits of a Polisher – someone who refines and perfects work to a high standard.
- Craftsmanship: his collaboration with producers like Tony Visconti and Brian Eno highlighted his commitment to crafting a polished, high-quality product. Albums like *Low* and *Station to Station* are testaments to this dedication to excellence.

Play Maker

- Collaboration and teamwork: while Bowie often took centre stage, he was also a skilled collaborator, working with artists like Iggy Pop, Lou Reed, and Queen. As a Play Maker, he facilitated creative collaborations that brought out the best in those he worked with. His ability to bring together diverse talents and create something greater than the sum of its parts is a hallmark of the Play Maker role.
- Band leadership: even as a solo artist, Bowie led various bands and projects, coordinating the efforts of others to achieve his artistic vision. His leadership in these collaborations often ensured that everyone's contributions were harmonised into a cohesive whole. This extended beyond the musician's team. In a recent webinar I listened to someone, who worked with Bowie as part of the backstage crew, talk with equal fondness of connection to everyone in the team in terms of putting on the show, musicians and road crew alike. He intuitively understood the role that every member of the team needed to play in a show and was appreciative of all. From the experience of the person leading the podcast

who had worked with many musicians, Bowie's approach was not always replicated in other bands.

Implementer

- Executing ideas: while Bowie was more often the visionary, he also had the ability to bring ideas to life, a trait of the Implementer. His ability to take abstract concepts and turn them into finished albums, tours, and performances demonstrates an understanding of how to execute ideas effectively.
- Discipline and work ethic: Bowie's prolific output over his career, especially his ability to work across multiple mediums (music, film, fashion), shows the discipline and work ethic typical of an Implementer.

David Bowie's career can be viewed as a blend of GC Index roles, with a strong emphasis on the Game Changer due to his relentless innovation and impact on culture. However, his success also depended on strategic thinking, meticulous craftsmanship, collaborative skills, and the ability to execute his visionary ideas. Understanding Bowie through The GC Index framework highlights how his diverse strengths contributed to his legendary status as a musician and leader in the music industry and beyond.

For me, Bowie was also a great example of the how the leadership lenses I described earlier in this chapter can really catalyse The GC Index proclivities.

Bowie showed a level of consciousness about his role as a leader in the music industry as well as a musician. His focus was beyond himself extending to a consciousness about who he was as a person and also his opportunity to lead in the world of music and the arts. He also had a strong connection to his values and to the possibility to impact the system in terms of the leadership influence that he had in his position. He was incredibly **curious** and experimental, embracing the unknown, even finding a way in his last album, *Blackstar*, to explore his art right up to the end of his life (*Blackstar* was released two days before Bowie passed). His valuing of **collaboration** was, as we have seen, legendary and his **compassion** for others both within and beyond music was shown in his campaigning, as well as in other aspects of his life.

Two examples stand out for me

Bowie was very aware of the potential of his position to influence, and his values displayed that regularly. There are many examples of Bowie talking about his values and what was important to him on social media. Two examples stand out for me. The first was hearing him address young musicians encouraging them to get out there and play their own music, the music that's in their heart and not to be a copy of others. In the second example, I saw footage of Bowie taking an MTV presenter to task about the lack of black music and musicians on MTV: at the time the leading channel for music globally. This was Bowie literally calling out racism in his industry irrespective of the impact that this might have had on his own career, and at a time when many other white musicians were 'burying their head in the sand' about the situation. Both of these examples are, for me, acts of compassionate leadership aimed at changing the system and supporting his fellow musicians to connect the dots on what was possible for them.

The point for me here is that Bowie showed, in the way that he lived his life, how our self-leadership, how we appear in different situations, can really bring The GC Index energies to life for ourselves and for other people around us.

Looking at my own band, Rebel and the Banned, I want to highlight some key aspects of how we work together to create music and how we manage both our GCI profiles and leadership to get the best out of each other.

So, it may be helpful to start with the context and the profile of The GC Index band profile.

This is Rebel and the Band's aggregate GC Index profile (see Figure 1). As you can see, based on highest individual profile scores, there is a heavy leaning towards Game Changer and three of the five band members scored Game Changer as their highest proclivity (see Figure 2 for individual GC Index profiles). We can hypothesise that in a creative group we might expect to see a disproportionate amount of Game Changer energy.

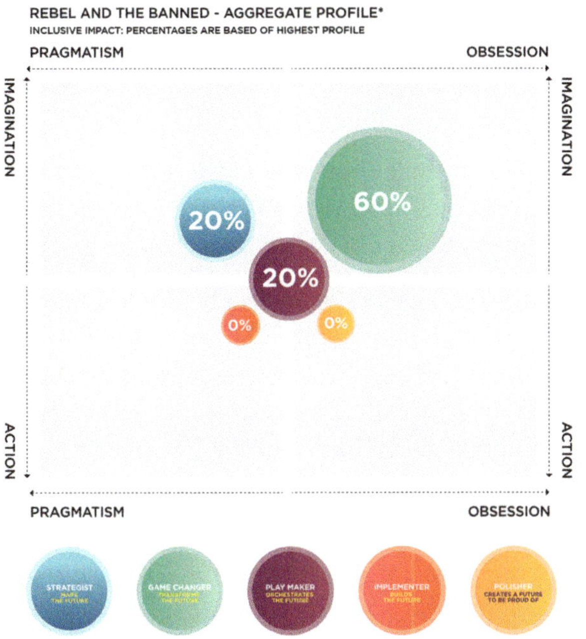

Figure 1: Rebel and the Band's aggregate GC Index profile

REBEL AND THE BANNED - INDIVIDUAL THE GC INDEX PROFILES

Figure 2: Individual band members' GC Index profiles

If we look at this aggregate picture of the band alone then the other energies seem unrepresented by comparison, in particular Implementer and Polisher.

However, if we look at the individual profiles, we can see something of a more balanced picture of the band with all the proclivities represented to a reasonable degree across the five-person group.

For example, what becomes more evident here is the energy for collective endeavour and collaboration as represented in the Play Maker scores. I would suggest that this Play Maker energy supports the Implementer energy by acting as a good counterbalance or moderation to the energy of the high Game Changer scores.

So, when we look at a 'potential impact' aggregate profile (see Figure 3) we can see again that the risk of dominance from the Game Changer energy is toned down considerably and the team looks more balanced. And this is certainly my lived experience as a member of the band.

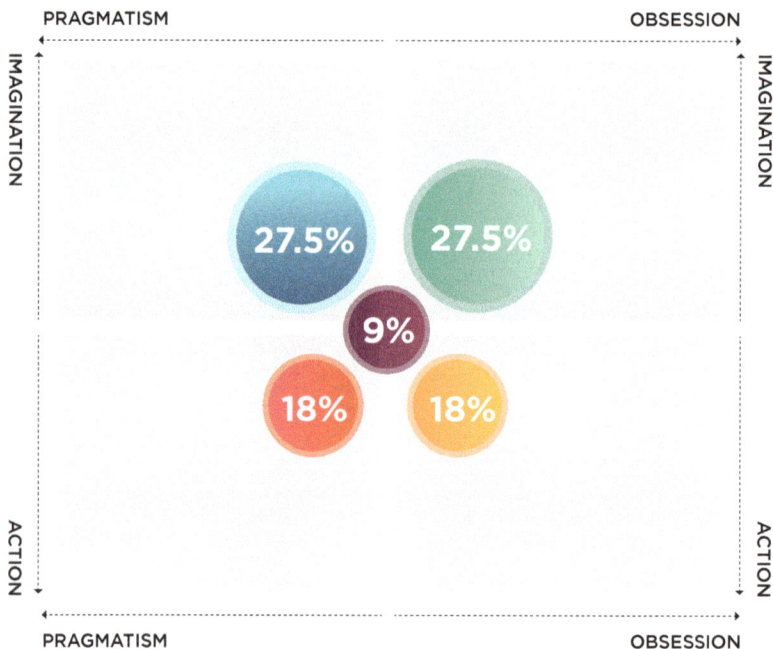

Figure 3: The band's 'potential impact' aggregate profile. (Potential impact profiles take account of all proclivities with a score of 6+.)

Of course, the reality is more complicated and nuanced than a picture of these profiles on their own can reveal. So, it's useful to look at how both the profiles and the leadership lenses also impact on the reality of our team working.

In terms of a shared purpose and vision, the band is quite purposeful about this aspect of ways of working. At the start of each year we spend time thinking about what we want to achieve in the year musically, but also check in with each other on why the band is important to us and what we have taken from the previous year both personally and collectively. It's also a time to celebrate what we have achieved in the previous 12 months.

So, a look backwards and a look forwards in terms of our intentions for the year ahead. The different energies in the band mean that the discussion can be very broad, the Game Changer energy in this situation can really play! But we can also come back to the pragmatism inherent in the Strategist and Implementer energy and agree on what we are actually going to do. Because we came together around a common purpose, using our art to highlight and raise awareness about key issues of social and climate justice, we also take time to review and reflect on how we have connected to that over the year in the music we have created, the gigs that we have played, and the collaborations that we have started with other like-minded groups.

The GC Index provides a way of highlighting our different working styles and strengths, and, combined with the leadership lenses helps us to anticipate and manage the way that we collaborate and manage conflict effectively. Being conscious of the fact that there are differences while also appreciating that these arise from our different strengths rather than personal disagreements helps us to resolve conflicts constructively.

I can't say we always get it right; we don't! Conflict when it happens can be challenging and not all the band members are comfortable in that situation. For example, the recording process in the band attracts different energies and, therefore, different creative tensions. The energy to produce a new track and to make it brilliant (Game Changer and Polisher) does, at times, butt up against the energy to create something that is good enough and get it on a streaming platform to build the band's brand (Implementer and Strategist). So, being conscious of that tension, being able to articulate it as well as leaning into the Play Maker energy, which looks for collaboration, is a key part of our creative process. Not to do so would lead to resentment and potentially under-performance in both the studio and on stage.

This is where strong interpersonal relationships and focusing on what connects us rather than what might divide us in that moment, helps. When we get it right it is also a moment where we all lean into our leadership in the sense of being curious about the divergence of ideas and compassionate for other band members' points of view; suspending judgement and believing that we are safe to have an open and frank discussion that will combine ideas, build trust and create great music.

The quality of our communication and conversation is really important. Great conversations facilitate great performance. Just as we need to stay in sync on stage, so we need to, as much as possible, stay in sync off stage. We talk and share a lot of ideas. And the Game Changer energy in the band means that there are a lot of ideas and sometimes those ideas can be fiercely defended! Great conversations happen when bands feel safe with each other; safe to say what is in their heart and their head. They literally create the space for the Play Maker energy to do its job of facilitating collaboration.

A successful rock band, like a team, is built on mutual trust and respect. Each member must trust that the others will perform their parts well and respect each other's contributions to the group's success. Trust is the rock on which most high-performing teams are built. And a rock band is no different.

Trust can be delicate. And, as band members, being aware of what contributes to and withdraws from each other's trust accounts is critical. For example, in my band, I have noticed that we collectively need to be conscious of the power and impact that a strong creative vision, inspired by Game Changer energy can have on the band. It is critical to ensure that it does not overpower by creating a supportive space in which everyone has a sense of ownership of what we are working on and feels empowered to make their individual creative musical contribution.

Our band, like any other team, is a collection of amazing people with many different talents and energies to offer. The trick is to create a culture which enables all of that diversity and the confidence to breath and grow while having great fun along the way. It's easy to just focus on what we do, creating music; and yet it is so much more satisfying to also connect on how we do it and why it's important to us. We can do that more effectively if we really understand the energies we have in the band and how we can use our leadership to really make those energies dance.

So, what might we take from this story?

The title of the chapter is 'Keeping the Band Together', and I suggested at the start that the band can be within ourselves, within a team or within a system. I believe what ultimately keeps any band together and enables them to thrive is their purpose and what's important to them: the culture they create in the band and how they work and interact with each other in pursuit of that purpose. And this is facilitated by creating the space to explore the diversity in a team using tools like The GC Index and the leadership lenses.

Perhaps, therefore, using the metaphor of music I can pose a final question for reflection. How is your band at the moment, and what kind of music are you creating?

Bibliography and References

Dalai Lama, *The Art of Happiness*, Hodder Paperbacks, 1999

Feynman, Richard P., 'The Value of Science', A public address given at the 1955 autumn meeting of the National Academy of Sciences

Frost, R., 'The Road Not Taken', *Atlantic Monthly*, August 1915

Harari, Yuval Noah, *21 Lessons for the 21st Century*, Vintage, 2019

Syed, M., *Rebel Ideas: The Power of Thinking Differently*, John Murray, 2019

Chapter 11

The Origin of Energy
in Work Teams

High-performing teams are those that recognise and cultivate individual and collective energy with a focus upon a shared ambition to thrive as a team, not just survive.

Ruth Baily

Introduction

Much has been written on the concept of 'high-performing teams', a plethora of systems, maps, processes and dysfunctions, on what it takes to navigate a route to 'high performance' and success.

All of the organisational development theory that I was taught and experienced throughout my career, centred around the principle that performance processes require individuals to align to an organisation's vision for growth, via a set of values, a vision, some strategic objectives and targets, all of which waterfall into a 'personal development plan'.

The high-performing teams' systems are, typically, built to serve this alignment. This performance dogma is so deeply entrenched, that, to challenge it, may generate a little discomfort but observing these traditional performance systems throughout my career and seeing them celebrated, yet falling short of personal growth, led me to explore another way.

My discoveries about personal growth have been strongly influenced by the science of emotion and the impact emotions have upon how we 'show up' and ultimately perform.

Along my own growth journey I have gained much insight and beliefs that now form my practice with teams, and it is this that has caused me to challenge traditional organisational performance theory, doctrine and systems.

In this chapter I offer, for your consideration, an alternative way of thinking, a proposition that builds upon existing views of the characteristics of high-performing teams but then aims to inspire a world where we can go further than performance, to a symbiotic and more sustainable growth path for individuals and teams.

In this proposition there is a balance to observe, where both the organisation and the individual grow and perhaps more importantly thrive. The vehicle for cultivating this mutuality is an understanding of the science of emotion and mood and how we use this understanding to inform the part we all play in teams that thrive.

Leadership impact in a nutshell

To explore this new paradigm, we first need a shared view of 'leadership impact' inside and outside organisations.

The diagrams below (Figures 1 and 2: Organisational impact in a nutshell) is typically how we all perceive the layers of impact within organisations. In this model, the perception is that individuals are 'housed' at the centre of the organisation, the team that they are placed in determines what they need to do to have impact and the 'team of teams' is where their team takes nuanced direction from, e.g. a sector team, a professional capability team, an executive director's team and so on; and all of these leadership layers are housed within the organisation's shell where the strategy, operating model, and value chain objectives influence all the layers within it.

Simultaneously, we may also visualise that this outer shell is how the organisation connects its value to the market and the customers it serves, and influences the wider ecosystem of stakeholders on the outside. This is the perception upon which our performance systems are built, however, I would argue this model does not reflect reality.

How we perceive Organisational impact

The reality of how our impact is experienced

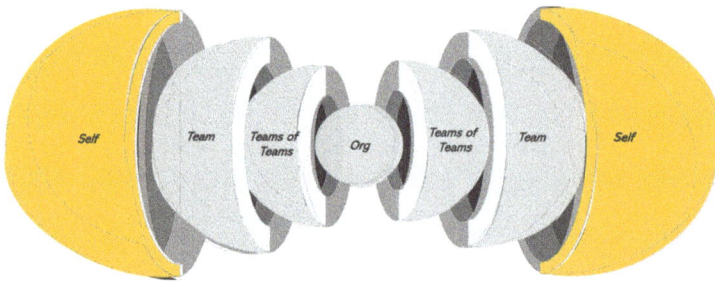

Figure 1 and 2: Organisational impact in a nutshell: perception and reality

The reality of how impact actually manifests itself is starkly different and reframing thinking in this area is one of the key shifts and points of our 'unlearning'.

In our alternative model, the 'self' layer is in fact the nutshell: the external world of customers' and markets' experience, the impact of an organisation – its people, their leadership, behaviours and so on – through the individuals that they come into contact with. The market exists in the 'white space' outside the nutshell and this rich ecosystem of clients, suppliers and so on are, in fact, all influenced by an organisation's people.

If you consider for a moment all the touch points your people have with the external landscape surrounding your organisation, it matters how that customer feels after an interaction with them; it matters what stories they tell, it matters how they 'show up' on good days and on the not so good, it matters how they manifest an organisation's culture and values, its operating model. All these interactions coalesce and directly influence how the organisation is itself experienced.

Your customers or clients and competitors, don't feel your organisation's operating model, organisation structure or strategic objectives and governance, they experience your individual people and who they are, how they are feeling today, influenced by mood, emotions, sleep, food, workload, etc., and if you've done a good job at inspiring your people with an emotional vision and purpose then they will carry this torch from the 'inside to the outside'.

Embracing a new way of thinking here and unlearning traditional doctrines can help individuals and teams wake up to why they need to consider specific practices to grow into their own leadership style: how visible they are, how self-aware they are, how they self-manage and the opportunities this brings. It helps them to take targeted action and consider their impact in a very focused way and this is an important key that opens a door to the success for leadership growth and for teams that thrive.

Leadership of ourselves

Imagine a future where organisations are designed intentionally for mutual growth, where business operating models offer not just the technical capabilities that deliver the commercial value chain but also the framework for leadership growth. By this I mean your individual growth that goes beyond your professional expertise and experience, your 'WHAT'.

In our vision your 'HOW' takes on equal importance of how you lead yourself and live and thrive in your role, and where you intentionally bring these two parts of you together you ignite a personal purpose: your 'WHY' becomes the place beyond how you perform, it is your place of impact, flourishing and thriving.

Leadership impact of Self

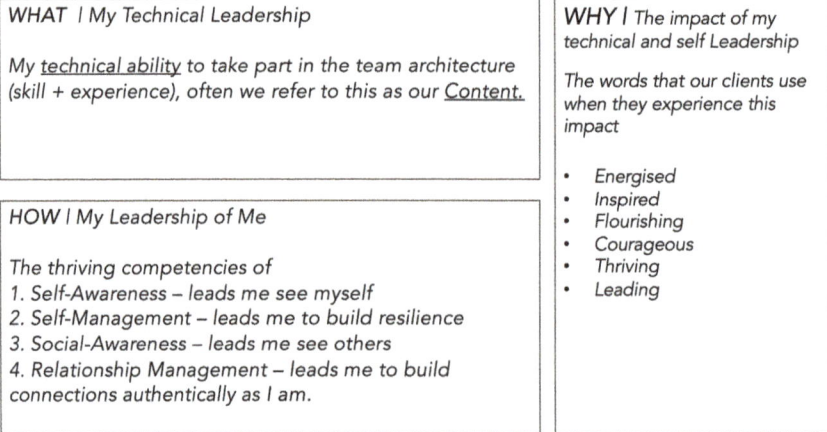

WHAT I *My Technical Leadership* *My <u>technical ability</u> to take part in the team architecture (skill + experience), often we refer to this as our <u>Content.</u>*	**WHY** I *The impact of my technical and self Leadership* *The words that our clients use when they experience this impact* • *Energised* • *Inspired* • *Flourishing* • *Courageous* • *Thriving* • *Leading*
HOW I *My Leadership of Me* *The thriving competencies of* *1. Self-Awareness – leads me see myself* *2. Self-Management – leads me to build resilience* *3. Social-Awareness – leads me see others* *4. Relationship Management – leads me to build connections authentically as I am.*	

Figure 3: Leadership impact of self

In Figure 3, Leadership impact of self, the WHAT we will all recognise: your CV filled with your technical/professional content and here many organisations can often help you deepen this expertise over time, with, for example, support through the stages of competency development in your field.

The HOW, is what we call 'Leadership of Self' and is possibly the least well-established development area. In this vision, each one of us takes ownership for our emotional well-being, for who we are and how we interact with others in the team.

What we find in our clients is when the WHAT and the HOW combine together, a powerful transition happens, that typically intangible thing called 'purpose' emerges from the inside. Our clients tell us is that what they experience is much more than performance: they speak about living inside a 'new version of themselves' that fuels action, 'doing'. This art of 'thriving' has in it a practice of growth, which helps us and those around us prosper, succeed and flourish.

thrive

/θrʌɪv/ verb

to grow, develop, succeed. it is to prosper; to flourish.
to be your best self.

Figure 4: Dictionary definition of thriving

So, this has become our vision at The Cause Effect, our vision is about getting to the art and heart of leadership. Inside our leadership and coaching programmes, we help client teams not just to be excellent at their WHAT – in general they really do know this – we support them to discover how to thrive in the process.

The key starting point is self-awareness, and we open this up to clients with introducing them to their impact today, where their individual energy lies and how unconsciously they direct it to their WHAT and the impact this has, and how others experience them.

We always begin this intervention with The GC Index. The GC Index is a powerful tool that safely opens the door to greater self-awareness and presents a very distinct moment of opportunity that is so much more than a diagnostic. The GC Index offers clients a mirror, that they can either choose to notice for a moment and then look away with some insight that, yes, that image feels like them or, they choose to look longer and deeper in the mirror to see much more of who they are. Those who do, experience an important 'tipping point' towards the landscape of thriving, and the insights on how to get to there. This tipping point is a vital step-on from self-awareness, it's what we call self-management. Figure 5, below, points to how The GC Index can be used in the context of self-management.

Self Management looks like :

"With this insight into my proclivities, rather than "I am a Gamechanger Playmaker", consider much more consciously how to adapt. "How can I focus on leading myself to make best use of my energy, for myself and for others today / or in this next meeting"..

"My natural tendency will be to apply my game changing energy, I will do this when I am on autopilot, busy, stressed, low mood, hungry etc. because visionary and novel ideas and bringing others together keeps me energised" – This may be my preference, but what alternative strategies may this next meeting need?, which other proclivities mat I need to dial-up"

"I am watching how my directional push for purpose impacts my team positively and negatively and questioning am I keeping myself out of delivery because it is tedious and I'd rather be distracted by playmaking, bringing people together and helping others"

Flow / order of Proclivities / energy

"My game changing and playmaker focus may bring others together around ideas which helps our collective focus, but my individual work suffers when I give all of my focus elsewhere, away from my own list of delivery. This impacts me and anyone waiting for me to achieve a task, and when I do prioritise this over my preferences, I, infact experience a high, maybe even higher degree of energy".

* Gamechanger
* Playmaker
* Strategist
* Polisher
* Implementer

Figure 5: The GC Index in the context of self-management

So, in our partnership with The GC Index, we work to help clients lead and perform beyond their technical abilities; being excellent at leading in their particular professional area is one thing, be it project manager, chief executive, teacher, systems engineer, PA, whatever their content area, but to thrive is to couple that with HOW they do their job. Ultimately this is about being a great leader of yourself, all of which helps individuals perform higher and find (noticeably) more meaning and fun as they go! Wrap all this into a verb and we call this **thriving.**

To thrive – the action of growing vigorously and flourishing in teams

When teams are at their best, when their impact is felt, when the individuals inside are integrating, in flow, when they are consistent, confident in landing their promises, handling the bumps in the road as growth; these teams are thriving. Most importantly, though, as they prosper, their impact is felt well beyond their invisible architecture and into the ecosystem of their intended purpose. So, in our vision for the future of teams we want all of this. To get to these conditions, we need to first describe the state of the individuals within them.

Inside these thriving teams there are individuals that have cultivated:

Self-awareness

- They learn about their strengths and where their energy lies.
- They discover what's in their 'blind spot'.
- They understand the patterns of how and why they get triggered and their subconscious behaviours that emerge when they are on 'autopilot'.
- These patterns that were once invisible to them on 'autopilot', begin to come into view.

This self-awareness is powerful and can generate a lot of reflection, but back to the action and verb of thriving, here is the key: self-awareness is not enough. To be self-aware and stuck doing the same thing is even worse than being on 'autopilot'. The individuals in thriving teams make a conscious choice to **take action** to do something different and effect better outcomes for themselves, their teams and their organisations.

When they do this they are taking a conscious step in making a change, adapting their practice. In early years education you will hear this referred to as 'self-regulation' and in adults as 'self-management', but essentially it's the same thing. People who practise self-management make friends with the proclivities they may have once avoided, they actively 'unlearn' their subconscious behaviours and move to more intentional ones and, in so doing, are quite literally changing the shape of their brain.

Whilst it may be tough at the start, with practice, it gets easier, calmer, and even inspiring! These individuals take ownership of the controls to navigate a new path, creating a vision and a map of where to go next, what we call individual purpose.

Conscious or not, this active piloting of themselves knits a contentment with who they are: the high and lows and vulnerabilities and the courage to be all of this. It turns out that to have purpose is not to search outside ourselves for the right vocation, job, partner or geography that we perceive will make us happy or bring meaning. What we see in our clients is that the flourishing of purpose comes from uncovering all of who we are, where our energy lies, how our pattern of learned personality drives us, the stumbles, the 'rabbit warrens' as well as the performance and the success.

Now bring into that vision a team, with multiple pilots who also take ownership of their controls in the cockpit. These people also have lower self-orientation, by this we mean, they are leading themselves well, they are aware of who they are and how they show up and they know how to manage their mood and emotions, because they go beyond self-awareness and practise self-management.

The inspiration they find within themselves, helps them to see others with greater empathy, most likely because they see that their own perfection is a fallacy thus relaxing their autopilot image of others. They are more open and have built the courage to be curious about one another's experience bringing diversity of thought into view.

As they learn more about each other, they look out for one another; this team begins to bind together, and in this team of pilots, the individual purpose strengthens the collective organisational purpose into a strong fabric for this team. Intimacy grows, team members find out more about each other and they choose to spend time together; it is noticeable that they 'have each other's backs', there is safety, stability and resilience to withstand any weather, good and bad. They don't press on head down, doing what they always do, and trudge through that bad weather, they stand firm scanning the horizon for what's coming next and when the 'storm has passed' they regroup, listen to each other, learn, creating momentum to go again.

This team knows its success can only be collective; it has credibility because, collectively, it has all interdependent skills to get the job done. It is reliable, because in pulling together the team can do what they say they will. All of these things (low self-orientation, credibility, reliability, intimacy) cultivate trust and that feeling that you belong, are safe and can really be your whole self (WHAT and WHO) whether you are at work or home.

So, in summary, the granular individual insights of those who lead themselves well and their commitment to self-manage generates a powerful energy and when connected to others in a team the collective generates a collective thriving, creating much greater impact for both themselves, the team and the organisation.

Two big ideas to help teams thrive

Developing a 'Leadership of Self' practice that ignites the energy in teams comes from having a self-management practice, and here we describe how to inspire energy for a new way of development.

How amazing would it be to ditch the work mask, to let go of the never achievable work-life balancing act in service of just living better? Two big ideas follow that we work on with our clients, leadership teams and leaders, people and families. We combine these practices to help us individually have more impact, own our individual energy, connect to others, build greater well-being and be at our best in life and with others in teams. Remember this is not performance, this is thriving.

Idea 1 – grow all of the domains of emotional intelligence

So, our vision for individuals and organisations focuses upon the development of all stages (domains) of emotional intelligence. We see this an essential step when cultivating good leadership of ourselves for thriving in teams.

There are countless examples of organisations that have lost sight of the impact their people can have, unaware of the impact in the nutshell, and this has had a significant impact and big consequences for their brand.

There are also those organisations that recognise that who and how their people are matters. I would go so far as to say, how their people **are**, is their brand. The energy that the teams in these organisations generate delivers outcomes that are so powerful, it's no surprise that they have a healthy workplace culture and often the bottom line follows. The obvious examples would be Google and its Search Inside Yourself programme, Johnson & Johnson and their Energy for Performance Programme, focusing on self-regulation. Microsoft now offer emotional intelligence training to build more empathy into their diverse workplace. Patagonia have led from the inside with the core values of authenticity and integrity, and woven it into the fabric of their culture, individuals live the shared values as they are encouraged to bring their whole selves to work and to engage in open and honest communication in teams.

The four emotional intelligence competencies designed through extensive research by Daniel Goleman and Richard Boyatzis in 1998 are described by the diagram in Figure 6. As we detailed at the start, in teams that thrive the following four distinct leadership competencies are actively lived. (See footnote[30])

Figure 6: Competencies for thriving

While emotional intelligence (EI) development is not completely new, in most organisations, leadership development often only focuses on the two 'social' domains to the right of this picture, **social-awareness** and **relationship-management** developing growth in empathy, influencing skills, good team coaching, how to handle conflict, how to bring teams together successfully and so on.

---

[30] Key Step Media. 'The Emotional and Social Intelligence Leadership Competency Model is a unique framework developed by Daniel Goleman and Richard Boyatzis, identifying the 12 specific, evidence-based competencies that are the building blocks of emotional and social intelligence in leadership. Leadership is not defined by formal roles within organizations, because we all have the capacity to lead at any level in our personal or professional lives. Hence this model has deep and wide application.'

What these programmes often miss is that when the domains of **self-awareness** and **self-management** are not considered then we fail to understand, unlock and leverage the individual self: the beliefs, values, emotional back catalogue that is completely unique to each of us and directly impacts our mood, decisions, behaviours and all the interactions we have with others in every moment of every day, work and home. So, organisations can invest all they like in social-awareness and relationship management, but it will not have a sustainable impact, without development first on self-awareness and self-management. Bringing the four domains to life is detailed below in Figure 7.

COMPETENCY	LOOKS LIKE ...
SELF-AWARENESS	I understand my mood, emotions, proclivities, I understand what triggers me and rather than act on it or knowingly bury it, or remain in a state where unknowingly these things lurk in my blind spot. I use my mood, my energy, my proclivities as data, as a guide. The GC Index is a window into this competency, what energises me and what do I have low energy for or perhaps actively avoid.
SELF-MANAGEMENT	Equipped with data from profiles and coaching that helps me to see my story, my proclivities and emotional triggers, I record and notice when and how this emerges in me and in what circumstances. Akin to building a muscle or an inner observer, I build expertise and courage to not just find it interesting, but to take action and decide what I want to do with it, here we notice inspiration, the container for the energy, actions and leadership we want to be famous for.
SOCIAL-AWARENESS	Armed with awareness that helps me see more of myself, I begin to see others differently, I am curious to what their proclivities might be and what they do with this knowledge, this is at the heart of empathy. It comes from having done the work on ourselves and helps us to understand and weave connection with others.
RELATIONSHIP MANAGEMENT	I have a gravitas emerging that develops from being open and authentic, developing from my self-management work not for the sake of it but because I can share more of what makes me tick. I develop relationships more easily and they go beyond the technical content. My coaching and mentoring skills are being honed through my curiosity, and from the self-management skills that help people see more of me whilst not focussing on myself. I am not resistant to handle difficult moods and emotions as sometimes I see that they need to surface and that there is a better place beyond them.

Figure 7: Full descriptions of the four EI domains that help teams thrive[31]

At The Cause Effect, our 'Leadership of Self' methodology uses these competencies as the spine that runs throughout our programmes and we support clients to build a practice across all the EI domains. Whether their focus is at the individual, team or organisational layer, this work supports

---

[31] Four competencies of Emotional Intelligence, Ruth Baily, The Cause Effect, 2023.

them to move simultaneously across the layers of the 'nutshell' with agility and confidence. The reality is to have our best impact, we must work and thrive across multiple layers not just one, and this is the art of it all.

Idea 2 – cultivate a deep curiosity of your mood

When individuals take the opportunity and have the courage to become more self-aware, they find their own threads of purpose and, here's the magic of it, when they take this and turn it into the tools of self-management (the second EI domain), we see a tangible change to their leadership. Those who commit to this active work begin to experience themselves differently. It does take time and focus, like learning to play an instrument, a language, or learning to drive but thanks to neuroplasticity: (the brain's ability to change and adapt, reorganise, or grow new neural networks) anyone can absolutely alter their experience.

Until recently, the adult brain was widely accepted to no longer change once fully developed, however, every single person is unique, and their brains are no exception. Modern neuroscience offers an inspiring perspective that our brains are much more dynamic, all types of brains, neurodivergent or neurotypical, change in every moment by both internal and external factors in us all. These processes are referred to as neuroplasticity, which is crucial for understanding our health, recovery and resilience.

So contrary to popular belief, our brains do not stop growing after childhood, or adolescence, but are shaped every single day by our own unique individual experience and learning from others' experiences. You may be surprised to learn that your emotions don't happen to you based on external triggers, but they are instead actually made by you, based on your previous experiences, your 'back catalogue' if you like. And all these emotions and experiences blend into what scientists called 'affect' or more simply put, your day to day, meeting to meeting, minute by minute, 'mood'.

So, the 'magic bullet' to self-management is literally understanding your own mood. This often gets referred to as 'mindset', but actually this is a full body experience, but either way it is a fundamental leadership skill. Your affect and, therefore, what you have energy for and why, matters to your well-being, your relationships, your team and family and your performance. No one else is responsible for it, just you. When people are not awake to this, they will often allow their 'affect' to run the show on complete 'autopilot'.

Our brains most important job is to keep us alive and healthy, essentially our own 'motherboard' for energy efficiency. To achieve this our brains constantly make guesses about what is best for our bodies. Might we need a meal? Water? Sleep? Dr Lisa Feldman Barrett Ph.D[32], a psychologist and neuroscientist whose life's work demonstrates that there are not emotion circuits buried in the brain that have been handed down to us, that all map on to each other's emotions. Instead Feldman Barrett demonstrates that 'emotions that seem to happen to you are actually made by you' and learning to manage your mood (affect) is the best way to lead yourself.

Self-management is the skill we all need to power up ourselves to perform well. The GC Index tool offers us a wonderful perspective here on the impact we have on our world, work and home. The map of proclivities shines a torch on where we unconsciously put that energy, and its data is a massive clue to how we are experienced by others in our lives.

But we need to be careful to not wear this as our badge. It offers us hard data for our self-management practice: it is what we do to observe it and how it drives us that will give us and our team members, the biggest rewards. After a day or two of understanding our GC Index profile of proclivities it's down to us individually to own and act on it.

'We do not see things as they are, we see things as we are.'

These are the words of author, poet and essayist Anais Nin and describe the science of 'affect' beautifully. Affect or mood-coloured glasses is the way we see the world, even if we try to tuck our emotions and mood away, it reveals itself again and again; the chapters of our story leak out in

---

[32] Lisa Feldman Barrett, *How Emotions are Made: The Secret Life of the Brain*, Houghton Mifflin Harcourt, New York, 2017.

the rise and fall of our emotions, politics, behaviours, parenting, attractions and the biases, things or people we may choose to avoid.

So as you begin to observe your mood as a barometer, get really inquisitive about where your energy is today, what it is made from and why it might be that way. Use this as a key to self-management and looking at your GC Index profile will highlight how you naturally show up; pause long enough throughout the day and interrogate your mood, allowing you to adapt how that can be used to your best advantage. Owning your mood and energy and how to deploy it is the single most important job of leadership.

Dr Dan Siegal, clinical professor of psychiatry at the UCLA School of Medicine and executive director of the Mindsight Institute shares:

'Where (our) attention goes, neural firing flows and neural connection grows. This not only helps us understand how psychotherapy practice works and how parenting works, but also how our societies shape our minds as well ...'

and that goes for work cultures, teams and projects too.

Summary: interdependence builds the jigsaw of thriving

We have learned that interrogating our mood to regulate ourselves is vital because our mood and, therefore, the energy we have in one moment to the next regulates others, we literally connect together, this is the work of the third EI domain – social-awareness.

We each have mirror neurons in our brain that are a fundamental mechanism for empathy and social understanding. When we observe someone else's actions or emotions, our mirror neurons fire, enabling us to 'mirror' or resonate with their experiences. This process helps us understand and empathise, essentially, we internally simulate the other people's experiences as if they were our own. Mirror neurons play a crucial role in social cognition, allowing us to recognise the emotions and intentions of others, bringing forth social connection and communication, compassion and empathy and it is this integration that drives our collective energy. This is why you can impact the energy in a team that you walk into, you don't even need to say anything, your brains and theirs work fast to assess and predict the affect in the rest of the group. This processing can help us connect easily and also to judge easily, and so being conscious and managing low and high mood will both impact and affect those around you.

So, this is how self-awareness and self-management unlock energy, because even if there are others who are wildly different to us in our team, by looking at our own mood and where it comes from, we develop a competency of being attuned to social cues, such as body language, verbal cues, and being able to interpret them and respond appropriately.

Socially aware individuals are skilled at navigating social situations, building and maintaining relationships, and demonstrating empathy and compassion towards others.

In GC Index terms, these are our natural Play Makers but this can also be cultivated too, and teams that have these individuals in them don't judge the differences in, for example, age, gender, race, neurodiversity and education, what they experience is their team members' affect or mood. They appreciate their stories, and styles and notice them in perhaps ways they didn't before. They don't respond to a behaviour in the same way as they did when they were on 'autopilot' because they have a genuine curiosity for what lies behind the behavioural pattern of the person they are with.

The empathy we build for ourselves in self-leadership helps build **social-awareness**, appreciating the others in our team, by using The GC Index to understand their energy profile, and also being curious about their mood (or affect), having empathy for how they act and lead and behave.

This social-awareness brings us closer and builds momentum and lasting relationships, and here is the fourth domain: relationship management an emergence of lasting and inspirational relationships, getting the best from each other in the team, a sense of how to influence people and projects for the best outcomes.

So hopefully as we close this chapter, we leave you with a dose of inspiration:

- That by learning from the past we can choose a different way, there is a meaningful alternative. While we may only be in the foothills of artificial intelligence it is already in the landscape of our lives, so for this reason understanding our own emotional architecture is of paramount importance. To navigate our emotions and mood, to remain adaptable and agile are just a few examples of the emotionally intelligent competencies that AI cannot effectively replicate.
- The combination of EI competencies and The GC Index self-awareness form the foundations for us to manage and apply our energies, in ways that help us to thrive as individuals and in teams and organisations.

The good news is we are all more than capable of developing these skills: 'We do not see things as they are, we see things as we are.'

So, if we want to thrive in our careers, teams and lives to be our very best selves, we will, indeed, all need to take the lead.

Section 4:

How Impactful Leaders Channel Energy into Organisational Performance

Chapter 12

Leadership and the Expression of Energy

The link between leadership and energy and why energy matters. Key insights from research and practice with practical pathways to translate insight into individual and organisational impact.

Andrew Dyckhoff

Why energy matters

We live in turbulent times. Just as organisations emerged from the impact of Covid-19 they entered a new period of uncertainty driven by world events and the consequent inflationary pressures. After two years of lockdown, organisation energy levels were already depleted. The need to digitize, create new ways of working and manage disrupted supply chains to survive has resulted in huge project workloads on top of business-as-usual responsibilities.

This combination of uncertainty and long working hours has led to initiative fatigue and going forward we will have to 'do more with even less'. Organisations are grappling with new ways of (hybrid) working. All this adds up to a 'perfect storm'.

Business impact of organisational energy

Dame Carol Black, distinguished clinician and author of *Working for a Healthier Tomorrow*, once said to me 'You do realise that as a CEO you can do more for the health and well-being of people than I can as a clinician!'

Organisations with high levels of positive energy are resilient and consistently deliver great results. Highly energised employees are happier and more fulfilled.[33] There is a clear win/win for business and society if we can create business environments that foster energy.

Organisation energy drives performance

Intuitively we know that energy matters. The evidence supports this intuition. Leadership energy levels correlate with financial performance.[34] Energy fuels organisations' success. Data from a global survey of 250+ companies showed that high-energy leaders were approximately four times more profitable than low energy leaders.[35]

Thus, the well-known formula Strategy + Execution = Results might better be cast as:

$$(\text{Strategy} + \text{Execution}) \times \textbf{Energy} = \text{Results}$$

The difference energy makes

Levels of energy correlate with performance levels and systems consistently display symptoms associated with differing levels of energy. Low/negative energy environments typically manifest a strongly hierarchical approach to leadership in which the leaders seek to control people and outcomes. High/positive energy environments manifest an approach based on trusting people to perform in a collaborative environment. This is illustrated below:

---

[33] Michael Cole, Heike Bruch and Bernd Vogel, 'Energy at work: A measurement validation and linkage to unit effectiveness', *Journal of Organizational Behavior* 33, 2012, The energy of individuals can manifest as a higher-level, collective construct positively associated with three collective attitudes – units' commitment to goals, the organization, and overall satisfaction, pp. 445–467.

[34] Heike Bruch and Bernd Vogel, *Fully Charged*, Harvard Business Review Press, 2011, How an organization's energy affects its performance, pp. 11–13.

[35] https://www.kennedyfitch.com/KFwebsite-new/wp-content/uploads/Employee-Experience-How-to-Build-an-EX-Centric-Organization.pdf accessed 08.04.2024

High

High energy
High performance

- Innovative
- Teamwork
- Trust
- Engagement
- Candour
- Respect
- Customer focus
- Competitive
- Profitable

Low energy
Low performance

- Hierarchy
- Bureaucracy
- Politics
- Fear
- Low trust
- Compliance
- Command and control
- Don't change meta-rule

Performance

Low

Low   System Energy   High

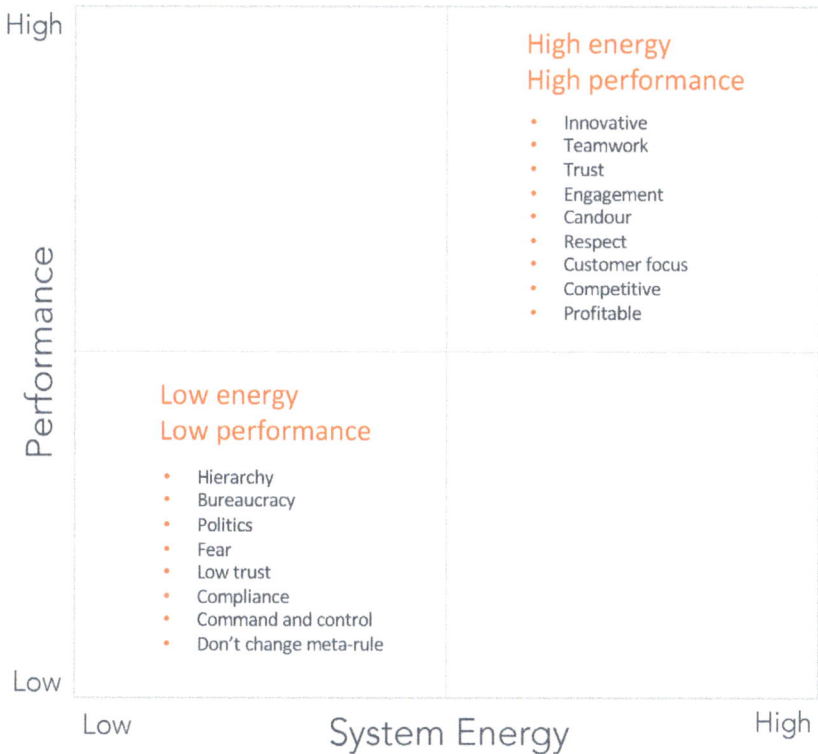

We want our leaders to energise us

Zenger Folkman has researched[36] the key attributes of leaders that deliver exceptional business results. As part of their research, they sought to understand which leadership traits are most valued by employees. In two hundred and fifty thousand 360-degree surveys Zenger Folkman asked 1.6 million raters to state which of 19 competencies that drive business performance is most important for their manager to have, to be successful in their role.

The standout number 1 ranked competency was 'Inspires and motivates to high levels of effort and performance'. The link with energy is because two of the three items used to measure this relate to the leader's capacity to energise others.

[36] John Zenger and Joseph Folkman, The New Extraordinary Leader, McGraw-Hill Education LLC, 2020.

Leader's capacity to energise

When we look at the results in the global database of 130,000 leaders, it would be reasonable to anticipate that scores for 'Inspires and motivates' should benchmark somewhere in the middle of the 19, on the basis that some leaders will score highly and some not. The sad reality is that it comes out at the bottom of the rankings. Leaders are generally least capable in inspiring, motivating and so energising their people.

This speaks to an energy gap across our organisations.

Organisation as a 'vehicle'

Using the metaphor of organisations as a vehicle, the results from the Zenger Folkman research show that we are great at building the vehicle and demonstrate the associated leadership traits.

Vehicle building activities include setting the strategy, building the product, hiring people, setting and driving KPIs. This capacity is reflected in high scores across the global database for technical and professional expertise, effort and driving for results. Where we fall short is in creating the fuel that drives the vehicle: organisation energy.

Bridging the energy gap

Leaders are the catalysts of action. As a mentor once taught me, as the leader it is 'always all my fault'. This reflects the power that we have as leaders to influence the environments we create for our people. The starting point is to recognise that leadership is about our followers and that we need to create the conditions in which they will do great work. Recognition leads us to focus on how we create roles and delegate tasks in such a way that our people are energised.

Rather like a hot-air balloon, organisations need to be constantly re-energised to maintain their altitude and if they are to go higher the energy levels must be substantially increased. To increase results, you need to increase the level of leadership energy, which in turn shifts the organisation energy leading to higher levels of customer service and profitability. See diagram below:

Leadership 'levers' for success

The Zenger Folkman research has identified the two most powerful leadership competencies (levers) as 'Drives for results' and 'Inspires and motivates others to high levels of effort and performance'. These are displayed by exceptional leaders, defined as those who deliver results in the top 10% of results in their industry. To understand what this means in practice it is helpful to look at the measures for each of the levers:

The measures for 'Drives for results' are:

- Does everything possible to achieve goals
- Achieves the agreed goals within the time allotted
- Follows through on objectives to ensure successful completion

The measures for 'Inspires and motivates' are:

- Energises people to achieve exceptional results
- Inspires others to high levels of effort and performance
- Brings to the group a high level of energy and enthusiasm

Leaders and energy – the power of 'and'

Organisations value leaders by the results they deliver. We promote leaders who give their all and follow through on the 'vehicle building' traits, but we rarely ask ourselves what the leader's impact on energy levels might be.

When we look at the data the strongest results are created when both 'Drives for results' and 'Inspires and motivates' are deployed. Statistically, if a leader has only one part and not the other at a top quartile level, the chances of delivering top decile results are approximately 12%. However, when the two are combined the chance is not 24%, but 74%!

Given the tendency for most organisations to focus on the vehicle building levers such as driving for results, it is likely that our organisation's results, however good, are suboptimal. Focusing on creating more energy to fuel the vehicle we can create a positive shift not only in the results of the business but the employee experience at work, which in turn positively impacts the health and well-being of our people.

Energy is the SPICE of life

It is important to recognise that energy means both the capability to do work and use power actively. Without doing (enactment) energy is latent potential. The feeling and experience of being energised applies in both cases but results only come from action.

We recognise that energy comes in different forms and that there are different drivers of energy for people and organisations, which lead us to commit energy, spiritual, physical, intuition, cognitive and emotional.[37]

---

[37] Nita Cherry, *Energising Leadership*, Oxford University Press, 2015, pp. 26–27.

S: spiritual energy is the power of connection with deeper values and sense of the purpose of human life.

P: physical energy is the fitness of our bodies, not just of muscles and limbs but thinking, feeling and spiritual connection.

I: intuition energy is the power of coming to know without conscious effort, of imagination and spontaneous creativity.

C: cognitive energy is the power associated with thinking. Through making intellectual sense of things, recognising and realising things, analysing and critiquing things, seeing patterns and finding the way through.

E: emotional energy is the force of positive feelings such as happiness, confidence, optimism and eagerness. It can also derive from negative feelings such as anxiety, fear and sadness.

These different types of energy are reflected in the drivers of energy for people and organisations. We commit energy based on elements such as our:

- beliefs and sense of purpose
- emotions (hopes and fears)
- care for people and things
- imagination, interests and preferences
- reserves of physical energy.

In addition, other elements such as the organisation culture, values alignment, the levels of trust or ethical behaviour influence our willingness to give our energy to the endeavour.

> *'Leadership exists to create an environment where success is inevitable.*
> *The core purpose of energising leadership is to mobilise enough collective human energy, for long enough, to achieve what we aspire to do or put right.'*

The work and practice of energising leadership is to use our own energies, individually and collectively, to intentionally influence the energies others are prepared to commit to organised effort. This involves mobilising, focusing, refreshing and refocusing energy.[38] Energising leaders:

- mobilise energy by creating awareness in others that things are worth doing and building confidence that they can be done.
- focus energy to ensure energies are aligned with desired outcomes and avoid waste.
- pay attention to energy levels and refresh and regroup rather than pressing on regardless (with the associated costs in terms of well-being and effectiveness).
- as priorities change, they detach and refocus energy.

Leaders and energy in practice

There are three areas to look at when thinking about energy and leadership. To be effective in maintaining and increasing the organisation energy, leaders need first to pay attention to their own energy levels, 'personal energy'. This creates the capacity to energise others, particularly the teams they lead, 'interpersonal energy'. Leaders at every level have the power and resources to influence the energy across the whole organisation, 'systemic energy'. The three areas are represented below:

ENERGISE SELF   ENERGISE OTHERS   ENERGISE THE ORGANISATION

Personal:
- Own Energy – Mental, Physical, Spiritual, Emotional
- Capability and Suitability

Interpersonal:
- Energise others (authentic leadership)
- Build Capability – Individual, Team, Organisation

Systemic:
- Engage at a system level
- Develop organisational habits with multi-order impact

---

[38] Nita Cherry, *Energising Leadership*, Oxford University Press, 2015, The energy cycle, pp. 85–109.

1. Personal – energise self

Leaders need to take care of their own energy: mental, physical, spiritual and emotional. In turbulent times this can be difficult to do. The pressures of work and demands of home life often mean that personal care suffers. Whilst it is possible to survive in the short and medium term, extended periods of stress lead to a long-term decline in performance.

Post-Covid, organisations have become much better at paying attention to the well-being of their people. There is a wide range of help available … the secret is to take action to avail yourself of the help.

Energy is also about capacity and capability. Focusing on playing to strengths and continuing to invest in learning to develop new skills, disciplines and habits creates new energy to input into the system.

Creating clear and compelling personal goals and ensuring these are aligned with their role in the organisation underpins the capacity to energise the organisation.

2. Interpersonal – energise others

Since leaders are the primary catalysts in determining the level of organisation energy, they need to be able to inspire and motivate and energise the people they lead in an authentic way. This means the leader needs to invest in understanding and being able to articulate what makes them special, their 'superpowers'. Psychometric instruments are helpful in both revealing what these are and giving a language for expressing them in words that are both accurate and accessible to others.

When deployed across a team, it is possible to create a shared language that supports effective collaboration. In our experience it is rare that leaders and teams take the time to deeply understand each other's motivations and sources of energy. If we imagine members of a team as 'cogs' that mesh with one another, a lack of understanding means the cogs rattle against each other, losing energy in the process. By investing in creating genuine understanding and mutual appreciation, team interactions become more efficient and effective, leading to better decisions made more quickly.

To achieve this desired outcome it is possible to use data to pinpoint the strengths of a leader and the members of their team. The Strengths Unleashed Triangulation approach uses three different lenses to bring the individual into clear focus (see diagram below):

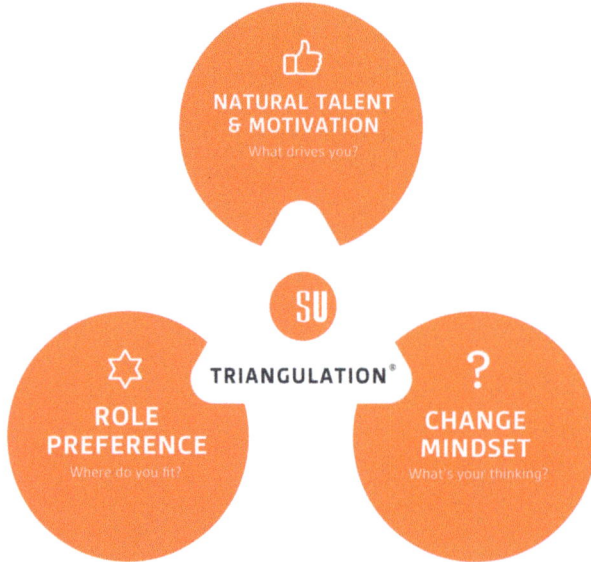

We calibrate:

- what drives them
- what they are thinking
- where they fit.

What drives you?

Energy and drive come from the use of our natural talents in pursuit of our goals. Leaders who know what drives them remain energised no matter what the challenge.

Mapping the leader's natural talent set and finding out what motivates them to come to work helps them identify the top 10 strengths they should play to and pinpoint the source of their energy and drive.

What are you thinking?

The leader's mindset is mission critical. Everyone has embedded, unconscious patterns of thinking that show up in their behaviours. When seeking to make things happen, these patterns are at play. If aligned with the leader's energetic strengths – and with the needs of the business – great things happen. Misalignment frequently leads to underperformance and a failure to create the desired impact.

The Zenger Folkman research identified the importance of inspiring leadership in energising people to high levels of effort and performance. The GC Index is a uniquely powerful organimetric instrument, which surfaces the leader's unconscious thinking to reveal their proclivities for energising the organisation. There are many ways this can happen. The different ways in which leaders engage for impact have been mapped in The GC Index Multidimensional Leadership matrix shown below. Leadership is, in GC Index terms, shaped, primarily by an individual's strongest proclivities. Moreover, most exhibit two of the five proclivities as their strongest, giving rise to the leadership combinations presented here:

MULTI-DIMENSIONAL IMPACT

STRATEGIST / PLAY MAKER
Aligns teams to common goals
They are at their best when they articulate a compelling picture of the future and align others to common goals that can achieve that future.

STRATEGIST / GAME CHANGER
Evaluate creative ideas through a strategic lens
They are at their best when assessing creative possibilities that can shape and support the achievement of their strategic vision. They will evaluate new ideas through a strategic lens.

STRATEGIST / IMPLEMENTER
Shape actionable strategic plans
They are at their best when they are clarifying actionable plans. They shape strategic objectives and plans to deliver them, bringing direction to action and structure to delivery.

GAME CHANGER / PLAY MAKER
Influence others' views on creative possibilities
They are at their best when they engage and enthuse others with creative ideas. They will influence others' views on what is possible when it comes to transforming the future.

GAME CHANGER / POLISHER
Creatively driving new ideas
At their best they understand what it will take to deliver creative ideas to the highest possible standards. They creatively drive progress recognising that others may not always see what they see.

PLAY MAKER / STRATEGIST
Facilitate the strategic debate
They are at their best when they are facilitating the strategic debate in teams, helping people to determine, and align to, shared objectives. They are inclusive and involving.

GAME CHANGER / STRATEGIST
Create ways to achieve strategic goals
They are at their best when they focus their creative thinking upon the enrichment of strategic objectives, bringing transformational possibilities to that endeavour.

IMPLEMENTER / STRATEGIST
Make strategy happen
At their best they bring a purposeful focus to aligned action. The 'why' of action matters to them. They get things done in a way that supports the achievement of strategic goals.

PLAY MAKER / GAME CHANGER
Facilitate the process of creativity and invention
At their best they facilitate the process of creativity and invention. They are alert to new ideas and possibilities that can transform the future and seek to align others to those possibilities.

POLISHER / GAME CHANGER
Relentlessly progressing ideas
At their best they are open to new ideas and possibilities. They value creativity and innovation and will bring energy to relentlessly progressing ideas. They will want to deliver to a high standard.

To illustrate how different constellations of proclivities create energetic impact, we look here at three frequently found examples using GC Index profiles. The level of their Energy for Impact is measured on a 1 to 10 scale where high scores represent strong energy.

This first example is that of the 'Inventive Leader'.

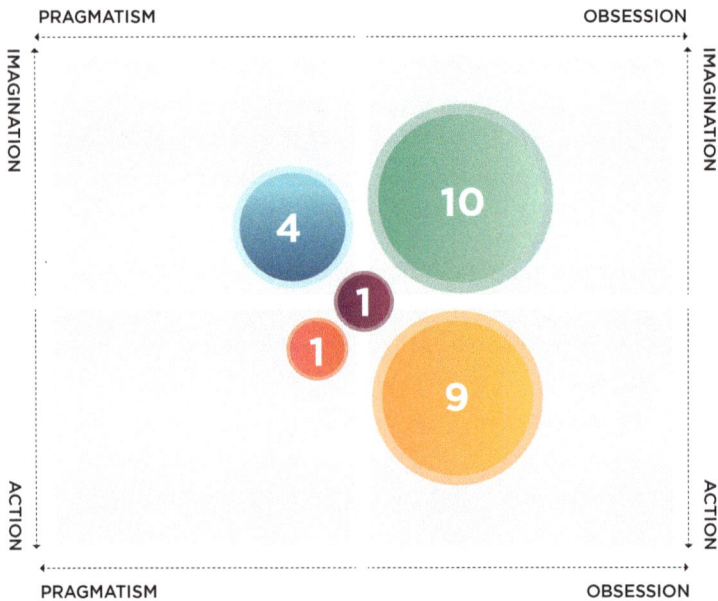

A 10 score for Game Changer and 9 score for Polisher speak to high energy for creating new possibilities that have the potential to change the landscape of their world. Leaders who do this inspire and energise us through the impact of their new ideas and their passion for seeing their ideas come to fruition. Not surprisingly this combination of proclivities is the most common amongst people who start their own businesses.

The second example is that of the 'Pragmatic Leader'. A 9 score for Strategist and a 7 score for Implementer speaks to high energy for creating clarity about what we are seeking to achieve and the tasks that will achieve the goal. They inspire and energise us by bringing purpose, energy, direction and focus to action. This is a common combination of proclivities amongst senior leaders in large, hierarchical organisations.

The third example is that of the 'Leader by Example'. An 8 score for Implementer and a 7 score for Polisher speaks to high energy for focused effort and operating to high standards. They inspire and energise us by their capacity and commitment and because they would never ask for anything that they would not also do themselves.

To achieve the goals of an organisation we need to ensure the right energetic mix. By surfacing the individual styles and collective proclivities of teams we can be consciously competent in assembling teams that will have a highest chance of delivering their goals. The GC Index model below shows how the different proclivities relate to the business cycle.

Where do you fit?

There is a persistent myth that strong leadership means being good at everything.

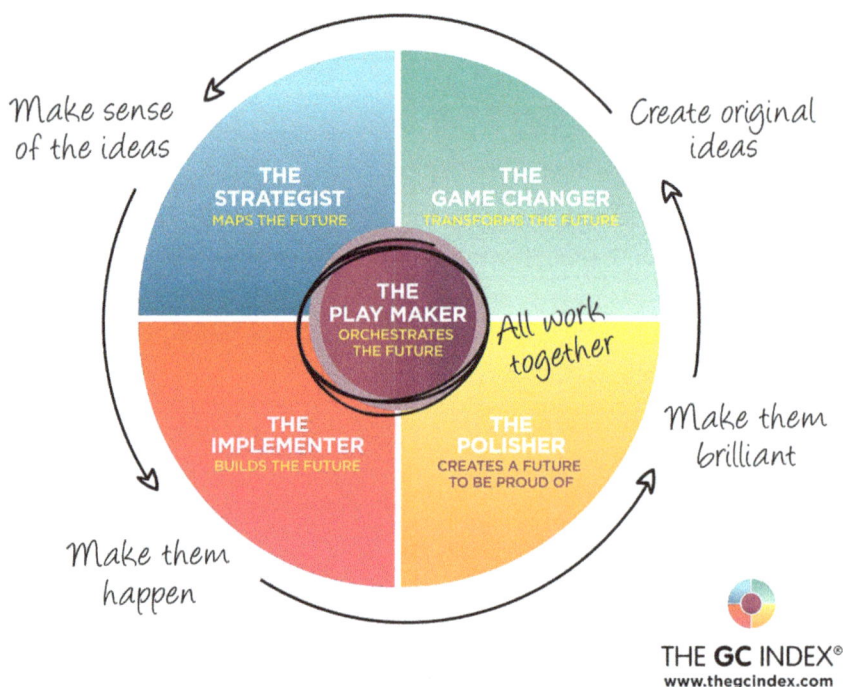

The Zenger Folkman research data shows that great leaders are exceptional in a few areas and know how to leverage these strengths to deliver results. This translates into a strong preference for a particular role in the organisation or a certain part of the business life cycle.

By mapping leaders' preferences across possible roles in different stages of the business cycle we can identify where they perform at their best and then help them to maximise their contribution within their preferred role. Game Changers create the new possibilities. Strategists are the architects who translate possibilities into plans. Play Makers create consensus. Implementers execute and Polishers improve.

The leadership roles that align with this continuous cycle are shown below, divided into roles that are either task or people orientated:

	GAME CHANGER	STRATEGIST	PLAYERMAKER	IMPLEMENTER	POLISHER
TASK	ENTREPRENEUR Business Ideas	DESIGNER Organisation requirements	ORCHESTRATOR Direction to action	OPERATIOR Consistent delivery	IMPROVER High standards
PEOPLE	EVANGELIST Enthusiasm for ideas	ADVISOR Relationship building	COLLABORATOR Inclusive leadership	ORGANISER Leadership for Execution	MOTIVATOR Galvaniser of others

In practice it is, of course, possible to show both task and people orientation, though leaders often have a strong preference for one or other.

Engaging with intent

Leadership is a 'contact sport'. By this we mean that it primarily takes place when we engage with others, face to face in the room or online. Leadership is reciprocal, you only get to influence others if others allow themselves to be influenced (and vice versa). This means that energising leaders must be adept at engaging with others.

This matters because it affects how people:

- make sense of things together
- share ideas
- make decisions.

Leaders who are effective in engaging others do this intentionally. They have developed conscious competence in exercising their talents and skills in an authentic way. They take the time and make the effort to really get to know the people they lead. The use of data brings precision to this engagement and when deployed across teams and teams of teams it creates a shared language that accelerates the capacity to make better decisions, faster.

Intent vs content

As leaders we tend to judge ourselves by our intentions. Others judge us by our content, that is, how we actually 'show up'. As human beings we mostly assume that what inspires and energises us will also inspire those with whom we interact and this can reduce the impact of our good intentions.

We can measure the degree of alignment through using tools such as the GC 360, which compares our own thinking with the perceptions of those we lead. On occasion the differences can be significant. When this happens the power of the insight is highly diagnostic and unlocks hidden potential for performance. We look first at the highest scores to reveal what is going on. In the following example the leader's view of self is dramatically different to those of his direct reports (self-score on the left):

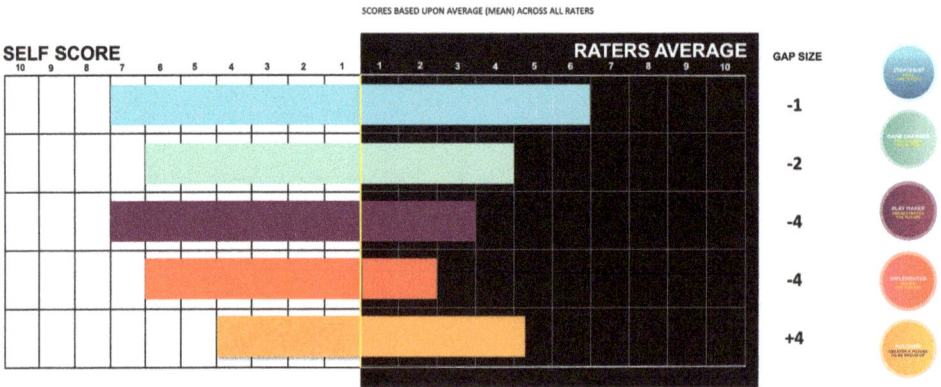

SCORES BASED UPON AVERAGE (MEAN) ACROSS ALL RATERS

The self-score indicates a 'contemporary leader' (Strategist/Play Maker) who, at their best, will be in engaging hearts and minds, involving and including others in shaping the future. The 360 score shows a leader who is perceived by their colleagues as an 'out and out' Polisher. To bring greater understanding of what is happening we also look at the differences of view at the average scores level.

There is only a small difference in views of the Strategist proclivity, however, the big differences lie in the Play Maker and Polisher scores. The conversations with the top team triggered by this data explained to the group why they were not growing the business at the desired rate. The leader was encouraged to 'let go' of both their perfectionist approach and the need to be in control of the whole business, which has subsequently thrived.

Developing others

Leaders who energise others also recognise the importance of developing capability in individuals, teams, and the wider organisation. Leaders who focus on making their people more successful command loyalty and foster high levels of discretionary effort.

Finding the 'sweet spot'

Research from Zenger Folkman (Zenger, J., and Folkman, J., 2020) shows that there is a sweet spot for individuals, teams, and organisations where competence, energy and a compelling goal intersect. It is therefore vital that others also have individual and collective goals that align with their role in the organisation.

1. Systemic – energise the organisation

Without energy organisations cannot function, yet we do not typically design our organisations to deploy energy efficiently and effectively. Indeed, the common experience of leaders is that they must spend time and energy compensating for organisational features that waste, divert and disconnect human effort.

Energising leadership is therefore distinctively different from general resources management, project management, time management and human resources management, etc. The desired result of leaders as catalysts is an energised and capable organisation, aligned behind a shared ambition, delivering results today, whilst transforming for the future.

First know where you are

Leaders therefore need to measure the impact they are having on the organisation before they seek to make changes. Whilst it is common to assess individual leaders' impact through assessment, 360 etc. organisations do not often look at the whole system impact of the leadership.

At the system level, leaders need to ensure that the vision, purpose, and mission of the organisation is both compelling (energising) and fit for purpose in volatile and rapidly changing circumstances. They also need to ensure that resources and effort are directed at both delivering results today and simultaneously reinventing the organisation to remain competitive and meet their customers' evolving needs. Thirty years of research and practice by Quanta Consulting have identified seven key elements that correlate with high levels of performance.

These are:

- Customer service
- Organisation climate
- Achievement focus
- Innovation
- Systems and processes
- Leadership – direct manager
- Senior leadership.

Deploying organisation-wide surveys reveals the energy narrative, which in turn allows senior leaders to clearly identify the areas that require catalytic intervention. One highly effective way to show the energetic profile of the organisation is The GC Index organisation impact survey (OIS).

Effecting change

In a world where people and organisations live in a state of semi-permanent overwhelm, large-scale interventions are rarely successful. We need, therefore, to think differently about change. In recent times there has been an increasing recognition of the power of small shifts that create big impact over time. Books such as *Atomic Habits* (James Clear) and *Tiny Habits* (B. J. Fogg) reflect this new understanding and approach. With our partner Quanta, we have adopted a distinctive and highly effective approach to change called 'energy fractals'. A fractal is an infinitely complex pattern that is self-similar across different scales consisting of simple building blocks which, with repetition, evolve into complex systems.

An energy fractal is a new behaviour that, when consistently repeated, has a powerful impact on the system. To take an example from daily life, if you want to get fit the fractal might be to exercise three times per week. The first order impact is improved fitness. The second order impact goes far beyond this. See illustration below:

Exercise 3 x per week for 6 months

Unfit

Fit

1st Order Impact

- Improved Fitness

2nd Order impact

- Energy Levels?
- Stress management?
- Employee relationships?
- Customer service?
- Profitability?

Experience shows that simple behavioural shifts specifically designed to address issues diagnosed in organisation-wide energy surveys have powerful positive effects. If we take, for example, communication (an area that frequently requires attention) an energy fractal to address this might look like this:

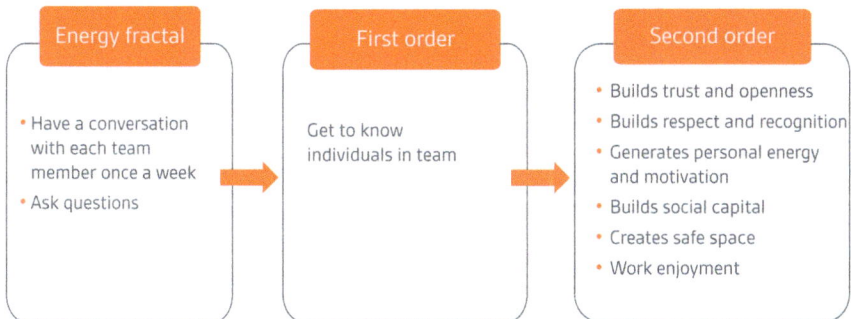

Energy fractal	First order	Second order
• Have a conversation with each team member once a week • Ask questions	Get to know individuals in team	• Builds trust and openness • Builds respect and recognition • Generates personal energy and motivation • Builds social capital • Creates safe space • Work enjoyment

A simple habit (have a conversation with each team member once a week) has the capacity to deliver multiple benefits at the personal, inter-personal, and the systemic level.

Closing reflections

Business typically is driven by self-interest. It is in the interest of organisations to have high levels of human energy committed to the realisation of their ambitions. The reality, however, is that most working environments are not highly energised or if they are, it is frequently a negative energy.

Organisations that focus on positive energy as well as driving for results are more likely to thrive in turbulent times. Leaders who inspire and motivate their teams re-energise them. Employees who are energised in pursuit of a compelling goal rarely look outside the organisation and bring elevated levels of discretionary effort to their work, which leads to higher levels of profitability.

The focus on energy as the fuel that propels the organisation is a powerful unifying idea that focuses on the 'so what' of leadership, in delivering exceptional performance. As we continue to face new challenges, understanding and acting on the insight that leaders have the capacity to catalyse new levels of energy, a 'win/win' exists where energised people in energised organisations deliver profitable results in a context where they truly thrive.

As a result, what is good for business is good for society.

Chapter 13

The Drive for Business Growth

Understanding the energy that drives business growth. A practical approach for business leaders, teams and organisations to employ in order to effectively achieve their chosen business growth strategies.

Peter Donovan

Who wakes up with the Energy for Impact to drive business growth?

You might ask or be curious to know what kind of person wakes up in the morning with the Energy for Impact to drive business growth?

Who are those people that want to contribute to the achievement of their company's goals and make a difference in the world as part of a team or organisation?

Clearly, they include not only business leaders, owners, boards, and investors, but also those employees who are drawn to teams and organisations with a purpose they believe in and want to be part of the journey to make their clients or customers successful.

These are the people who thrive in environments where they can collaborate with others, unleash their full potential, and create positive change. They find fulfilment in working towards a greater purpose beyond just personal gain.

As for me, I wake up every day with a passion to make my clients more successful, helping them do good in the world, delivering game-changing leaders and increasing their business growth and market capitalisation. As a business owner, I know that if I get this right our company will continue to flourish, we will work better with our clients' teams, be motivated to collaborate across our partnership team and continue to innovate.

Have you ever noticed a pattern, that your most impactful moments tend to coincide with times of high engagement and energy? It's a common observation. We each possess a unique Energy for Impact, which drives our ability to make meaningful contributions. It's this impact that The GC Index measures at an individual, team, and organisational level. High skills plus high energy equals high impact.

Consider this, if you're working at a for-profit company or non-profit organisation and find that your passion for making a difference isn't aligned with driving business growth and contributing to your team or company's goals, then you are probably not doing your best work.

This is where The GC Index can be particularly valuable for leaders and organisations. As you'll discover later in our section on post-hire activities, The GC Index empowers everyone to make a game-changing impact, facilitating the celebration and leveraging of individual differences and contributions and alignment of 'collective energy' towards impactful outcomes and a shared vision.

To bring all this together, the capacity to awaken with the enjoyment, sense of purpose and drive, resides in not just a few, but within all of us. This intrinsic motivation serves as a powerful catalyst for channelling our efforts towards fostering positive change in driving business growth and in championing the success of our teams and organisation.

What is this chapter all about?

As the proverb says:

> 'If you want to go fast, go alone. If you want to go far, go together.'

Transformational things happen on teams and in organisations when everyone's Energy for Impact is working well together.

It's this collective Energy for Impact where The GC Index becomes an organimetric (organisation metric), a measurement framework and language that identifies individual and collective impact and how people contribute to the achievement of organisational goals and business growth.

In our experience, where The GC Index has differentiated itself from other assessment tools and frameworks, is it goes beyond the individual to the empowerment of a team and an organisation to realise their full potential. It's this collective Energy for Impact that can influence how we make a difference in the world and help organisations work through disruptions to stay on the tracks to continued *sustainable* and profitable business growth.

If you work at a for-profit business or non-profit organisation or provide them with a service or solution, then this chapter is for you. Other chapters in this book will describe the dynamics of 'collective energy' in relationships and groups.

In this chapter, we'll delve into tangible examples highlighting how The GC Index organimetric framework and language can effectively channel the Energy for Impact within leaders, teams, and organisations, to drive business growth. How both 'for-profit' and 'non-profit' companies have used this to help take their organisations to the next level.

While these examples of driving business growth are insightful, the deeper learnings to help you apply this to your team and organisation will come from understanding how we got there. We will cover that journey in the following sections:

- About Top Gun Ventures and how we use The GC Index
- Selecting the right business growth strategy
- The level of organisational change required to achieve a company's chosen business growth strategy
- The ideal team specifications and profiles to make it all happen and real-world examples of the drive for business growth.

About Top Gun Ventures and how we use The GC Index

We are pathfinders in sourcing visionary and transformative leaders and assembling high-achieving teams. We specialise in helping organisations in growing industries that are driving or defending against new business models and disruptive technology.

As a retained executive search firm, we bring more than 20 years of delivering TGV GameChanging Leaders and teams that have taken our clients to their next level of business growth. Each of our partners in the firm brings extensive business leadership experience as well as executive search expertise to each client engagement. It's this combination of experience and expertise that has allowed us to help our clients thrive through the many up and down business cycles from the dot-com crash, through the financial crisis, to the growth in digitalization, Covid-19's remote work adjustments and now to the transformative opportunities from artificial intelligence (AI).

Along the way we have always sought out best practices and this is where in 2017 we discovered The GC Index, had all our Partners certified as GCologists and TGV became a GC Partner.

In our opinion, The GC Index (aka The Game-Changing Index) is an organimetric that empowers organisations to drive performance and achieve innovation by creating GC Index game-changing leaders, teams, and cultures. It is a radical rethink of how organisations identify and nurture key talent; identifying how people at all levels in organisations can make their best impact.

At Top Gun Ventures we are all about delivering TGV GameChanging Leaders to our clients. We do more than fill open leadership positions. Our approach assures time-tested TGV GameChanging Leaders with the experience, adaptability, drive, and cultural fit to help organisations accomplish ambitious goals, overcome difficult challenges, drive business growth, and explore new strategic directions. As such, the framework and language of The GC Index and its assessment method-ology that reveals how 'every team member' can make a GC Index game-changing contribution was a perfect fit for our toolbox and provided essential data to support our approach.

There are three phases to the recruitment process: Pre-hire, Hiring and Post-hire. We use The GC Index in all of them but in different variations to bring our clients the best candidate to deliver their chosen business growth strategy. We have found The GC Index to be equally, if not more, helpful to our clients at the Pre-hire and Post-hire stages so we will expand on these less obvious phases in the details below.

Pre-hire

- Firstly, we actively listen to our client's needs and what they are asking for in a new leader.
  - However, when a senior position needs to be filled the typical response from companies is to look at the job as it is currently structured and try to fill it as soon as possible. Ideally, the hiring executive, HR leader, or the interview team would bring the near- to long-term needs into the discussions. Realistically, they are often consumed with short-term issues and so they opt for the simplest course of action: replacing the job as it currently is. This is not ideal, it's just the natural thing to happen. It is indeed what often happens.
  - Our purpose and value add at the pre-hire phase is to help determine what is the right business growth strategy to get our client from where they are now to where they need to go next. As you will see later in the section on 'Selecting the right business growth strategy' we ask a series of questions to flush out the right strategy for their next level of business growth and what role the leader and team will play in achieving that strategy. From this we identify the 'Must Have Requirements' and 'Measures of Success'.
- We most often start out with a GC Index assessment of the hiring executive and in the debrief introduce the language of the five proclivities: GC Index Game Changer, Strategist, Implementer, Polisher and Play Maker.
  - These are action-based words used in everyday business discussions and help the hiring manager to think through where they need to go next and what type of leader they need for the tasks, challenges, and business growth strategy ahead. Often, and perhaps more helpful, is identifying what type of leader they don't want and which, based on their own profile, they will work best with.

- For example, if you already have the right strategy and just need to execute better, quicker, and more efficiently, then you don't need a GC Index Game Changer leader, no matter how prestigious or well known in the market, as they are energised to change the world. Likewise, if you need to be more innovative, to find new ways to grow in new markets, you don't want an Implementer leader that is only energised by getting things done and possibly resistant to new ideas and new business practices they are not familiar with, no matter how great a track record of performance they had in the past.
- The most pre-hire GC Index assessments occur with C-Level hires to the Senior Leadership Team (SLT). Many of our US clients are global and we have completed in-county leadership hires across a wide range of cultures such as Europe, South America, India, the Middle East and Japan. Regardless of country or culture, the four most critical 'Best Fit' relationships for success are noted below and this is where the individual and team GC Index insights can help with making the best hiring decisions.
- Candidate 'Best Fit' relationships with:
  - Their boss
  - The leadership/peer team they are part of
  - The team they will be leading
  - Their Energy for Impact proclivity profile for the role and tasks they need to accomplish.
- For example, we ran 20 GC Index assessments with one of our clients, Authentix, when replacing a Chief Operating Officer (COO) who had exited the business.
  - It was a critical hire because the founder CEO had moved to Chairman of the Board and a newly promoted CEO, Kevin McKenna, had taken over. Bringing in a new COO from outside the company to match up with a newly appointed CEO had to be right first time. The CEO and COO relationship needed to be a strong and complementary fit that could gain rapport quickly. The COO was accountable for keeping the day-to-day contractual commitments and activities on track and making the big decisions when the CEO was not available. This meant that the

COO had to have great working relationships with the senior leadership team (seven heads of functions, plus the CEO). Additionally, the COO led the operations team (eight direct reports), from engineering to product operations (hardware, software, services, and manufacturing). We also ran assessments on our four shortlist COO candidates.

◻ By having these individual and team GC Index proclivity profiles it helped us, along with our other candidate assessment techniques, to evaluate the best fit COO for the tasks ahead and all three relationships, the CEO, senior leadership, and operations teams. However, and not surprising in hindsight, this data helped the client to understand that what the founder COO had covered was really two jobs and trying to get another COO to cover this was always going to be a compromise in some aspects of the business. This insight resulted in a change of strategy. We hired our COO candidate to be Senior Vice President Engineering and added a Chief Sales and Marketing Officer, and they have both excelled in their positions.

◻ The newly appointed CEO, Kevin McKenna, and these two new senior leadership team executives are still working together five years later and firing on all cylinders. Just imagine what poor decisions (albeit well intended and based on incomplete insights) might have been made without the many GC Index individual and team profiles and insights to prompt us to ask the tough questions upfront, and how that would have impacted the desired business growth to be. We are currently doing the same again with another C-Level replacement hire.

◻ More importantly, this is a successful company with a culture that thrives on teaming and collaboration and lives up to its values every day. With this best practice approach, you can see how they have been able to sustain and build on this winning culture when bringing in new, and highly influential, senior executives to the organisation.

- We will go into more details later, on how to select the right business growth strategy, identify the business drivers and intensity of change needed to attain your strategy and the profiles of leaders and teams to make it all happen.

Hiring

- We utilise The GC Index as a diagnostic tool, akin to a doctor's MRI, to gain deep insights into senior executives. This assessment provides an 'inside view' of their inherent drive and strengths in catalysing business growth, and is based upon the constellation of their proclivities as Game Changers, Strategists, Implementers, Polishers, and Play Makers.
- This comprehensive understanding illuminates how potential candidates are motivated to act and their preferred methods of making an impact. When combined with our expertise in executive search, this tool serves as an additional data point, our MRI equivalent results, enabling us to assess the suitability of senior executives for specific roles and best fit for the tasks and business growth strategies ahead.

Post-hire

- Attaining business growth in today's unpredictable markets is much harder. It takes both great leaders and great teams to embrace the uncertainties, seize new opportunities and navigate the way forward to grow the business.
- As such, we offer to run, as part of our onboarding activities, our TGV GameChanging Leadership Team Workshop with our newly hired leaders and their new team. This is powered by The GC Index assessment, framework, and language.
  - When you get a new boss and you are told they are a TGV GameChanger brought in to save the day, everyone is suspicious, and 'rejection' can kick in: some team members worry if they will have a lesser role in the new team or have the energy for a new direction or way of working. Likewise, the new leader is energised with the task and challenges ahead but does not know what motivates his new team members or how to align

their collective Energy for Impact so they can do their best work to meet the new organisational goals and drive business growth.

- ❑ Right up front, we establish with our clients the three major imperatives for business growth, and these are turned into the objectives of the team workshop. We then design a series of breakout sessions for the team to better appreciate what each team member contributes most, where collaboration can make them stronger and clarifies a new purpose for each team member aligned around the business growth goals. This gets the new leader up to speed much quicker and the team energised straight away to go after the new goals and feeling potent and purposeful for the tasks ahead.

- Our three-hour GC Index powered TGV GameChanging Leadership Team Workshop has proved so successful in energising and aligning teams to do their best work and make a bigger impact that our clients repeatedly ask us to run these workshops with other teams or across their organisation. We gained global recognition for this work in 2022 by winning, along with our client Spirent Communications, The GC Index Organisation GEMS award for the most impactful organisation programme.

- We will share later several real-world examples of how companies have achieved their chosen business growth strategies, how they have used The GC Index and how you can do the same with your teams and organisation.

Where we fit in The GC Index organimetric classification matrix

The GC Index organimetric has numerous applications in both business and non-profit sectors. We utilise, as described in our recruitment process above, five of its twenty applications, focusing on pre-hire (business strategy, sales and growth), hiring (recruitment), and post-hire (leadership and team development), as noted in Figure 1 on page 266.

THE GC INDEX APPLICATION	STRATEGY & BUSINESS	ORGANISATION & CULTURE
PRE HIRE	BUSINESS STRATEGY	CULTURE TRANSFORMATION PROGRAMMES
	MANAGEMENT CONSULTING	EQUALITY, DIVERSITY & INCLUSION
	MARKETING & BRANDING	OPERATIONAL IMPROVEMENT
	MERGERS & ACQUISITIONS	ORGANISATIONAL DESIGN & DEVELOPMENT
PRE HIRE	SALES & GROWTH	WELLBEING
	TALENT MANAGEMENT & DEVELOPMENT	CHANGE & TRANSFORMATION
POST HIRE	LEADERSHIP COACHING & DEVELOPMENT	CHANGE MANAGEMENT
HIRING	RECRUITMENT & ONBOARDING	DIGITAL TRANSFORMATION
	PERFORMANCE MGMT & SUCCESSION PLANNING	INNOVATION PROGRAMMES
POST HIRE	TEAM IMPACT DEVELOPMENT	PROJECT & PROGRAMME MANAGEMENT
	YOUNG PEOPLE DEVELOPMENT	TECHNOLOGY & SOFTWARE SOLUTIONS

Figure 1: The GC Index organimetric classification matrix

Transforming teams across the globe with GC Index insights

To date, as a GC Partner, we have conducted over 600 individual GC Index assessments, had 20 GCologists certified and run around 70 team profile snapshots to take organisations, product business units and sales teams to their next level. Workshop attendees have come from the Americas, Europe and Asia.

The GC Index leadership team have commented that they see us as 'leading edge' thinkers grounded in the challenges that our clients face and committed, as trusted advisers, to helping them find a way through these challenges.

The benefits of The GC Index continue to evolve with new tools such as GC Translate, an AI assisted proclivity translation engine and most recently ChatGCT, an AI assistant chatbot. We stay up to date by participating in the monthly GC Index group activities to learn from other GC Partners and share our successes. This enables us to find new ways to apply The GC Index insights to impact the business outcomes of our clients.

Selecting the right business growth strategy

Understanding the array of strategies for business growth is crucial groundwork for navigating the journey towards success. Achieving the alignment of collective energies to attain an organisation's chosen business growth strategy, as we will see in later examples, is where The GC Index is at its most powerful as an organimetric and adds most value to ambitious organisations and teams.

We have a unique vantage point on business growth

As executive recruiters, we have a unique vantage point to observe where companies are thriving, surviving, or failing and get early visibility on the impact of latest trends, such as artificial intelligence (AI). We also get to discover the different business growth strategies that companies adopt to meet their challenges and opportunities and how, in the end, the people side of their business always determines their success, underperformance, or failure.

For-profit businesses

In the for-profit world the five most common business growth strategies for organisations are:

- Flat growth
- Incremental growth
- New growth
- High growth
- Sustainable growth.

In all cases, companies are looking to do this as efficiently and profitably as possible. Measures of business growth success are typically revenue, market share, customer delight and market capitalisation. In many companies, they will have more than one business growth strategy underway or all five at the same time in different parts of the organisation, be that at the company level, or within functional or regional divisions.

For example, especially in unpredictable times, when revenues are declining due to reduction of customer spend and buying behaviours are changing, holding as close to *flat business growth* is a success and essential for survival to stay around to grow another day. Furthermore, if you are not disrupting the market then you are being disrupted and when companies find their very existence under threat, they need to find a new path to *sustainable business growth.* This may involve developing a new strategic offering, reinventing, or repositioning the business to meet the future market and customer needs.

Non-profit organisations

When it comes to non-profits their business growth is about:

- Expanding services to extend support to a larger number of individuals requiring assistance.
- Offering new prevention services towards eliminating the issues they are addressing.
- Expanding and growing volunteers and employees to meet the increase in services.
- Maturing and growing funding mechanisms to pay for *new business growth.*

You might say that their business growth is not just about putting out fires but preventing them in the first place and covering as many fires as possible. Business growth can also be a mix of services and prevention activities offered. Most non-profits start with 100% of services to address the issues but this inevitably reaches a stage where there will never be enough resources to meet the demand and increasing the percentage of prevention programmes becomes the path to *sustainable growth*.

A lot of complexities that need to be managed well

As you can see from the above, business growth consists of various strategies depending on where an organisation is currently and where it needs to go next and what it sees as its endgame. This brings a lot of complexities into play that need to be aligned and managed well. This is where The GC Index organimetric framework and language can help harness leaders', teams', and organisations' Energy for Impact to find the ways to work together to achieve their chosen business growth strategy.

Let's look next at how to select the right business growth strategy, the levels of organisational change required to achieve the chosen strategy and then the ideal profiles of leaders and teams to make it all happen.

Selecting the right business growth strategy

As executive recruiters and trusted advisers to our clients, we often get involved when the time comes for business strategy. Below are the questions we advise Boards and CEOs to explore to flush out the right strategy for their next level of business growth, but these also apply to any team leader or team member in any type of organisation. The starting point is to determine what is the right business growth strategy to get you from where you are now to where you need to go next.

- Questions to determine your business growth strategy:
  - **Endgame:** What is the endgame, the long-term business growth strategy, and where is the company heading next in its growth cycle (accelerating, high growth, launching new growth areas, or transformation, etc.)?
  - **Impact:** What role will the leader and team members play in achieving that strategy?
  - **The Must Haves:** What kind of capabilities and experience do the leader and team members need to succeed in this newly defined role? What unchartered areas do they need to be able to navigate through? Can the leader and team members inspire and energise their organisation, in their current culture, to deliver exceptional results? What are the 'Must have Requirements' to set the bar for success?
  - **Measures of Success:** How will we know if the leader and team are succeeding after three months, end of year one, end of year two, at our endgame? What is the success criteria? How would we measure this and how confident are we that the leader and team can achieve this in the time frame needed?
  - **Business Growth Strategy:** Based on the above, what is the right business growth strategy, what is the level of organisational change needed for success and what is the ideal leader and team profile?

The most common business growth strategies that CEOs and Boards choose are the following and, as mentioned earlier, you may have all three going on within the same company, at an organisational level or within a function or regional division:

- Driving incremental business growth
- Driving new business growth
- Driving sustainable business growth.

The level of organisational change required to achieve a company's chosen business growth strategy

We need to look first at the drivers of business growth and causes of success and failure. Then how we can unlock business growth through the lens of change, and why we have chosen three business growth strategy examples to look at for the ideal team profiles to make it all happen:

- Driving *iterative change* to attain *incremental business growth.*
- Driving *innovative change* to attain *new business growth.*
- Driving *transformative change* to attain *sustainable business growth.*

What are the drivers of business growth and causes of success or failure?

We have talked with hundreds of successful business leaders, board members and investors and continue to do so at every opportunity and all agree that there are four main areas that impact a company's success or failure: capital, markets, technology (solutions) and people.

We ask them, in hindsight, to think about a failure they have experienced, and proportion blame across the four areas. On reflection and to their surprise, they assign as much as ~60% of the blame to the people side of the business and ~40% split across capital, markets and technology. Next, we ask them to look at underperformance and the people side goes up to 80% and 20% on capital, technology, and markets.

Finally, we ask them to look at the four areas and think about where they see themselves as experts and where they spend most of their time and it is a complete reversal, 20% on the people side and 80% on capital, technology and markets.

This is an 'Ah-ha moment' for many business leaders because they had been saying all along that the people side of the business was the most important but had not comprehended the size of impact it had on success or failure or how little, compared to the other areas, they had spent studying the people side of the business.

Now, if you can imagine the bigger impact that the people side has on business success, then just imagine the impact that TGV GameChanging Leadership and GC Index powered TGV GameChanging Leadership Teams can have on business growth.

Based on our observations, people-related issues occur when motivation and interest declines. The most recent Gallup polling[39] shows that only 23% of people around the world are engaged at work, 62% are not engaged and 15% are highly disengaged. Most advice on how to address this problem is aimed at managers and organisational leaders. However, research by HBR's Professor Boris Groysberg and Research Associate Robin Abrahams on HBR readers and HBS executive education participants[40] showed that it is possible for individuals to take steps to sustain their motivation or recover it.

They note that one of the ways to do this is to 'reframe' your thinking about work in two ways. First, by asking yourself who you are in your job and to concentrate on the higher-order purpose, e.g. a mindset shift where one man is laying bricks, and the other is building a cathedral. Second, by considering what role your job plays in your life, how you may help others inherently by doing your job or just being a better breadwinner for your family.

This is where The GC Index can really help individuals find a new purpose on the team related to their natural proclivities, revitalising the motivation and passion for their work. Also, how leaders and organisations can make a bigger impact on the people side of the business to steer away from failure and underperformance.

---

[39] https://www.gallup.com/workplace/349484/state-of-the-global-workplace.aspx
[40] https://hbr.org/2024/05/advice-for-the-unmotivated

Based on our work with clients and industry research these four areas: capital, markets, technology and people have evolved into *six drivers* that business leaders can manipulate to impact business growth:

- Leadership and strategy
- Employees and teams
- Organisation and processes
- Technology and solutions
- Markets and customers
- Capital and M&A.

Other companies and consultancy firms will have a similar framework so use these with our examples below if you prefer. The principles are all the same; when it comes to business growth you need to determine how heavy you need to push and pull each driver of business growth lever to make it happen to achieve your chosen business growth strategy.

Unlocking business growth through the lens of change

In today's ever unpredictable and opportunistic markets, and transformations ahead with artificial intelligence (AI), the best way to look at business growth is through the lens of change. When it comes to pushing and pulling these *six levers*, it's all about how much change you need to make in each of these drivers to have the desired effect on business growth. Change and transformation can be broken down into three levels – *iterative*, *innovative* and *transformative* change:

- **Iterative** change – Doing things better, faster, more efficiently or at scale.
- **Innovative** change – New things to add new value.
- **Transformative** change – New things that make old things obsolete.

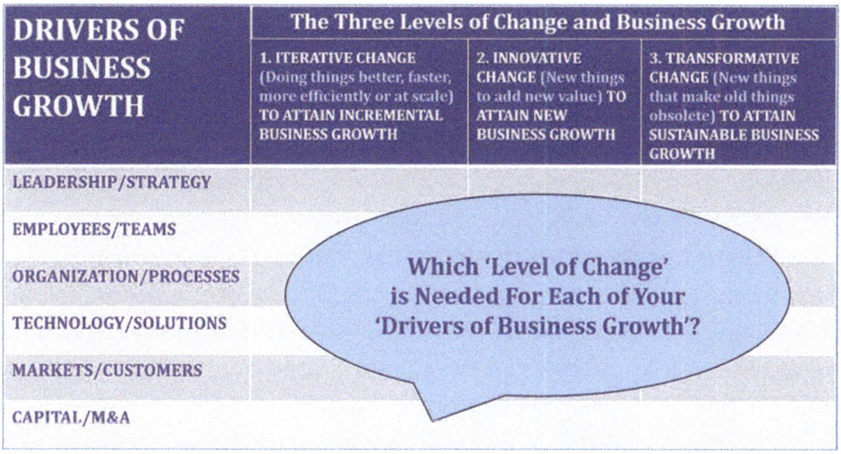

DRIVERS OF BUSINESS GROWTH	The Three Levels of Change and Business Growth		
	1. ITERATIVE CHANGE (Doing things better, faster, more efficiently or at scale) TO ATTAIN INCREMENTAL BUSINESS GROWTH	2. INNOVATIVE CHANGE (New things to add new value) TO ATTAIN NEW BUSINESS GROWTH	3. TRANSFORMATIVE CHANGE (New things that make old things obsolete) TO ATTAIN SUSTAINABLE BUSINESS GROWTH
LEADERSHIP/STRATEGY			
EMPLOYEES/TEAMS			
ORGANIZATION/PROCESSES			
TECHNOLOGY/SOLUTIONS			
MARKETS/CUSTOMERS			
CAPITAL/M&A			

Which 'Level of Change' is Needed For Each of Your 'Drivers of Business Growth'?

Figure 2: Unlocking business growth through the lens of change

As you can see in Figure 2, for the *six drivers* of business growth, it may take a different type of leader and team to be successful at each of these three levels of change, *iterative*, *innovative* and *transformative*.

We have found that while some leaders and teams say they are good at all three levels of change most will do their best work at just one as that's where their Energy for Impact to drive business growth strategy is strongest. Some will say they are good at a couple of these, but they always want to start with one level of change first. For example:

- In the case of *iterative* change, a new leader and team brought in to tackle a challenge will say that they don't want to make any major investments straight away as they want to see first how they can get the best out of the people, processes and technology and then look to invest in any gaps, at which point they will move to *innovative* change.
- Another leader and team that sees that they need a *transformative* level of change to attain their business growth strategy will want to make changes straight away with new solutions and set the company on a *new strategic direction* to meet the future demands of customers and assure a *sustainable* path of business growth. Once this major transformation has been achieved, they like to

institutionalise it and keep it moving forward with *iterative* and *innovative* updates. We will see an exemplary illustration of this later in the real-world examples of the drive for business growth.

When leaders and teams embark on addressing the complexities of maximising the *six drivers* of business growth and determining the appropriate intensity of *iterative, innovative*, or *transformative* initiatives to align with their chosen business growth strategy (*incremental, new* or *sustainable*), understanding their team's capabilities and motivations becomes pivotal. This insight, as shown below in Figure 3: Team workshop profiles, can be gained through an analysis of their team's collective Energy for Impact and proclivity mix profile, encompassing Game Changers, Strategists, Implementers, Polishers, and Play Makers, as defined by The GC Index. Unlike personality assessments and psychometrics that are not linked to impact or performance, The GC Index organimetric provides 'people data' that you can make business decisions on. We share, later, several real-world examples of how organisations have used The GC Index Team Workshop to help achieve their chosen business growth strategies.

DOMINANT SCORES

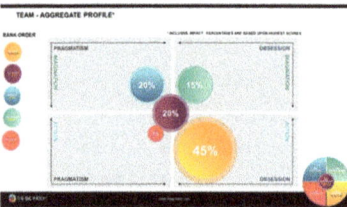

POTENTIAL SCORES

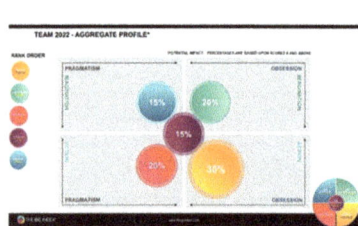

INDIVIDUAL THE GC INDEX PROFILES – SHOWING NAMES

1) **How does The GC Index Team Profile help or hinder us from achieving our business growth objectives?**

2) Who on this team might you call upon to support you with elements of your own individual objectives and why?

3) Are there any current or future projects/processes where The GC Index data can help us make more informed decisions?

Figure 3: Team workshop profiles

Likewise, when senior leadership teams and organisations embark on this understanding of what's needed to attain their company's business growth strategy, understanding the capabilities, motivations, and alignment of Energy for Impact for *all* their teams becomes critical for success, especially on the people side of the business. This is when we would use The GC Index's Organisation Impact Map (OIM) workshop. The OIM provides a map of each team's overall GC index proclivity profile (as well as individual team members) in the format of the company's organisation structure (or flow of teams in a project assignment or business process).

These insights, as shown in Figure 4 below, reveal how each individual and each business entity within an organisation makes an impact, and is then used to understand the current level of performance and alignment in an organisation and identify areas and relationships in the organisation that can be improved to attain their business growth strategy and take the company to the next level.

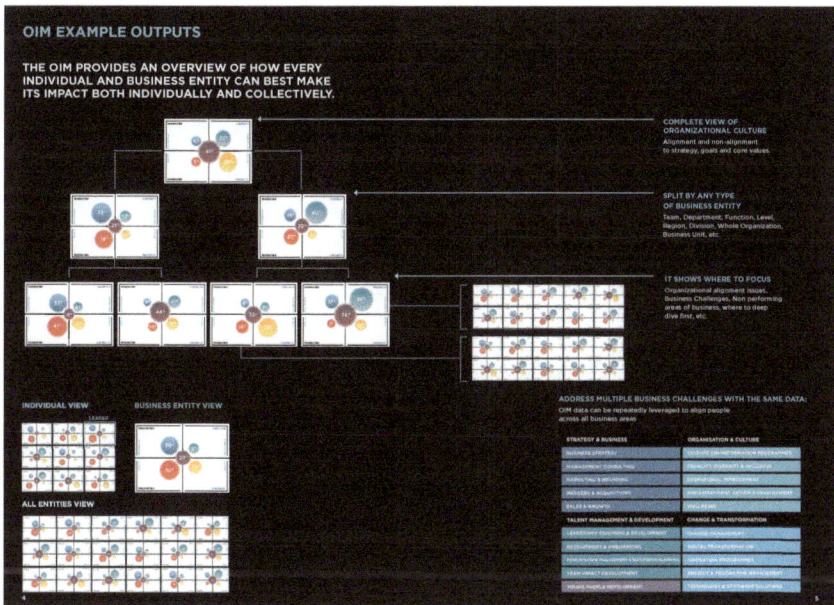

Figure 4: Organisational Impact Map (OIM) workshop profiles

Unlocking business growth requires innovative and creative leaders, cohesive teams, and aligned organisations. They masterfully orchestrate business growth drivers, calibrating the levels of change needed of these drivers to impact a company's chosen business growth strategy.

Next, we'll explore the three most common combinations of change and business growth, followed by example team profiles to navigate these journeys:

1. Driving *iterative* change to attain *incremental* business growth.
2. Driving *innovative* change to attain *new* business growth.
3. Driving *transformative* change to attain *sustainable* business growth.

The ideal team specifications and profiles to make it all happen

As business consultants and executive recruiters, we consistently enquire whether our clients possess the requisite leaders and teams with demonstrated profiles capable of executing their selected business growth strategies.

If the response is negative, we encourage them to first explore internal avenues such as networking, promotions, succession plans, or reorganisations. Should suitable leaders or teams prove elusive, as is often the case, we step in to facilitate external hires, introducing TGV GameChanging Leaders or orchestrating TGV GameChanging Leadership Workshops to align and invigorate the team.

In both leader and team scenarios, we leverage The GC Index assessment tool, in conjunction with our other evaluations and executive search expertise, to deliver the most qualified individuals for the tasks ahead.

Today, leaders and teams need a trifecta of competencies to successfully drive business growth: functional expertise, specific domain knowledge, and proven leadership of change and transformation:

- Functional expertise: The necessary leadership or functional experience and track record of success.
- Domain knowledge: Specific domain expertise and know-how for the company's chosen solutions.
- Driving change: Executives and teams that bring proven successes at leading change-driven *iterative*, *innovative*, and *transformative* levels of change to make it all happen and deliver on the company's chosen growth strategies.

When developing a leader or team specification, we look to identify the ideal backgrounds and change-driven growth profiles that can deliver on the client's chosen business growth strategy.

Below is an example of the team specifications for our three example business growth strategies: *incremental*, *new* and *sustainable* growth. You may have a similar specification for your teams, but we share our examples here so you can see later how we use The GC Index to identify the ideal team profiles.

Business Growth Strategies	Background	Change-Driven Growth Profiles
1. Driving ITERATIVE Change for INCREMENTAL Business Growth	Teams with a proven background of accelerating business growth and financial performance by getting the best out of people, processes, and technology. Invests in relationships and builds cohesive teams. Stays task driven and not distracted by new ideas	They make an impact by streamlining operations, optimizing workflows, and increasing efficiency through AI driven enhancements and are invaluable assets to their organizations. They understand that achieving sustainable growth requires continuous refinement, and that adopting and leveraging AI is critical to achieving that goal
2. Driving INNOVATIVE Change for NEW Business Growth	Teams with a proven background of launching a new product, service, or capability inside an existing company that drives new growth and revenue streams, can help teams work better across the organization, enters new markets with creative and/or disruptive solutions	In a world where innovation is the lifeblood of sustained success, these teams make an impact by driving change across the business. They not only identify new AI driven market opportunities but also create them, driving growth and revenue streams that set their organizations apart. They are the visionaries who understand that staying competitive means pushing the boundaries of what's possible with AI
3. Driving DISRUPTIVE Change for SUSTAINABLE Business Growth	Teams with a proven background of transforming a company to deliver a new strategic offering, reinventing, or repositioning the business to meet future customer needs, and establishing a new path to sustain continued growth. Building relationships and transitioning their team to new ways of working	For these teams staying relevant often means leaving behind legacy systems and capabilities and embracing new technologies as well as new business models. They make an impact by being at the forefront of reshaping industries, and their ability to be among the first to market with entirely new AI driven products, businesses, and industries

Figure 5: Example team specifications to drive business growth strategies

The background and change-driven growth profiles specifications above describe what a team needs to deliver for each of the three example business growth strategies. This specification represents the collective Energy for Impact that a team needs for success.

Part of The GC Index tool set is an AI-assisted translation engine known as GC Translate. This can discover the Energy for Impact proclivity profile within any written content such as team job profiles, LinkedIn bios, communication statements, project objectives, strategic plans and much more, including the background and change-driven growth team specifications in Figure 5 above.

We have run each of the three business growth strategy examples above through GC Translate and the resulting GC Index team profiles are shown below in Figure 6.

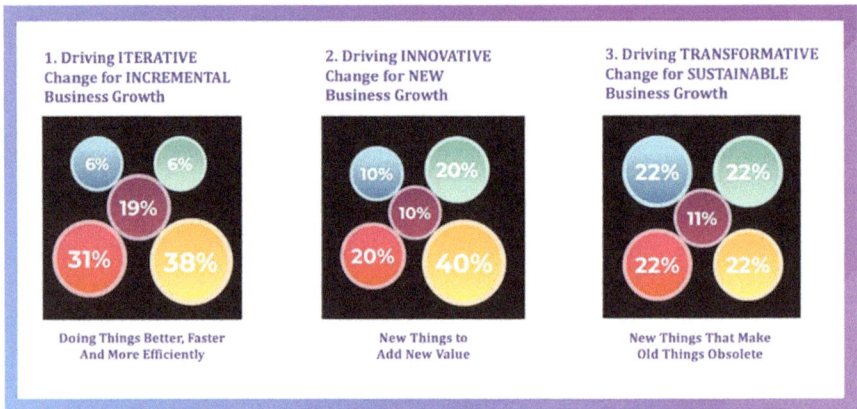

Figure 6: Example team profiles to drive business growth strategies

Moreover, this profile assertion gains additional validity from looking at the numerous GC Index team assessments and workshops we've conducted, and by aligning the known successes and reputations of these teams against the three business growth profiles above. We share further proof of this validity in our later section on real-world examples of the drive for business growth.

Every business growth strategy situation will be different, but these three example profiles are most common and allow for a deeper discussion with clients to determine the ideal leader and team needed to achieve their chosen business growth strategy.

We share below how each of the five GC Index proclivities can make a GC Index game-changing contribution to each team in Figure 6 and the ideal GC Index Multi-dimensional leadership profiles to lead these teams.

1. Leading *iterative* change to attain incremental business growth

Doing things better, faster, more efficiently or at scale

- These teams will have a business background of accelerating business growth and financial performance by getting the best out of people, processes, and technology.
- This is where we need teams with Energy for Impact as strong Polishers, Implementers, and Play Makers, and this is where they will do their best work.
- What we don't need are any new strategies or new ideas that distract our efforts or take us in a different direction.

Everyone can make a GC Index game-changing contribution to the team

- In these unpredictable and opportunistic markets strategy can change overnight. As such, in this scenario, what we need from our Strategists is for them to keep looking at the market and competitors to see if anything changes to make sure this is still the best strategy.
- For our GC Index Game Changers, we need them to direct their energy internally; we are not looking to change the world just yet, but we do need their new ideas on how we can think outside the box to implement better, faster, more efficiently and to continually improve our solutions. This is what we term 'disciplined Energy for Impact' versus the 'natural Energy for Impact' we have been talking about so far. We provide an exemplary illustration of 'learned Energy for Impact' later in the real-world examples of the drive for business growth.

The ideal leader for this team

- A task-driven hands-on 'leader by example' (Play Maker Implementer) would be ideal for this role as would a 'leader as a coach' (Polisher/Implementer).

2. Leading *innovative* change to attain new business growth

New things to add new value

- These teams will have a business background of launching a new product, service, or capability inside an existing company that drives new growth and revenue streams, enters new markets, and/or defends against disruptive innovation from new entrants.
- This is where we need our GC Index Game Changers to come up with new innovative ideas and Implementers and Polishers to make it happen to a high standard.
- Again, we don't need a Strategist with a new direction to look at because we are trying to achieve our current strategy by offering our customers new things that add new value and open *new* business growth opportunities.

Everyone can make a GC Index game-changing contribution to the team

- Again, in a business world of rapid change, we need our Strategists to keep an eye on the market and competitors to make sure our strategy is still valid. While we don't need a Play Maker to find consensus as we have already decided to deliver *innovative* solutions, we do need them to help us all work better together, especially across the interfaces between product, operations, and sales.

The ideal leader for this team

- An 'inventive leader' (GC Index Game Changer/Polisher) that can turn ideas into reality and get things done to a high standard would be ideal for this role as would a 'creative problem solver' (GC Index Game Changer/Implementer) that can bring new ideas and see better ways of doing things. Also, a GC Index Game Changer that can work well with strong Implementers and Polishers.

3. Leading transformative change to attain sustainable business growth

New things that make old things obsolete

- These teams will have a business background of transforming a company to deliver a new strategic offering, reinventing, or repositioning the business to meet future customer needs, and establishing a new path to sustain continued growth.
- This is where we need our GC Index Game Changers to come up with 'out-of-the-box' new ideas and our Strategists to determine the new solutions and direction for the company to go in to meet the new demands of customers and ensure we have a continued path to *sustainable* business growth. Plus, we need strong Implementers and Polishers to make it happen with a sense of urgency, new ways of working and to a high standard.

Everyone can make a GC Index game-changing contribution to the team

- We have already decided that we need to transform the company towards a new direction, so we need a healthy conflict of views to navigate the best way forward. As such, we are not looking for our Play Makers to find consensus. Rather we need them to help us transition to a new way of working.

The ideal leader for this team

- A 'visionary leader' (GC Index Game Changer/Strategist) that will bring creative ideas and possibilities to shaping future purpose and direction would be ideal for this role as would an 'aspirational leader' (Strategist/Polisher) that can 'see the big picture' that's built upon a rigorous attention to detail, works well with GC Index Game Changers and will inspire a creative team to do their best work. Also, an 'inventive leader' (GC Index Game Changer/Polisher) that can turn ideas into reality, get things done to a high standard and collaborates well with a strong Strategist.

In the next section we will share real-world examples of how businesses and non-profit organisations have used The GC Index to help take their organisations to the next level of business growth.

Real-world examples of the drive for business growth

We will share a variety of examples from three real-world organisations on the drive for business growth. They operate in different theatres but have all found ways to work well together to attain their business growth strategies. Additionally, they provide a wide array of lessons learned that we can all benefit from as we look to drive business growth in our teams and organisation:

- IKEA: A household brand that is respected internationally.
- Spirent Communications: A global client serving 100% of the world's top network companies.
- All Community Outreach (ACO): A local charity supporting a million-plus people.

For each of these real-world examples we will provide details on:

- Company overview and leadership
- Energy for Impact to drive business growth
- Attaining business growth
- Key takeaways.

IKEA – A household brand that is respected Internationally

Company overview and leadership

IKEA's vision is 'To create a better everyday life for the many people.' Their business idea is to offer a wide range of well-designed, functional home furnishing products at prices so low that as many people as possible will be able to afford them.

IKEA is owned by the Ingka Group and led by CEO Jesper Brodin (a former IKEA executive). Jon Abrahamsson Ring, CEO Inter IKEA Group, leads IKEA's 12 franchisees and more than 200,000 IKEA co-workers around the world. Jon says that he has learned that the success of any organisation lies in leading business through people.

Energy for Impact to drive business growth

Founder Ingvar Kamprad said, 'IKEA is not the work of one person alone. It is the result of many minds and many souls working together through many years of joy and hard work.'

Jon Abrahamsson Ring, CEO IKEA, says:

'IKEA is in my heart, and I strongly believe in our vision to create a better everyday life for the many. I'm passionate about transforming business and people for the better. That means making great products and services available for as many people as possible. And it means keeping things simple even as you scale a global brand. Most of all, it means working together towards a shared and common goal.'

Ingka CEO, Jesper Brodin's emphasis is on togetherness, saying:

'The power is where the people are. Believe in yourself and your strengths, but don't forget to rely on other people's strengths, too. Because we're truly stronger together.'

This is an example of a company that has the leadership and a purpose that many people believe in and want to be part of the journey to drive business growth and in championing the success of their teams and organisation.

Attaining business growth: leading *innovative* change to attain *new* business growth (see Figure 6, example 2).

IKEA innovated to grow a new interior design function that has achieved significant business growth and added a new segment of customers:

- In 2021 IKEA launched Billie, their 7/24 AI chatbot, that has handled 47% of customers' queries to call centres in the last two years. Rather than laying people off, at the same time as launching Billie, IKEA trained 8,500 call centre workers as interior design advisers and launched their interior design business which has since grown to $1-billion plus.

- If you wanted to start an interior design business, where would you hire your people from and how would you familiarise them with the uniqueness of your business and customer needs? What better training could you provide than having them start as call centre workers and learn what customers really need and the gap where they need help with designing their interiors? This is a great example of recognising the unique talent of everyone in the company and leveraging their 'natural Energy for Impact' to grow further and feel potent about what they can achieve together as a team in a new growth part of the organisation.

- In 2022 sales by phone or video of products and services through Ingka's remote interior design channel accounted for $1.4 billion and 3.3% of its total revenue. By 2028 it expects that to grow to 10% of revenues as part of a push to appeal to future Gen-Z customers. Now that's a successful *new* business growth strategy that came out of an *innovative* level of change.

- Asked if the increased use of AI was likely to lead to a reduction in headcount at the company, Ulrika Biesert, Global People and Culture Manager at Ingka Group said:

  'That's not what we're seeing right now and we're committed to strengthening co-workers' employability in Ingka, through lifelong learning and development and reskilling, and to accelerate the creation of new jobs.'

- I'd say, the way they managed the people side of their business was also *innovative* and a key contributor to driving *new* business growth.

Key takeaways

This is a real-world example of an *innovative* change that has attained *new* business growth. You can see above in Figure 6, example 2, how the Game Changers and Polishers would bring you 'out-of-the-box' ideas and new possibilities that you had not thought of before and your Implementers could operationalise new strategy and get it done.

With the right leader and team profile you can do the same at your organisation and The GC Index can reveal how *everyone* can make a game-changing impact on the team.

Spirent Communications: A global client serving 100% of the world's top network companies

Company overview and leadership

Spirent helps keep their digital world in check by providing tools that test if their networks, devices, cybersecurity, and positioning systems are working properly.

However, five years ago, its business sustainability was under threat from the fast-moving real-time digitalizing world. Test and measurement in the lab was not going to be enough any more and they needed to find a way to get the company back on the rails of *sustainable* business growth. Eric Updyke was brought in as CEO to reposition the company in a new strategic direction to meet the future needs of their mostly telecommunications service provider customers and the demands of the marketplace.

Test and Measurement used to be done once in the lab before new network products were released to the market but with the new types of programmable networks, the future demand would be for test and measurement to be automated and checked continuously as live networks were reconfigured in real-time and assigned client service level agreements. Spirent's customers needed an assurance that the level of performance they had promised to their customers and billed for was being delivered.

Eric knew that to make this work they had to completely change the way they went to market, provide new services for their global customers and to build a new set of automated solutions covering the full life cycle of Test and Assurance from lab to live network. To drive this initiative forward, he wasted no time in bringing on board two seasoned leaders: Manuel Zepeda, tasked with overseeing Global Sales and Services, and Doug Roberts, entrusted with leading Automated Test and Assurance Solutions. We will hear shortly the real-world examples from these front-line leaders on how they successfully transformed these areas and their usage of The GC Index.

To provide a north star to help navigate this new journey Eric reset the company focus with a new purpose and commitment to every customer: 'Your promise assured – we stand behind your promise to deliver a new generation of technologies to your customers, from lab to the real world.'

Additionally, for the company to stay on the rails of sustainable business growth Eric made it clear to everyone in the company that they had to accomplish these business goals profitably.

Bringing us into the present, Eric, Manuel, Doug, and the Spirent team have delivered innovation, creativity, and a sense of urgency to drive a new sustainable business growth strategy. Spirent has doubled their market capitalisation value over the last five years, and by virtue of the future value embedded in these new automated services and offerings, a competitor company, Keysight, has stepped forward with a billion-dollar plus acquisition proposal, underscoring the allure of the company. This larger and more industry diverse company will bring an abundance of resources for the next phase of Spirent's sustainable (and profitable) business growth journey and the capital to realise the full potential of artificial intelligence (AI).

We will hear next the real-world examples and insights from Spirent's key front-line leaders, Manuel Zepeda and Doug Roberts.

Manuel Zepeda, Executive Vice President, Global Sales and Services, Spirent.

Manuel's Multi-Dimensional leadership profile (Polisher/Strategist), as shown in Figure 7, is that of an 'aspirational leader'. At his best he can 'see the big picture' that's built upon a rigorous attention to detail and likes things to be properly 'thought through'.

Figure 7: GC Index profile – Manuel Zepeda

Energy for Impact to drive business growth

Manuel learned early in life that change is constant and adapting to it was, and is, imperative to success.

He says:

'Being the tip of the spear for change excites and ignites every sensory organ I have. Spirent has given me the opportunity to implement change, observe, learn, and quickly modify to produce the best possible outcome to drive business growth.'

Attaining business growth: leading *transformative* change to attain *sustainable* business growth (see Figure 6, example 3).

Manuel's initial task was to completely change the way they went to market and offer new innovative services to their global customers, a task metaphorically akin to replacing the engine of a car while travelling at top speed.

Manuel was successful because he tackled this transformative change with the approach of 'fast evolution' as he comments here:

'When I joined the company, I quickly realised that we were too down in the trenches with the technocrats and not discussing business issues. I realised quickly that selling bits and bytes or features wasn't going to generate sustainable growth. We started with arming the commercial team by understanding who knew how to tell a story then created collateral for them to tell it. Over time, we had to make some difficult choices to upgrade our people skills to take the next growth step. This was certainly not a revolution but rather a fast evolution of trying new methods, failing fast and retrying until we had a winning formula.'

Manuel says that

'The GC Index allows management to have a different perspective on our team members. It helps us align a person's natural strengths with the job at hand to monetize our solutions while creating value for our customers and our employees. We continue to leverage The GC Index in some of our most critical people decision making opportunities and we have increased collaboration within Spirent, thanks in part to The GC Index.'

To provide the people data for Manuel and his global team we ran three GC Index powered TGV GameChanging Team Workshops. Each of these teams (17–20 attendees) was a cross-section of regional and functional leaders, covering most all Vice Presidents and Directors.

Every team workshop was geared toward achieving the same business objectives and outcomes. Employing the same workshop format across all groups facilitated output comparisons; the convergence of messages across workshops emphasised the need for decisive action.

Business objectives:

- Leading and propagating collaboration across the entire company.
- Top three business priorities:
  - Managed solutions growth (services)
  - End-to-end solution selling
  - Urgency (install it in everything we do)

Outcomes from this workshop:

- Learn what our strengths and gaps are as individuals and as a team.
- To be able to leverage the strengths and address the gaps.
- Understand what 'impactful collaboration' would look like in this team and across the entire company.
- Leverage a language and framework to align people and make better business decisions to achieve our business objectives.

We've conducted approximately 70 team profile snapshots, revealing that in many instances teams exhibit weaker performance in one or two of the five GC Index proclivities, hindering their ability to scale or drive business transformation. However, the profile for Manuel's Sales and Services Team showcased a remarkable abundance of strengths across all five proclivities at the global level (refer to Figure 8 below).

Proclivity	Global	CPEs	Americas	EMEA	Asia	NEMs	Channels	Ops	HR	Execs
Game Changers	15	6	2	2	3	1	2	-	1	-
Strategists	13	2	1	3	4	-	2	-	1	1
Implementers	20	3	7	5	3	-	1	2	2	2
Polishers	13	1	3	5	2	-	2	1	1	1
Play Makers	18	4	1	4	5	3	1	2	2	-

Figure 8: Frequency of GC Index proclivities by region and function

With these insights, Manuel and his leaders encouraged collaboration within and across regions and functional teams. This helped with the business goals and from thereon, leading, and propagating collaboration across all Sales and Service Teams became the norm.

For example, the six Game Changers from the CPE (Customer Partner Executive) group, the leaders of their top strategic customers, were in great demand from the global regions (Americas, EMEA and Asia). As one of the CPE Game Changer leaders said:

'Some studies can make people feel like they are deficient in certain areas. The GC index makes people feel proud of their strengths and how they fit into a winning team full of different GC Index proclivity profiles. The GC Index is also powerful because it teaches leaders to think about problem solving and team building in terms of the optimal combination of profiles and roles.'

Following the three team workshops, 10 global HR executives became certified GCologists. This allowed Spirent to continue using The GC Index in everyday business activities and to support the action plans coming out of the workshops.

Here is what one of the HR executives said:

'The GC Index has been a "game changer" for us. It's really impacted the collaboration in the business, and I love the investment we've made in our people. I've seen people light up as they go through their debrief when they see how their profile resonates with them. We've helped people out of roles where the role didn't fit the person and their energy, and others into new roles we've opened – all using The GC Index as an indicator. The other benefit is that it gives us a great framework and common taxonomy from which to look at our strengths and have conversations – why things are working and why they may not be.'

Key takeaways

Pioneering transformative change naturally entails upheaval, often causing companies to take a step back before moving forward. However, as a sales leader, Manuel was not afforded this luxury, as it would have spelled disaster for the company. The market is ruthless when it comes to revenue downturns, regardless of the reasons or investments made for sustained growth. Therefore, Manuel's approach of 'fast evolution', of trying new methods, failing fast and retrying until they had a winning formula was clever and key to success.

The team workshops allowed Manuel to engage a bottom-up buy in and alignment of everyone's Energy for Impact behind the new business goals. The level of collaboration that was achieved in hours from the workshops may have taken many months to achieve with normal business activities.

The ripple that Manuel started with the three GC Index powered team workshops went on to gain recognition for Spirent (and TGV) by winning The GC Index Organisation GEMS award.

Importantly, as Manuel had set as his number one business goal, his Global Sales and Services group had taken the lead on propagating collaboration across the entire company.

Next, we will hear from Doug Roberts, a front-line executive, who leads all of Spirent's automated test and assurance product development and life cycle services from the lab to the real-world networks.

Doug Roberts, Executive Vice President and General Manager, Automated Test and Assurance, Spirent.

Doug's Multi-Dimensional GC Index profile is Game Changer/Polisher. At his best he will turn creative ideas into reality and get things done to a high standard. He will have developed the skills to engage and influence people to get them 'on board' with his ideas and expectations.

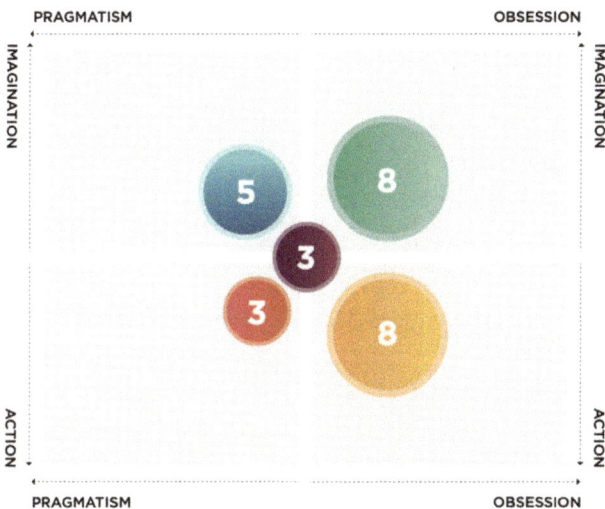

Figure 9: The GC Index profile for Doug Roberts

Attaining business growth: leading *transformative* change to attain *sustainable* business growth (see Figure 6, example 3).

As Clayton Christensen, famous for revolutionising innovation, noted, if you are not disrupting the market, you are being disrupted. When it comes to staying on the rails of *sustainable* growth you need to be the one that is disrupting the market and that's where Doug and his team are experts and why Spirent was one of a few companies that grew during the Covid-19 pandemic.

Doug's task is to develop the new *innovative* and creative products, services and solutions that meet their customers evolving needs and set Spirent apart from their competitors. It's also to institutionalise and make efficient these new solutions as they become mainstream.

To provide the people data for Doug and his global team, we ran a GC Index powered TGV GameChanging Team Workshop on his Senior Leadership Team. Here are the business and workshop objectives.

Business objectives:

- Solutions: Transform the business from just a product and support business into an outcome driven services portfolio business.
- Customers: Enable the go-to-market expansion from legacy lab tools to live operational solutions.
- Processes: Foster a collaborative team environment that allows us to maximise.
  - Product planning
  - Development
  - Delivery activities

Outcomes from this workshop:

- Understand what 'impactful collaboration' would look like in this team and across the entire LSA Business Unit.
- To be able to leverage our strengths and address the gaps.
- To apply The GC Index language and framework to align our collective impact and velocity of change on the tasks ahead to achieve our business objectives and accelerate our transformation to an outcome driven services portfolio business.

Below is the profile of Doug's Automated Test and Assurance Team back in 2021 (formerly LSA, Lifecycle Service Assurance):

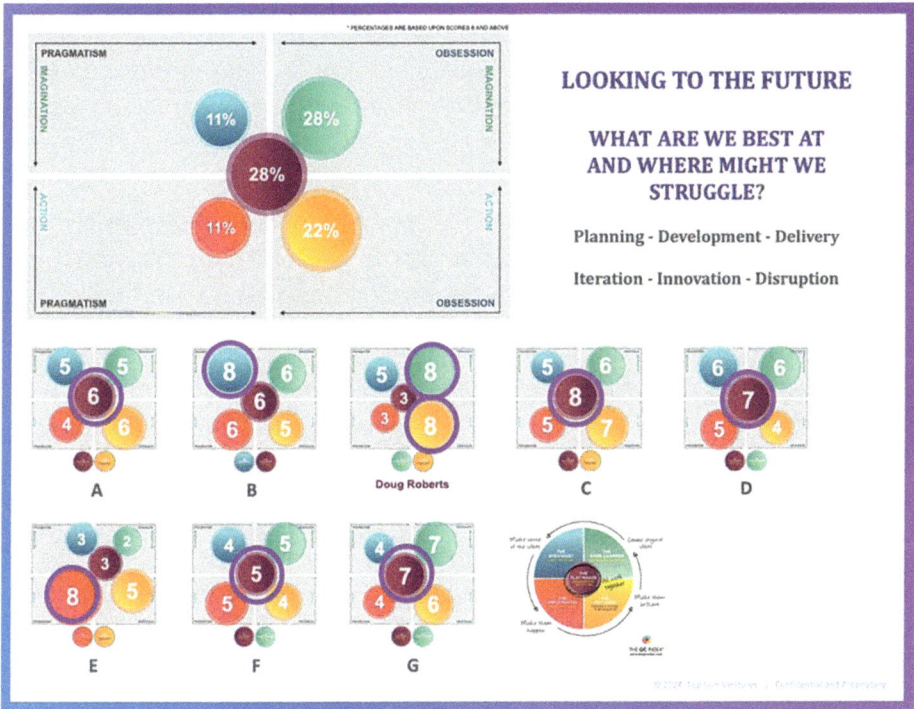

Figure 10: Above is the team profile for Doug's Automated Test and Assurance Team

The team profile, with strong Game Changers and Polishers, explained why Doug and his team had been so successful at coming up with innovative and creative solutions. Most leaders would have celebrated this finding and moved on but not Doug.

His takeaway, and life cycle mindset, was very insightful for the next phase of their business growth journey. He commented, 'We have a lack of Implementers on our leadership team.' This became a key item for the Business Unit that led to a transformation in the way they operated the business.

Doug had astutely observed, as depicted in Figure 10: Team profiles to drive business growth, that the absence of Implementer Energy for

Impact to operationalise strategy and instil a sense of urgency in execution leads to mere conceptualisation, ultimately stalling innovation, and business growth. His main concern was that while everyone was excited with the new solutions and services, they may miss the plan targets and delivery promises made to their customers, nor find the efficiencies to scale the products and services to bring them into mainstream offerings.

As Clayton Christensen also noted:

> 'The reason why it is so difficult for existing firms to capitalize on disruptive innovations is that their processes and their business model that make them good at the existing business actually make them bad at competing for the disruption.'

For Doug it was the reverse, the reasons why they were so good at capitalising on disruptive innovations may work against them in the next phase of their business growth journey as they bring these new products and solutions into mainstream business.

Once again, drawing from our analysis of 70 team profile snapshots and those of other GC Partners, it's a rare occurrence for a team profile to perfectly align with the ideal profile for where the company is going next and driving future business growth.

While there are numerous ways to address this gap, delving into them all is beyond the scope of our discussion here. One of the best ways is to add disciplined Energy for Impact to your team's *natural* Energy for Impact. We provided some brief examples earlier in the section on team profiles to drive business growth (Figure 6) and how everyone can make a GC Index game-changing impact, but the approach taken by Doug and his team stands out as the most exemplary we've encountered.

Additionally, navigating the way forward in business has many similarities to navigating an adventurous journey across land, sea, or air. The first thing navigators learn about their guiding compass is that north is not always north. There is the true north you are heading for and the magnetic north that the compass is pointing to. Periodically, navigators must stop to calculate the declination between magnetic north and the true north they are trying to get to and put actions in place to close the declination gap.

- True north – chosen business growth strategy
- Magnetic north – the *natural* Energy for Impact of the team
- Closing the declination gap – the disciplined Energy for Impact actions to build on top of the team's *natural* Energy for Impact to get back on track to true north.

Here, Doug shares insights on the disciplined Energy for Impact that he and his team put in place to instil discipline and foster transformation in their business operations, effectively compensating for the absence of inherent Implementer Energy for Impact within his leadership team:

'While we had several Polishers and Play Makers on the team it was the identified gap in implementation that led to a directed action to create an implementation plan for our annual strategy. We collectively agreed to take our annual operating plan and break it down into what became known as our L2 Action Plan. This action plan became a monthly rubric by which we would run our business or "implement" our plan! Effectively, it was a reversed engineered task sheet that itemised each task to be accomplished, with assigned ownership, that would have to get done if we were to accomplish our plan.'

Further, Doug added:

'The L2 Action Plan became the operational dashboard by which we managed our monthly Business Unit operations meetings. Over time we were able to digitize this plan via API connections with key systems to track our progress, i.e. Research and Development project data, Product Line Management (PLM) strategic plan data, Support customer request data.'

Key takeaways

Although we could have provided numerous insights into Doug and his team's success in crafting inventive products, services, and solutions to shake up the market and captivate their customers, we believed the more significant takeaway for those interested in driving business growth within their teams and organisations was the concept that Doug identified and exemplified of disciplined Energy for Impact.

In actuality, there's invariably a disparity within the team's composition concerning the ideal profile for the direction you're aiming to pursue next. Achieving this entails a combination of natural and disciplined Energy for Impact.

Doug concluded by saying:

> 'Some would say, why not just go to a platform like Monday.com in the first place? To which I would say, you have to first realise the team as a whole doesn't have the proclivity to operationalise and execute on a well-articulated plan before you jump to any conclusive action to fill that gap! This is where The GC Index was invaluable.'

As we can see from both Spirent real-world examples, leading *transformative* change to attain *sustainable* business growth includes the challenge of delivering new things that make old things obsolete, as depicted in example 3, Figure 6: team profiles to drive business growth.

All Community Outreach (ACO) – a local charity supporting a million-plus people

Company overview and leadership

ACO is a non-profit charity serving one million-plus people with a mission to help their neighbours to prevent hunger and homelessness while working towards financial stability.

ACO is led by Marjorie Vaneskahain Burr, CEO. Marjorie's Multi-Dimensional GC Index profile is Game Changer/Strategist as shown in Figure 11 is that of a visionary leader. At her best Marjorie will bring creative ideas and possibilities to shaping future purpose and direction. She will have developed the skills to engage people with her ideas, especially those who will make them a reality, her Implementer and Polisher colleagues.

Figure 11: GC Index profile – Marjorie Vaneskahain Burr

Energy for Impact to drive business growth

Here is what Marjorie says about her Energy for Impact to drive business growth in the non-profit world:

'Before my feet hit the floor each weekday morning, I've already reviewed our agency dashboard with the data that reflects the work and the impact our agency made the prior day, week and month. My first thought is what I can do personally to make an impact TODAY and change lives. That's when the ideas begin to flow.'

Attaining business growth: leading *innovative* change to attain *new* business growth (see Figure 6, example 2).

ACO had set themselves the task to expand from a few to all the towns and cities in their county of a million people and growth rate of 4%. As well as serving a significantly larger number of neighbours, they were starting up new services around education, employment, and finance management to take their neighbours in need from a financial crisis to financial stability. At the same time as they were moving into bigger facilities to offer more food and care pick-ups and better operations for donation drop-offs.

This was a major transformation for the organisation both internally and externally, but essential for their business growth to meet the increasing demands for help. Marjorie, being The GC Index Game Changer was looking for a new 'out-of-the-box' idea to help her top team of 14 become stronger leaders and work better together to transform their services and take their organisation to the next level. Marjorie heard about The GC Index powered TGV GameChanging Leadership Team Workshops we had run at for-profit companies and said, 'if it's good for them it's good for us non-profits'.

Below is The GC Index profile of the top team at ACO and one of the recommended actions coming out of the team workshop on applying The GC Index in their everyday work (see Figure 12). At the end of the workshop, we asked each attendee, 'Who are you going to call?' We asked them to share with the group what they had learned from the workshop, the one thing they will do differently and 'who they will call' to team up with to learn together how to apply The GC Index insights in the workplace.

It's never easy applying a new theory and framework to the workplace or changing how we behave and interact with others, but this session is where the students become the teachers. Hearing from their peers, the quiet ones that rarely speak up to the ones that never stop talking, who they want to team up with, why and what they hope to learn is very motivating for everyone and helps to create the mindset for change and confidence to leave the status quo behind.

This is where the true learning sinks in and provides the enjoyment and motivation to use this language straight away in their everyday interactions.

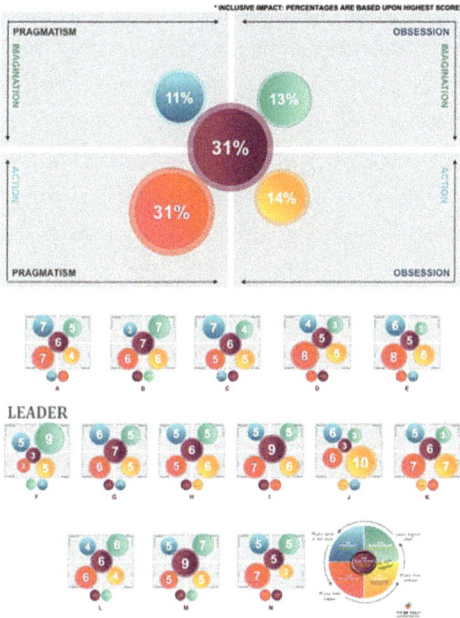

Figure 12: 'Who are you going to call?' – Where the students become the teachers

Several months after the team workshop Marjorie wrote a newsletter, shown below, that reflected the impact of The GC Index framework on the organisation with examples of how Marjorie and her top officers, the Quad team, were using the language in their everyday business activities.

ACO Newsletter – Who's in charge here?

- Some days I am the CEO of All Community Outreach! Other days, they just let me think I am … 'They' are the other officers that I work with each day that make up the team we call 'Quad'. I assure you that while I may have the ultimate responsibility, the four of us together are a powerful force with more than 50 years combined serving ACO.
- **Aaron Vaughn** serves as ACO's Chief Operating Officer. Today he leads our entire operations and finance departments. This includes

the total renovation project of our annex and expansion. I remember Aaron as a college student, working part-time at ACO in our donation operation. Over the last decade, he went from managing our warehouse operations and processing centre, then adding resale operations, and today overseeing all of our operations in every department. He is calm under pressure, is the voice of reason, brings cohesion to the team, and is fair and compassionate. Aaron is the Play Maker of the group, orchestrating ACO's future and keeping it running smoothly. He is amazing.

- **Rhonda Ptak** is the Implementer. It is her job to build ACO's future with a strong community base. She has the energy and drive of three people and can juggle multiple jobs at the same time. In fact, she does just that! When Rhonda and I first worked together in fund development, we planned exciting and profitable events to raise funds for ACO programs. With her 'can do' attitude, she then also jumped into the food pantry part-time to help when we needed her leadership. Like several of us, Rhonda left ACO to pursue other interests, but was led back to us at a critical time when the organization was expanding from 'Allen Community Outreach' to 'All ...' She accepted the position of Community Development Officer and has been instrumental as we expand our reach across Collin County. As if she was not busy enough, when the resale program needed management, she agreed to take on additional responsibilities to grow the redesigned and rejuvenated resale and boutique stores. Rhonda's tenacity, creativity and 'I can do it' attitude are key to the Quad.

- **Michelle Clough** serves as Missions Officer. I first met Michelle when she was a volunteer with our organization. We were hiring a food pantry manager when she came into my office and assured me that she wanted the position, even when I tried to talk her out of it. At the time I had no idea of the strength, compassion, and capacity this woman has to lead, organize, and implement anything that comes her way. Years later, after 'retiring' then coming back as the Volunteer Director before stepping into her current role, she is the driving force of our client services team.

Michelle is our Strategist. Without the mission and her amazing team, there would be no ACO. The rest of us are here to support them as they change the lives of families in need every day.

- **Let me be clear about who is really in charge …** it is the families who come to us with their critical needs. It is the volunteers who work side by side with us to ensure successful programs to support those families in crisis. And it is the donors who make it fiscally possible for us to continue the vital programs and services to create a stronger, stable community.
- One more thing … I am the [GC Index] Game Changer in the Quad. I bring vision and innovative ideas to the organization. Honestly, sometimes my ideas create some eye rolls from the staff, but they are open-minded. Working together we sift through ideas and plans, then implement and support the programs and services that prevent hunger and homelessness by creating a path to financial stability for families in Collin County.
- These labels [The GC Index proclivities] came from a wonderful leadership workshop that was held last fall by ACO volunteer, Peter Donovan of Top Gun Ventures with our top management team of 14. We are grateful to Peter and his team for making us better leaders and teaching us how to work with each other's strengths and talents.

Key takeaways

This is also a great example of the power of having a self-aware GC Index Game Changer as a leader. GC Index Game Changers bring new and innovative ideas that can transform the future, but they can't do it alone. You can see in Marjorie's newsletter message how she relies on the proclivity profile strengths of her other officers and how together every-one is making a GC Index game-changing contribution to take their business growth in the non-profit world to the next level.

Let's take a moment to visualise the gratification of being valued members within the contexts of these three organisations. Picture the start of each day filled with a sense of purpose and determination to contribute meaningfully to their triumphs, inspiring us to ignite similar enthusiasm within our own teams and organisation.

In summary

Just like my fellow GC Index Game Changers, I strive to unlock untapped ingenuity, and I hope this chapter has energised you to step outside of your comfort zone to be even more innovative.

Selecting the appropriate business growth strategy requires a deep understanding of organisational dynamics and market realities. Whether it's incremental, new, or *sustainable* growth, leaders must assess the level of change required and the ideal profiles of leaders and teams to execute the strategy effectively.

This journey towards business growth is best navigated together, harnessing the collective Energy for Impact within individuals, teams, and organisations. The GC Index provides a framework to understand and leverage this collective energy, enabling teams to channel their efforts towards common goals. By aligning individual strengths with organisational objectives, teams can drive impactful outcomes and propel *sustainable* business growth.

I'm confident, that with the knowledge of natural and *disciplined* Energy for Impact, we can foster a culture of collaboration and creativity, where every voice is valued, and we can navigate through the disruptions ahead to keep our teams and organisation on the tracks to *sustainable* business growth.

In these unpredictable times, it's good to remind ourselves that we all have the capacity to awaken with the enjoyment, Energy for Impact and a sense of purpose to drive business growth and in championing the success of our teams and organisation. When this occurs, we can be assured of doing our best work, feeling potent and fulfilled.

Section 5:

Channelling Energy for Effective Organisational Change

Chapter 14

Dynamic Flow and The GC Index

A breakthrough in productivity and energy management – the key ingredient to human engagement, impact and efficient productivity.

Simon Phillips

Introduction

Do you ever find yourself in moments of boundless energy and unstoppable drive, ready to take on any challenge that comes your way? Have you experienced those rare instances where everything seems to fall effortlessly into place, and you're completely immersed in the task at hand? As someone who's spent nearly three decades guiding individuals towards greater effectiveness and productivity, I've delved deep into the intricacies of human performance, sparking a re-evaluation of conventional time-management paradigms.

In this journey, I've come to realise that time, once perceived as a linear and measurable construct, is far more nuanced and multidimensional than we've previously imagined. Like threads in a tapestry woven by the hands of great philosophers, our perception of time evolves, giving rise to a profound shift in perspective. Instead of merely managing time, I've witnessed the transformative power of harnessing our energy – a shift that lies at the heart of true productivity and fulfilment. Join me as we explore the dynamic interplay between time, energy, productivity, impact, and flow, uncovering the secrets to unlocking our fullest potential and living life with purpose and passion.

From time management to flow

A: Rethinking time management

Time's elusive nature

You can't manage time. Indeed, some of the greatest philosophers are not convinced that time actually exists. It's just a perpetual flow of NOW. For example;

- Henri Bergson, a French philosopher, proposed the concept of duration, suggesting that time is subjective and experienced as a continuous flow rather than a series of discrete moments.[41]
- Roger Penrose, a mathematical physicist, has delved into the concept of time through the lens of quantum mechanics and the theory of consciousness. His proposition challenges the prevailing perception by suggesting that time might be intricately linked to the essence of human consciousness. In other words, Penrose proposes that time may not be a separate entity, but could be deeply intertwined with the fundamental nature of human consciousness itself.[42]
- Eckhart Tolle, author of the global best-seller, *The Power of Now*, suggests that time is largely a mental construct and that much of human suffering arises from an excessive focus on past regrets or future anxieties, rather than living fully in the present moment. He emphasises the importance of mindfulness and being present as a means to transcend the limitations imposed by time and access a deeper sense of inner peace and fulfilment.[43]

In contemplating the elusive nature of time, one is confronted with a profound philosophical enquiry that transcends conventional notions of past, present, and future.

The perspectives above invite us to navigate the enigma of time with

---

[41] Henri Bergson, 'Time and Free Will: An Essay on the Immediate Data of Consciousness', 1889.

[42] Roger Penrose, *Cycles of Time: An Extraordinary New View of the Universe*, Bodley Head, 2010.

[43] Eckhart Tolle, *The Power of Now*, 1997.

humility and curiosity, recognising it not as a linear progression but as a timeless journey of self-discovery. In short, it prompts a re-evaluation of our approaches to time management.

As we've seen already, the term 'time management' is a misnomer, we can certainly improve our efficiency in the moment, but we'll never create more hours in the day. Rather than attempting to control the abstract concept of time therefore, we'll make more significant gains if we focus on effective 'energy management'. In this light, being productive is all about how we manage our energy effectively so we can achieve the outcomes we seek.

All the time-management tricks, tools, tips and techniques in the world will not help if we fail to manage the energy we need to get things done.

This paradigm shift recognises that the allocation and utilisation of our energy resources play a pivotal role in achieving our desired outcomes. By redirecting our focus, we empower ourselves to navigate productivity with a holistic and sustainable approach.

B: The essence of productivity – defining productivity as effective energy management

Productivity isn't just about checking tasks off a list; it's about maximising efficiency and achieving meaningful results. It's the art of managing our energy resources to ensure we're 'firing on all cylinders' when it counts. By shifting our focus from mere time management to 'energy management', we unlock a more pragmatic approach to getting things done. This means understanding our individual rhythms and capacities, so we can allocate our energy where it matters most and maintain a steady flow of progress.

At its essence, productivity is about finding that perfect balance between input and output. It's about working smarter, not harder, and making the most out of the time and energy we have available. This requires a keen awareness of our own energy levels and working patterns, so we can optimise our efforts and tackle tasks with precision and purpose. Whether its prioritising tasks based on energy levels or taking strategic breaks to recharge, the goal is always the same:

'To accomplish more while preserving our mental and physical well-being.'

Ultimately, productivity is about achieving our goals in a way that's sustainable and fulfilling. It's about homing in on what truly matters and taking deliberate action to move closer to our objectives. By mastering the art of energy management and understanding the nuances of our own productivity patterns, we empower ourselves to navigate the complexities of work and life with greater ease and effectiveness. In essence, productivity becomes not just a means to an end, but a pathway to personal and professional growth and fulfilment.

C: Unleashing impact

The ripple effects of productivity

As we harness the power of productivity, the impact reverberates far beyond the completion of tasks – it permeates every aspect of our lives, shaping our relationships, our achievements, and our overall sense of fulfilment. Productivity isn't just about getting things done; it's about making a tangible difference in the world around us. When we optimise our energy and resources to achieve our goals, we unlock the potential to create meaningful change and leave a lasting impact.

One of the most profound impacts of productivity is the ripple effect it has on our relationships and interactions with others. By managing our energy effectively, we're able to devote more attention and focus to those we care about, fostering deeper connections and strengthening bonds. Whether it's spending quality time with loved ones, collaborating effectively with colleagues, or supporting our communities, our productivity enables us to show up fully present and engaged in every interaction.

When we consistently achieve our goals and make progress towards our aspirations, we build confidence in our abilities and cultivate a mindset of success. This new-found confidence spills over into every aspect of our lives, empowering us to take on new challenges, pursue ambitious endeavours, and reach heights we never thought possible. In this way, productivity becomes not just a tool for achieving specific outcomes, but a catalyst for personal growth, resilience, and self-actualisation.

D: The development of flow

Harnessing the power of optimal experience

Flow is a state of optimal experience where individuals are fully immersed and focused on the task at hand, experiencing a deep sense of enjoyment and fulfilment. When we enter a state of flow, time seems to stand still, and our actions become effortless and seamless. This phenomenon, first explored by psychologist Mihaly Csikszentmihalyi[44], highlights the profound impact of being fully engaged and absorbed in what we're doing. In essence, flow is the epitome of productivity, as it allows us to tap into our highest potential and achieve peak performance.

Achieving flow requires a delicate balance between challenge and skill – tasks should be neither too easy nor too difficult but perfectly matched to our abilities. When we find ourselves in this sweet spot, our attention becomes completely absorbed in the task, and distractions fade away. This intense focus not only enhances our performance but also brings a sense of joy and satisfaction to our work.

Whether it's writing a compelling article, solving a complex problem, or engaging in creative expression, flow enables us to unlock our creativity and tap into our innate potential. Moreover, while the benefits of productivity and impact are often measured in external achievements and contributions to others, the personal impact of flow is deeply intrinsic and profoundly transformative.

Experiencing flow on a regular basis can cultivate a profound sense of fulfilment, inner peace, and self-actualisation. It is a state where our deepest passions and talents converge, allowing us to tap into our highest potential and live authentically. In the embrace of flow, we find not only joy and satisfaction in our endeavours, but also a profound sense of meaning and purpose that permeates every aspect of our lives. Thus, while productivity and impact propel us forward in our external pursuits,

---

[44] Mihaly Csikszentmihalyi, *Flow: The Psychology of Optimal Experience*, 1990.

flow nourishes our soul and ignites the spark of our truest selves, guiding us on a journey of self-discovery and personal growth.

E: Embracing acceptance

The keystone to personal fulfilment

Acceptance stands as a cornerstone amidst this discussion on time, productivity, impact, and flow. To mix some metaphors, it serves as the linchpin that binds these concepts together. It offers a transformative pathway, not only in navigating the complexities of time and productivity but also in fostering meaningful impact and attaining the coveted state of flow. At its essence, acceptance beckons us to surrender to the unfolding of time, embracing each moment as it arises without resistance or judgement.

In the realm of productivity, acceptance emerges as a potent force, liberating us from the constraints of perfectionism and the incessant pursuit of efficiency. By accepting our limitations and imperfections, we create space for creativity and innovation to flourish, transcending the boundaries of traditional productivity paradigms. Moreover, acceptance infuses our endeavours with a sense of purpose and authenticity, allowing us to harness our energy and resources in alignment with our values and aspirations.

In addition, acceptance fosters a deep sense of inner peace and resilience. When we stop fighting against the current of life and surrender to what is, we tap into a wellspring of strength and fortitude that resides within us. This inner resilience empowers us to weather life's storms with grace and courage, knowing that we have the capacity to overcome any obstacle that comes our way. When we embrace acceptance, we find liberation and freedom, allowing us to live authentically and fully, in alignment with our true selves.

F: Introducing dynamic flow

The evolution of flow

In 2022, I introduced the idea of dynamic flow[45] to illustrate how the

---

[45] Simon Phillips, *Dynamic Time Management*, 2022.

notions of time, productivity, impact, flow and acceptance work together. Embracing what can and cannot be controlled is a fundamental aspect of fostering a productive mindset. Recognising the limitations of control allows for a more realistic and adaptive approach to navigating the challenges that life presents. It keeps our focus on the NOW which is the only 'time' we can exert our influence.

Understanding the intricate link between energy management and adaptability is paramount. Effectively channelling energy resources allows individuals to navigate change with agility, turning challenges into opportunities for growth.

Thriving on ambiguity through resilient energy management is critical for personal and professional success. Embracing the uncertainty inherent in change, individuals equipped with resilient energy-management skills find themselves not just coping, but flourishing, in dynamic and evolving environments.

Dynamic flow itself is all about balancing what we can control (our use of energy) and what we are wise to accept (things beyond even our influence). We can only access this state of dynamic flow when we act, and don't act, mindfully. This is why you often hear people talking about the power of saying 'No' in terms of personal productivity. It is just as important as the things we say 'Yes' to, when we prioritise our lists of things to do.

However, when it comes to getting things done, what *energy* are we talking about?

Enter stage right: The GC Index

A significant breakthrough

In my work on productivity and impact, I always felt there was a disconnect between the various personality assessments and how an individual achieves fulfilment. I may well make decisions with a mixture of 'thinking' and 'feeling', or absorb information utilising a combination of 'sensing' and 'intuition', but how does that relate to my bigger self-image? How does that help someone lacking in confidence and struggling to identify how they can make a difference within a team?

In 2015 I was introduced to The GC Index and immediately saw something different, something that could really help. The GC Index is a measure of someone's 'energy' for both contribution and impact. Through the lens of The GC Index, we can see that how individuals generate and express energy to contribute to their communities, workplaces and families varies widely and this revelation introduces a dynamic dimension to our understanding of personal productivity.

A revelation in energy management

The GC Index introduces a new layer of insight, unveiling the diversity in how individuals generate and express energy and thereby revolutionising our understanding of personal productivity.

The five proclivities identified by The GC Index explain why five extroverts can respond to the same task in entirely different ways:

1. One with excitement at the endless possibilities (Game Changer energy)
2. One with joy as they see how the task aligns and supports what has already been defined (Strategist energy)
3. One with frustration that the task has emerged right in the middle of completing the previously agreed priority (Implementer energy)
4. One with hesitation as they ponder the efficacy of this new idea (Polisher energy)
5. One with despair as they see the proposed task disrupt the harmony of the team (Play Maker energy).

To explore this a bit further, I invited some individuals with a lot of energy for one of the five proclivities to share when they recognise that they are in flow.

Game Changer energy

Game Changer energy is fuelled by a freedom of creative expression. Game Changers draw energy and inspiration from freely exploring ideas and possibilities. This proclivity reveals that creativity is not just an outcome but a dynamic source that propels individuals into a state of energised flow.

Generating energy through freely exploring ideas is the hallmark of a Game Changer. It's in the process of inventing something out of nothing that individuals with strong Game Changer energy discover their purest form of flow – a state akin to alchemy!

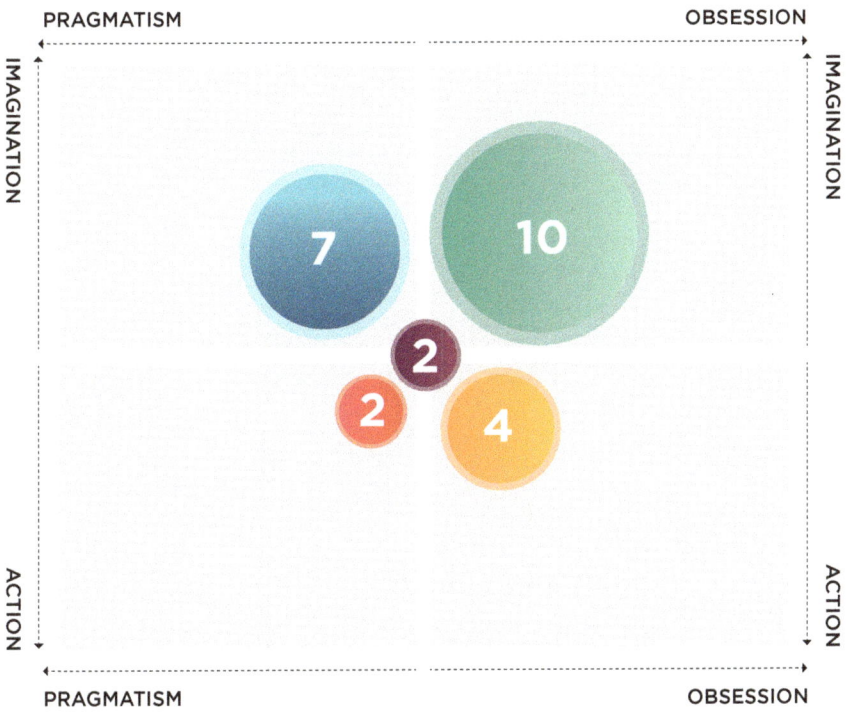

The stories below bring this Game Changer energy to life.

Game Changer energy in flow

Figure 1: Vanda North, co-author of *Mind Chi: Re-wire Your Brain in 8 Minutes a Day – Strategies for Success in Business and Life*

Figure 2: Jill Whittington, The Change Maker Group and Flow, Grow, Flourish

Q: What is flow?

VANDA:

'Flow is when I take the luxury of allowing myself to play.'

Q: When does it happen?

VANDA:

'Mostly I set myself, or someone gives me, an unsolved situation. If possible, I sleep on it first, and frequently dream a perfect solution, get up and capture it right away.'

JILL:

'My only "deliberation" was to be able to put it into words, so I let it soak and then it came to me.'

Q: *What does it feel like?*

VANDA:

'Even writing about it makes me feel the excitement of creating. There is also a bit of frustration as the perfection in my head is hard to express or achieve.'

JILL:

'I feel like a kid at Christmas who is peeping into an unopened gift. The sense of excitement and anticipation mounts as I see ways forward, like a sackful of enticing gifts.'

Q: *What types of activity trigger a sense of flow for you?*

VANDA:

'Wanting to look at something differently. And occasionally creating just for the fun of it.'

JILL*:*

'It can be triggered from totally random, left field, ideas out of the blue, generally whilst walking or doing something mundane.'

Strategist energy

Individuals with high Strategist energy thrive on understanding how things fit together. This energy type is a sustained force, as the individual aligns with the big picture, deriving energy from the clarity that allows them to instigate action and maintain a sense of flow.

Aligning with the big picture becomes more than a task for a Strategist; it's a source of ongoing energy. Their sense of flow emanates from the profound understanding of how individual elements synchronise to create a cohesive whole.

Strategist energy in flow

Figure 3: Andrew Tallents, author of *Self-Coaching for Leaders*, Managing Partner of The Tallents Partnership

'When I am in flow I never feel rushed. I feel I have space to think and experiment with a variety of potential plans that others will find easy to understand.

I find it easy to think back to the past to see what might work in the future. I then test the plan to see how robust it is and then need help in implementing it.

The triggers for me moving into flow are usually present when there is a lack of clarity about the future, and I need to find a pathway to get through it. This is when I create time to do the work that I am best able to accomplish.'

Implementer energy

Implementer energy is rooted in action – an energy source that finds fulfilment in uninterrupted task completion. For those with high Implementer energy, flow is achieved through the seamless movement through and between tasks.

Uninterrupted task completion serves as the marker of Implementer flow. A completed activity list or a successfully delivered project becomes not just an accomplishment but a manifestation of the individual's energy in motion.

Implementer energy in flow

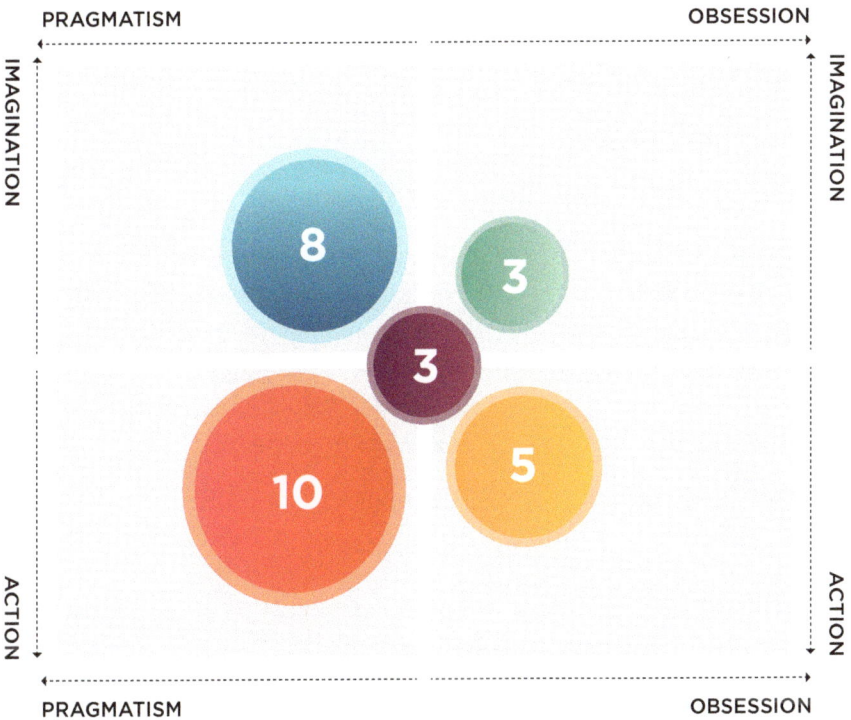

PRAGMATISM   OBSESSION

IMAGINATION   IMAGINATION

8

3

3

10

5

ACTION   ACTION

PRAGMATISM   OBSESSION

Figure 4: Alison Ball, Finance Training and Support Manager, PS Connect, University Corporate Services, University of Exeter

Q: What is flow?

ALISON:

'Flow for me is mostly linked to problem solving, achieving balance, and determining pathways to resolve grey areas. It's often more about this sense of control, resolving things, and creating order out of messiness rather than the task itself.'

Q: When does it happen?

ALISON:

'I can feel when flow mode switches on in my head, and I'm off, like I'm running in a race. The newness of something sparks my interest, but I often need a lot of self-discipline to see projects through to completion. I find it much easier to become engaged if a task has fully defined SMART objectives and I know my part.'

Q: What does it feel like?

ALISON:

'I'll want to start that project or task immediately and I find that sudden burst of energy and excitement almost addictive. I enjoy seeing people develop their own skills and become more confident with something they've been unsure of. I can get over-enthusiastic and/or over-commit to things, and as my initial burst of energy subsides, my energy for that task will often wane too.'

Q: What types of activity trigger a sense of flow for you?

ALISON:

'The task has to be about improving something for other people or for myself. I like autonomy and find it hard to become engaged if someone else has set all the parameters and there's no room for my own spin on something.'

Polisher energy

The pursuit of perfection is the engine driving Polisher energy. This tall order is met with a relentless pursuit of high standards, and though perfection may seem elusive, glimpses of alignment within their environment become powerful sources of energy.

Accepting imperfection while tirelessly striving for improvement, characterises Polisher energy. It's a delicate balance that fuels a continuous pursuit of excellence while acknowledging the reality that perfection may never be fully attained.

Polisher energy in flow

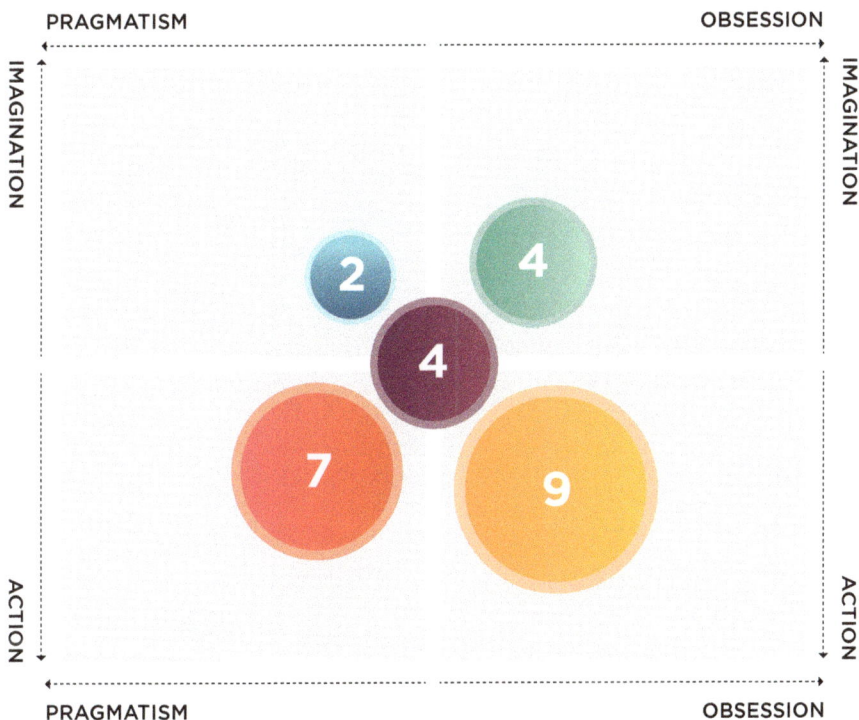

Figure 5: Nicole Rogers, Resident Polisher, The GC Index

Q: What is flow?

NICOLE:

'When I don't get distracted and get so caught up in something that I don't notice time. I become obsessed with finishing the task and can't stop myself even though I sometimes know I need to move on to something else.'

Q: When does it happen?

NICOLE:

'Normally when there is a big task to do, one which I have been putting off starting. Once I start it, I then can't stop until it is done.'

Q: What does it feel like?

NICOLE:

'It feels efficient and smooth, and I wonder why it took me so long to get started. I feel anxious sometimes thinking about starting a big task and so might put it off and just keep doing the smaller easier tasks first to tick them off the list. Then once I get into it and find the time and head space, I wonder why I didn't just get on with it, as it feels great to accomplish that task and I question myself as to why I didn't just get stuck in earlier.'

Q: What types of activity trigger a sense of flow for you?

NICOLE:

'I am not sure there is a specific task or activity.'

Play Maker energy

Play Maker energy is sourced from cohesion and collaboration. For individuals with high Play Maker energy, witnessing harmony within a group becomes a profound source of energy. Making an impact is not an individual endeavour but a collaborative achievement.

Making an impact through group harmony defines the energy landscape of a Play Maker. Coordinating a team where the team's success is prioritised over individual achievements is a true manifestation of Play Maker energy.

Play Maker energy in flow

Figure 6: Leigh Bezuidenhout, LeighB & Company Ltd

'Cultivating a state of flow is paramount for me in my work and personal life, often, it is ignited by elusive elements that resist easy expression. Every day, the task of assessing my daily responsibilities and compiling a comprehensive list often triggers a sense of overwhelming pressure and sometimes even chaos. The pivotal shift happens when I allocate time slots for each task and actively engage in meaningful conversations with those involved.

'In every endeavour, my approach is to understand the objectives of my team members or clients and align myself with their goals as well as mine. This deliberate process brings a clear sense of equilibrium, transforming my mental state from uncertainty to peace. The assurance that everyone is clear on their responsibilities, including me, fosters a great working and home environment. In return, I get to understand how best to support others around me, and they are aware of my needs to fulfil my objectives. Having this golden thread between myself and others brings flow and a great sense of belonging too.

'Achieving this is not always a straightforward journey, as some individuals may be hesitant to share their thoughts and feelings regarding their objectives openly either because they are 'too busy' or don't see the value in sharing their headspace for various reasons. Navigating through assertive personalities, particularly in male-dominated settings, poses challenges. Nevertheless, pushing through the initial resistance almost always brings a shared ground, allowing for the nurturing of meaningful connections and the creation of a harmonious work environment. Once the barriers are broken – if you are lucky enough to get that far, the value is experienced, reciprocated, shared, and the circle ultimately gets bigger.'

Integration of dynamic flow and The GC Index for personal productivity

The GC Index provides insights into diverse energy profiles, enabling a tailored approach to productivity strategies based on an individual's unique strengths.

Tailoring productivity strategies based on GC Index profiles transforms the one-size-fits-all approach, allowing for a more personalised and effective alignment of tasks with individual energy dynamics.

Aligning personal strengths with tasks creates a roadmap for achieving personal flow. It involves a conscious effort to understand how one's inherent energy aligns with the demands of various responsibilities.

Balancing different energy sources becomes the key to unlocking optimal productivity. By harmonising the diverse energy types identified through The GC Index, individuals pave the way for a more seamless and fulfilling work experience.

Dynamic flow and The GC Index – practical applications

A lot of the work we do involves helping our clients to match the energy individuals have to contribute with the type of tasks and processes being tackled. Here are some examples of the impact this alignment can make.

Innovation hub catalyst

I recently consulted with a team in an Innovation Hub, where we applied the principles of dynamic flow and The GC Index to revolutionise their approach to innovation. In our brainstorming sessions, I saw at first-hand how the team's Game Changer energy sparked groundbreaking ideas, while their Strategist energy ensured strategic alignment with our project goals. The result? A dynamic environment where creativity flourished, progress surged, and innovative solutions took shape. It was a testament to the power of harnessing the right energy for the task at hand.

Importantly, the team also established ground rules for the brainstorming activities to limit Polisher energy to an overview of lessons learned to date. This acceptance that, at this early stage, not everything is fully understood and ready for close scrutiny, was critical for the new ideas to be nurtured.

Agile project management design

Aligning individual strengths with specific project components under-pinned another recent assignment. The requirement was set out in a series of objectives to create an agile project management system that adapts to evolving requirements, fosters a pursuit of excellence, and leverages the collaborative spirit for optimal outcomes. We matched these objectives by utilising three individuals with Implementer, Polisher and Play Maker energy and the results were both rapid and astounding. Each person could 'play to their strengths' and everyone was energised by both the process and the outcome achieved.

Educational renaissance

In every educational setting, the students will have different needs in terms of how they engage with information and how they learn. When I introduced a group of tutors to The GC Index, they began to consider how they could tailor their programmes to match the energies of their students. The result was a dynamic and engaging learning environment where creativity thrives (Game Changer energy), strategic understanding deepens (Strategist energy), collaborative learning becomes a corner-stone (Play Maker energy), specific processes and goals are defined (Implementer energy) and a continuous improvement infrastructure is established (Polisher energy).

While these elements may be present in many educational approaches, the workshop delegates shared that they are seldom pursued consciously.

Resilient team dynamics in crisis response

Crises often occur when something happens which was not anticipated. The recent pandemic was a crisis no one in healthcare fully expected. Change within the healthcare sector can take time. Leaders are keen to set the right strategy, use the resources optimally and measure everything twice to ensure the best outcomes have been achieved. This Strategist, Implementer, Polisher energy can be seen consistently across the public sector.

However, a crisis requires a different energetic contribution – creativity and orchestration.

What we saw in the response to Covid-19 was a system tapping into Game Changer and Play Maker energy and, within weeks, IT infrastruc-ture was implemented which had been languishing in strategic papers for years, allied health professionals were deployed in ways far beyond their role definitions and medications were administered at a speed previously considered impossible. Everything switched from the usual protective, defensive, boundary-contained system to something that felt more like one team.

There was also widespread acceptance of what would need to be left 'undone' as everyone turned their attention to what they could control and influence in the now!

Establishing a hybrid workplace

The pandemic also introduced a way of working that has transformed the world of work. The lockdowns meant all office-based personnel were working from home, connected only by their digital communication platforms. At the time, we ran numerous online webinars supporting people to look after themselves and maintain their mental health and resilience.

Now, many organisations and workforces have opted to work in a largely remote way, venturing into the office only sporadically. Unfortunately, not many organisations have reflected the sense of isolation and disconnect this has created for many in their workforce.

However, one of our clients, a large government body, grasped the nettle and responded quickly, investing in human-centred hybrid working. It led to the establishment of numerous changes, tailored to the needs of each human being.

Importantly, the new environment focused on outcomes achieved and value delivered rather than processes followed. This led to a sense of freedom amongst the workforce as individuals were encouraged to apply their natural energies unhindered by the unnatural constraints first created in co-located offices.

It was also a real acceptance of what could actually be controlled at a centralised level. Offices are containers, with fixed routines, dedicated spaces and identifiable boundaries. Homes are fluid, expressive locations, open to the flow of families, friends, service providers and communities. They are complex environments that need to be navigated flexibly and attempting to apply rigid rules and processes demonstrates no empathy for the lives of your workforce.

These examples illustrate the versatility and transformative potential of integrating dynamic flow and The GC Index, showcasing how these concepts can reshape conventional approaches and foster innovation in real-world scenarios.

Conclusion

A: Recap of dynamic flow and GC Index principles

In essence, dynamic flow and The GC Index converge to redefine the foundational principles guiding personal and professional growth. Dynamic flow encapsulates a paradigm shift in understanding productivity, emphasising the fluidity of tasks, the balance of action and acceptance and the harmonious alignment of energy resources.

Simultaneously, The GC Index emerges as a revelation in energy management, offering a spectrum of energy profiles that illuminate the diverse ways individuals generate and express their vigour. From the creative prowess of Game Changer energy to the strategic alignment of the Strategist, the action-oriented Implementer, perfection-driven Polisher, and the collaborative harmony of the Play Maker, each profile contributes a unique dimension to the energy landscape. The synthesis of these energy dynamics becomes a catalyst for personalised productivity strategies, recognising and leveraging individual strengths for optimal performance.

B: Encouragement for readers to explore and apply these concepts

Consider this chapter an encouragement to embark on a journey of self-discovery and intentional application. Integrate dynamic flow into your daily rhythm, acknowledging the ebb and flow of tasks and embracing the concept of adaptive productivity. Delve into the intricacies of The GC Index, recognising your unique energy profile and those of your peers. The fusion of these concepts holds the promise of not just heightened productivity but a profound sense of purpose and accomplishment. As you immerse yourself in this thinking, you will discover new dimensions of resilience, creativity, and success, ultimately crafting a narrative of personal and professional fulfilment that reflects the vibrant energy within you.

C: The potential for transformative changes in personal and professional life

Productivity is no longer just a rigid pursuit confined by outdated notions of time. Instead, personal energy becomes a compass guiding you through diverse landscapes of creativity, strategy, action, perfection, and collaboration. This integration promises to be a game-changer, altering the very fabric of how individuals approach their daily tasks and navigate the dynamic currents of life.

In the professional sphere, the adoption of dynamic flow and The GC Index sets the stage for a paradigm shift. Individuals equipped with a nuanced understanding of their energy dynamics discover new depths of resilience, adaptability, and innovation.

Whether in the boardroom, the studio, or the collaborative workspace, the transformative impact is palpable. Dynamic flow allows for the seamless adaptation to evolving responsibilities, while The GC Index provides a roadmap for tapping into diverse and untapped energy sources, fostering a workplace culture rich in creativity and collaboration.

On a personal level, this integration becomes a compass for self-discovery and growth. As individuals align their inherent strengths with tasks, balance diverse energy sources, and embrace the fluidity of productivity, transformative changes unfold. The pursuit of perfection gives way to a more forgiving yet improvement-oriented mindset, and the collaborative spirit amplifies personal relationships and community impact. It's an opportunity that transforms the assumed boundaries between work and life, and leads us towards holistic well-being and purposeful living.

In essence, embracing dynamic flow and The GC Index is an invitation to embark on a transformative odyssey, where the potential for profound impact resonates far beyond our current self-imposed limitations.

Chapter 15

Harnessing The GC Index to Understand CIO Impact, a Case Study

The ways in which The GC Index can inform decisions when it comes to talent management within organisations. These decisions are crucial to the success and longevity of organisations large and small.

Georgina Pawley

Introduction

At Life Body Health, our mission is to harness data to drive individual and organisational excellence. We recently explored the impact of The GC Index with a core group of chief information officers operating within UK headquartered organisations.

Our focus was to use individual data to uncover insights into how chief information officers (CIOs) contribute to their organisations. This case study delves into the findings from our session, highlighting the diverse impacts CIOs can make and the importance of understanding these differences.

Background

Over 40 CIOs were involved in the session which began with an introduction to The GC Index, a unique tool that profiles Energy for Impact rather than traditional metrics such as expertise, experience, and personality. With my background in recruitment, I have often observed organisations failing to maximise the value of their people. For me in my world of work, The GC Index addresses this gap by focusing on how and where individuals are naturally motivated to make an impact, providing a fresh perspective on talent management.

The GC Index Framework

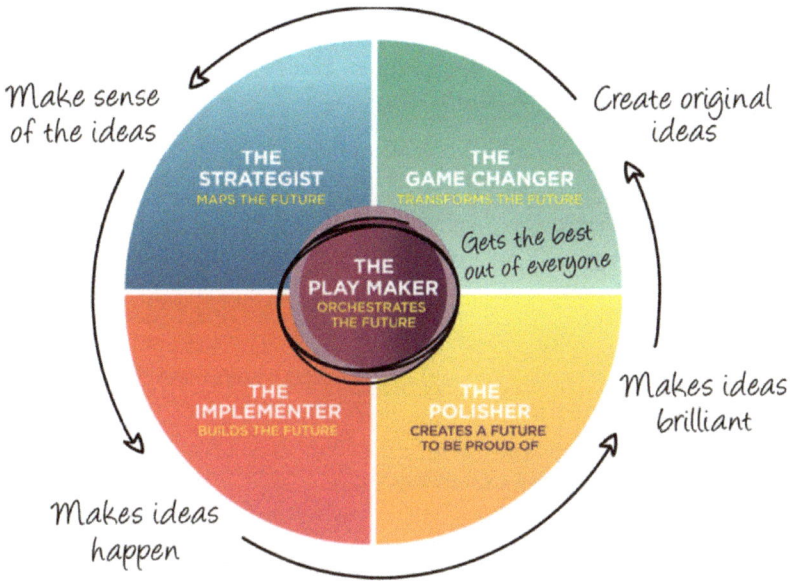

The GC Index profiles individuals across five key proclivities:

- **Game Changer**: Energised by exploring new, original ways of doing things.
- **Strategist**: Focuses on making sense of things and understanding the problem before starting.
- **Implementer**: Prefers to take action and get things done effectively.
- **Polisher**: Concentrates on incremental improvements and refining existing ideas.
- **Play Maker**: Helps people to work together effectively and that stakeholder interests are managed.

These proclivities offer a nuanced understanding of how individuals can best contribute to their teams and organisations.

Session overview

During the CIO session, we explained each proclivity in detail and demonstrated how to interpret individual profiles. For example, one CIO shared their GC Impact Profile (see Figure 1 below) highlighting a Strategist/Implementer combination. A Strategist/Implementer CIO brings energy to clarifying purposeful and actionable plans, shaping strategic objectives, and structuring delivery.

Figure 1: The GC Index profile for a CIO

We discussed the activities that energise and motivate individuals with such profiles, emphasising the importance of aligning roles with natural tendencies. Our assumption here is that, in any setting, when an individual is engaged by a task, they are more likely to apply themselves to that task and to developing the skills needed to achieve that task.

No such thing as a perfect CIO

In Figure 2 below, I have presented 10 of the anonymised GC Index profiles for our group. During this discussion, we shared the individual GC Index profiles of each CIO. You will note that no two individuals have the same profile, and this is true of all 47 CIOs in our group.

EXAMPLE CIO INDIVIDUAL GC INDEX PROFILES

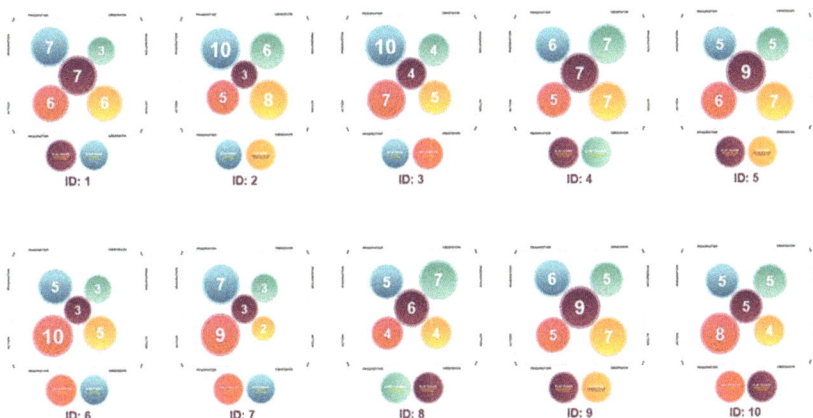

Figure 2: Selection of individual GC Index profiles for our CIO group

For example, a CIO with a strong Game Changer/Polisher (ID:3) proclivity excels in delivering creative ideas to the highest standards. Another CIO with a strong Polisher/Play Maker proclivity (ID:9) sets high standards to get the best from others, focusing on the pursuit of excellence.

These individual GC Index profiles demonstrate that being a successful CIO isn't one-dimensional. These differences help organisations to understand the subtleties of *how* an individual performs in their role; what's underpinned their success. This understanding, in turn can help individuals in talent management to create programmes that help individuals develop proclivity-related competencies so they can excel at their particular approach to leadership.

Taking the Polisher/Play Maker example above, these individuals would be encouraged to focus upon:

- The skills needed to be an excellent Play Maker, specifically, consensus-building skills and conflict management skills.
- Inspiring others with their high expectations as a Polisher, helping others to aspire to organisational excellence.

Through the individual GC Index profiles, we can demonstrate that being a successful CIO isn't one-dimensional and The GC Index data further helps organisations understand the impact they want from their CIO. More specifically, an individual CIO is more likely to thrive in a role when their proclivities are aligned to both the role, the structure and the culture of an organisation.

Take our Polisher/Play Maker individual as an example. They will thrive as a CIO in a culture that

- Values collaboration, inclusion and involvement – Play Maker
- Values those individuals who have the energy for managing boundary tensions by looking for consensus – Play Maker
- Values people who bring energy to continuous improvement and the pursuit of excellence – Polisher
- Values people who bring energy to getting the very best from others – Polisher.

Each of the CIOs in our session was able to reflect, in the most tangible way, upon the question:

'Where do I add most value in my role given my proclivities, and the nature of the role and organisational culture?'

The GC Index team data

We also presented team profiles and heat maps, providing a comprehensive view of collective impact within organisations. This holistic approach helps CIOs understand their teams' dynamics and identify areas for improvement.

Aggregate data insights

The session's highlight was the analysis of aggregate data from 47 CIOs who completed The GC Index assessment. I have presented the group's aggregate GC Index profile in Figure 3 below.

The percentage scores are based upon individual's highest individual scores, so 10% of individuals had a highest score for Game Changer, 30% a highest score for Implementer, 25% a highest score for Play Maker and so on.

The data revealed intriguing trends in how different proclivities are represented among CIOs.

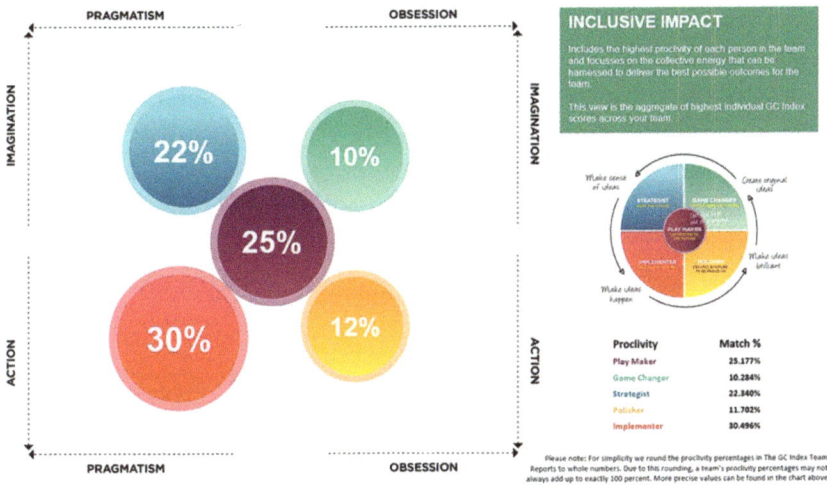

Figure 3: The aggregate GC Index profile for 47 CIOs

- Implementers: 30%
- Play Makers: 25%
- Strategists: 22%
- Polishers: 12%
- Game Changers: 10%

This distribution sparked a discussion on the typical CIO role and how it aligns with these proclivities. Participants reflected on whether these results matched their expectations and experiences.

Detailed findings

Further analysis of the data provided deeper insights into individual proclivities:

- **Play Maker proclivity:** 16 out of 47 CIOs had a leading Play Maker proclivity, highlighting the importance of collaboration and team cohesion in their roles.
- **Game Changer proclivity:** 6 out of 47 CIOs, indicating that fewer CIOs see themselves as generators of creative ideas and possibilities.
- **Strategist and Implementer proclivities:** 11 CIOs each, showcasing an energy for both strategic planning and execution.
- **Polisher proclivity:** 3 out of 47 CIOs, suggesting a lesser focus on refining and perfecting processes within this group.

These insights prompted group discussions about the benefits and challenges associated with each proclivity. Participants shared their experiences and strategies for leveraging their strengths and addressing their weaknesses.

What was clear throughout, was that this was not a discussion about *can* an individual do the job – they were, after all, all successful. It was a discussion about *how* they would go about their role and who they needed in their teams to be successful. All may recognise the importance of Polisher energy in their teams even though that may not be where their energy is.

Organisational and demographic trends

We also examined the data based on organisational size and gender, uncovering additional trends:

Organisational size

- **Companies with up to 10,000 employees:** Predominantly Play Maker/Implementer (16% Game Changers), indicating a need for collaboration and execution in smaller organisations.
- **Companies with 10,000 to 50,000 employees:** Implementer/ Polisher with low Play Maker (4%) and Game Changer (4%) representation, suggesting a focus on execution and refinement in mid-sized companies.
- **Companies with over 50,000 employees:** Strongest in Strategists (31%) and Play Makers (29%), with a low Game Changer presence (4%), highlighting the importance of strategic vision and the management of team dynamics in larger organisations.

EMPLOYEES UP TO 10,000 - 23
TEAM PROFILE – INCLUSIVE IMPACT VIEW

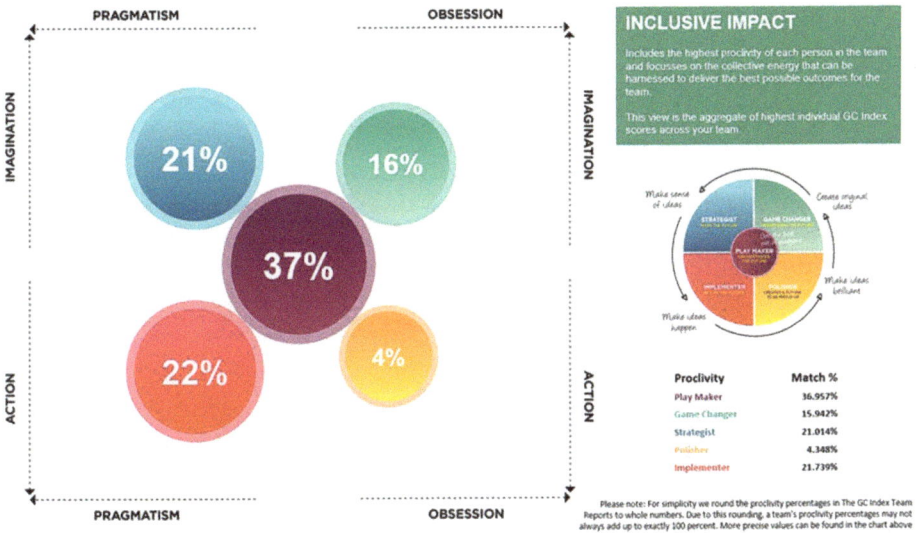

Figure 4: The aggregate GC Index profiles by company size up to 10,000 employees

EMPLOYEES 10,000 TO 50,000 - 13
TEAM PROFILE – INCLUSIVE IMPACT VIEW

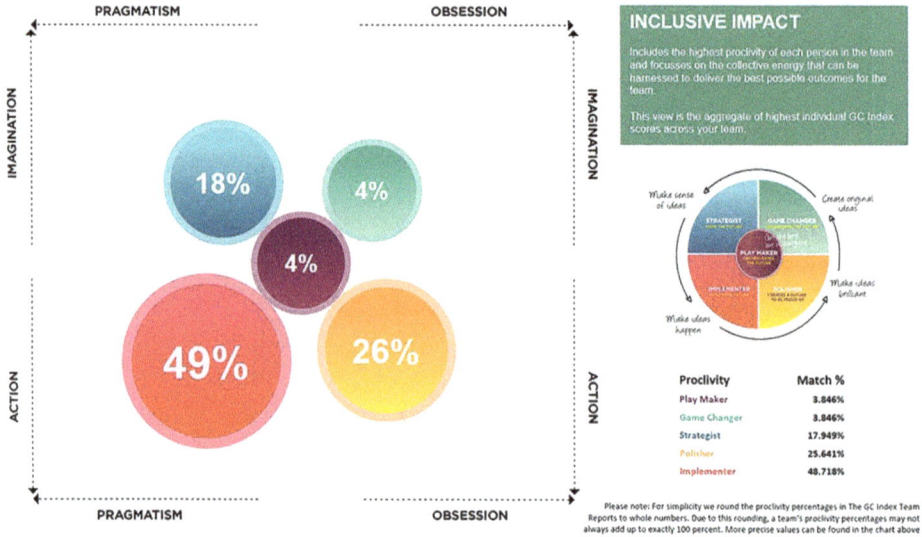

Figure 5: The aggregate GC Index profiles by company size 10,000 – 50,000 employees

EMPLOYEES OVER 50,000 - 8
TEAM PROFILE – INCLUSIVE IMPACT VIEW

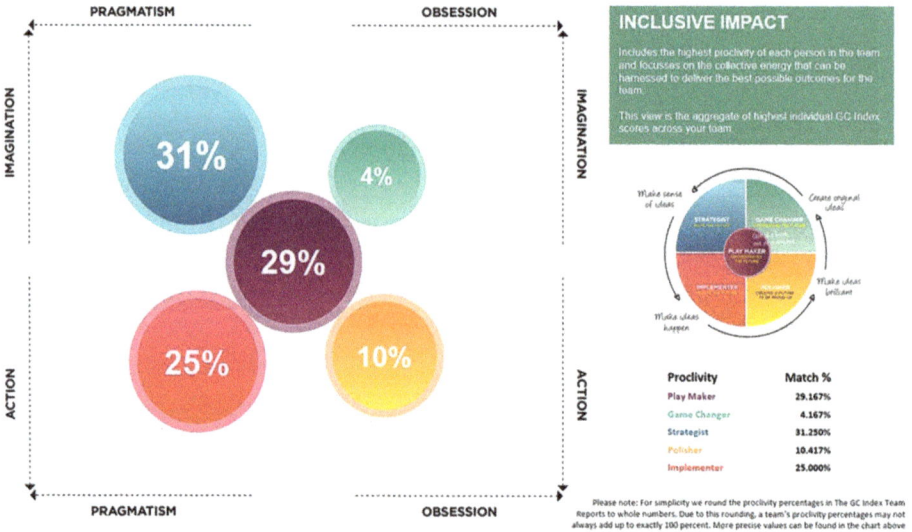

Figure 6: The aggregate GC Index profiles by company size over 50,000 employees

These trends suggest that organisational size influences the dominant proclivities among CIOs, with smaller companies favouring execution and innovation, while larger companies emphasise strategic planning and team cohesion.

Gender analysis

Gender analysis revealed notable differences in proclivities between male and female CIOs:

- **Male CIOs:** Were predominantly Play Maker/Implementers (31% Play Makers, 26% Implementers).
- **Female CIOs:** Predominantly Implementer/Strategists (45% Implementers, 36% Strategists) with low representation in Play Makers (6%) and Game Changers (5%).

ALL FEMALE COMPLETED LINKS - 11
TEAM PROFILE – INCLUSIVE IMPACT VIEW

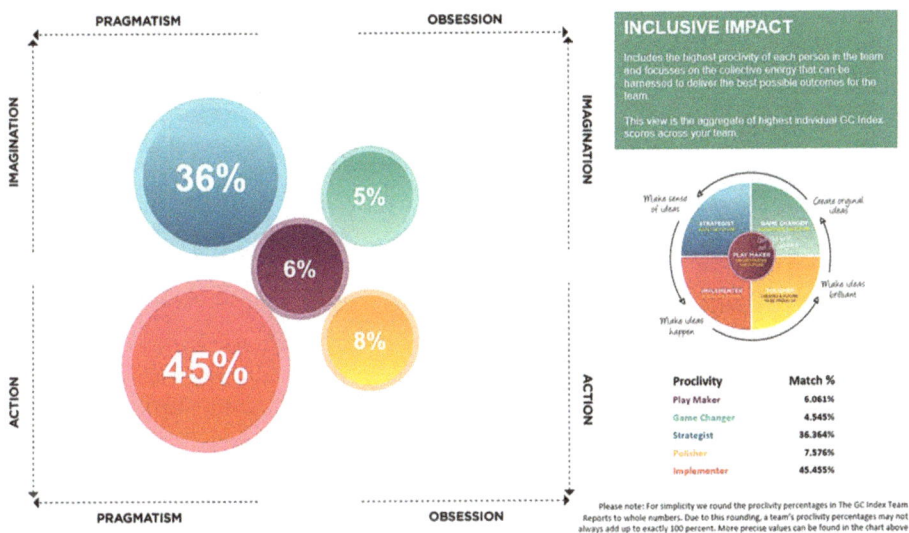

Figure 7: The aggregate GC Index profiles by gender – female

ALL MALE COMPLETED LINKS - 36
TEAM PROFILE – INCLUSIVE IMPACT VIEW

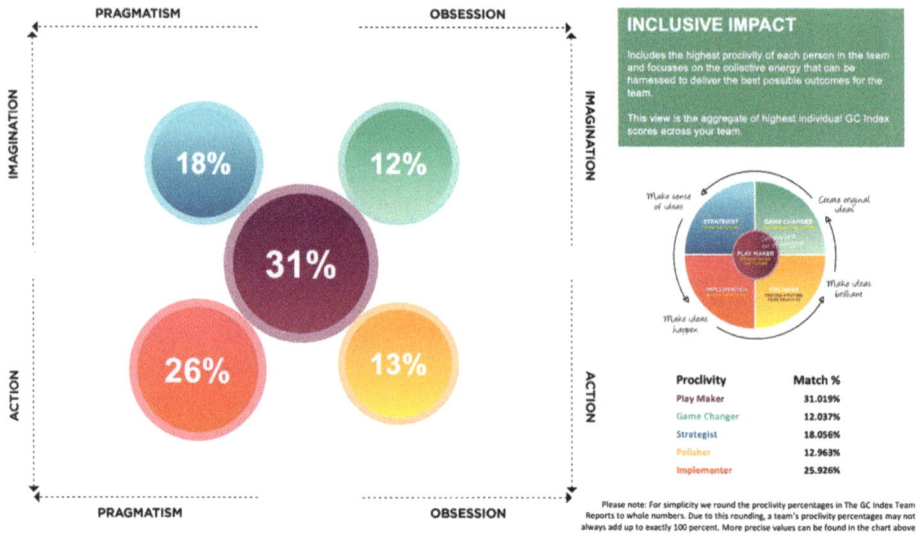

Figure 8: The aggregate GC Index profiles by gender – male

These findings led to lively discussions, particularly among female CIOs, about the perceived need to demonstrate productivity and the impact of gender stereotypes on their roles. Many women felt that to be perceived as strong leaders, they needed to focus on execution and strategic planning, which aligns with the Implementer/Strategist profile.

Implications and applications

The insights from The GC Index session have significant implications for CIOs and their organisations:

1. **Enhanced self-awareness:** Understanding their own proclivities helps CIOs develop and leverage their strengths and manage their weaknesses, leading to more effective leadership.
2. **Optimised team dynamics:** By recognising the diverse impacts within their teams, CIOs can build complementary high-performing teams, aligning roles with natural tendencies.

3. **Strategic alignment:** Aligning individual and team impacts with organisational goals ensures that technology initiatives support broader business objectives.

In summary

The GC Index data provides a powerful tool for unlocking the full potential of CIOs, fostering high-performing teams, and driving organisational success. By understanding and leveraging individual and collective impacts, CIOs can enhance their leadership effectiveness and contribute more impactfully to their organisations.

The strategic value of The GC Index goes beyond individual and team assessment; it fundamentally transforms how CIOs perceive and enact their roles.

1. **Tailored leadership development:** The GC Index enables personalised development plans that align with each CIO's natural proclivities. This leads to more engaged and effective leaders who can navigate the complexities of their roles with greater confidence and competence.
2. **Enhanced decision making:** CIOs equipped with insights from The GC Index can make more informed decisions about team composition and project assignments. By aligning tasks with individual strengths, they can optimise team performance and ensure more successful outcomes.
3. **Culture of continuous improvement:** The focus on proclivities encourages a culture where continuous improvement is valued. CIOs and their teams can regularly assess and adjust their strategies to better align with organisational goals, fostering an environment of agility and innovation.
4. **Benchmarking and best practices:** The aggregate data from The GC Index provides valuable benchmarks for CIOs. Understanding where they stand relative to their peers can help them identify areas for growth and development. Additionally, sharing best practices within the community can drive collective advancement and excellence.

5. **Empowering diverse leadership:** The insights into gender-based proclivities highlight the unique strengths that different leaders bring to the table. Organisations can leverage this diversity to create more inclusive and dynamic leadership teams, ultimately leading to richer perspectives and more innovative solutions.

6. **Future-proofing organisations:** By aligning CIOs' impacts with long-term strategic goals, organisations can better prepare for future challenges. CIOs who understand their natural proclivities can anticipate changes and proactively lead their teams through transitions, ensuring sustained organisational resilience.

The GC Index not only equips senior executives with a deeper understanding of their own impact but also fosters a broader organisational culture that values and leverages individual strengths. This holistic approach is crucial for driving sustained success in today's rapidly evolving business landscape.